Gender Justice and Contemporary Asian Literatures

A CASEBOOK

Gender Justice and Contemporary Asian Literatures

A CASEBOOK

Karen Laura Thornber

The Modern Language Association of America
New York 2024

85 Broad Street, New York, New York 10004
www.mla.org

To order MLA publications, visit www.mla.org/books. For wholesale and international orders, see www.mla.org/bookstore-orders.

The MLA office is located on the island known as Mannahatta (Manhattan) in Lenapehoking, the homeland of the Lenape people. The MLA pays respect to the original stewards of this land and to the diverse and vibrant Native communities that continue to thrive in New York City.

Library of Congress Cataloging-in-Publication Data

Names: Thornber, Karen Laura, author.
Title: Gender justice and contemporary Asian literatures : a casebook / Karen Laura Thornber.
Description: New York : The Modern Language Association of America, 2024. | Includes bibliographical references and index.
Identifiers: LCCN 2024002117 (print) | LCCN 2024002118 (ebook) | ISBN 9781603296601 (hardcover) | ISBN 9781603296618 (paperback) | ISBN 9781603296625 (EPUB)
Subjects: LCSH: Oriental literature--History and criticism. | Oriental literature (English)--History and criticism. | Women in literature. | Social justice in literature. | Social problems in literature. | LCGFT: Literary criticism.
Classification: LCC PJ314.W66 T46 2024 (print) | LCC PJ314.W66 (ebook) | DDC 895.09/3522--dc23/eng/20240425
LC record available at https://lccn.loc.gov/2024002117
LC ebook record available at https://lccn.loc.gov/2024002118

Contents

Acknowledgments and Dedication

The research and writing of *Gender Justice* were funded by a Competitive Research Grant from the Academy of Korean Studies (AKS-2021-R-017) as well as by Harvard University's Reischauer Institute of Japanese Studies and Faculty of Arts and Sciences. This publication was also subsidized in part by Harvard Studies in Comparative Literature. I'm thankful for the continued support of my transregional interdisciplinary books on interconnections among literature, configured broadly, and global challenges.

Research for *Gender Justice* was conducted during the height of the COVID-19 pandemic, and I'm thankful for the undergraduate and graduate students at Harvard who, despite everything, provided me with timely and skilled assistance: Fangdai Chen (now at Lingnan University, Hong Kong), Min Ji Choi, Aniket De, Alexandria Ho, Cookie Kunarattanapruek, Adi Kusnodi, Akhil Thomas, Seton Uhlhorn, and Bota Ussen.

I feel most fortunate to have had the opportunity to speak with many diverse individuals and groups on gender and justice. Feedback from faculty members, students, staff members, and other engaged individuals at Harvard and across the United States as well as at universities, alumni gatherings, and other forums in Europe and throughout East, South, and Southeast Asia has broadened and deepened my perspectives in many important ways.

I am thankful to James Hatch, my editor at the MLA, for his early interest in my work on gender and justice and for his expert guidance throughout; to the MLA Publications Committee for its astute recommendations; and to the staff members of the MLA publications program for their exemplary editorial and production care. Anonymous referees provided insightful feedback at two crucial stages of the project, for which I am most grateful.

Working on *Gender Justice*, particularly through the years of the pandemic, has helped me better appreciate my family's lived experiences across generations, oceans, and gender, ethnic, national, and other identities. Their unwavering commitment to justice has been an inspiration throughout. My husband, Tom Havens, was, as ever, an eager interlocutor, his love and thoughtful care beyond measure or description.

Gender Justice is dedicated to my students, past and present, whose commitment to challenging norms and pursuing justice of all types in a world that often compels silence and encourages injustice has been truly exceptional. I've been extraordinarily fortunate to have worked with so many undergraduates across the Faculty of Arts and Sciences and graduate students across the university and beyond, many of whom have faced significant gender injustice themselves, who take seriously the poet Amanda Gorman's caution that justice is not necessarily what "just" is (132)—and Gorman's insistence that "there is always light, if only we're brave enough to see it. / If only we're brave enough to be it" (134).

WORK CITED

Gorman, Amanda. "The Hill We Climb." *Call Us What We Carry*, by Gorman, Viking Books, 2021, pp. 132–34.

Note on Transliteration, Personal Names, and Titles of Works in This Volume

Given the intended audience of *Gender Justice*, titles of narratives discussed in the main text that were initially written in languages other than English that use the Latin alphabet are identified by the title of their published English translation, followed in parentheses by the original title and date of first publication. When a narrative was originally written in an Asian script, the title of the published English translation is followed by a transliteration of the original title, the title in the original script, and the date of first publication. When the title of the published English translation is not a close translation of the original title, the literal translation is given after the original title. The same convention, with the exception of the inclusion of Asian scripts, applies to titles of narratives discussed in notes. When there is no published English translation of a text, I provide my own translation in parentheses, following the original title.

Life dates for key writers discussed in the main text are given on first mention of that writer's name. I refer to writers by their pen name if that name is used more commonly than their birth name; in these cases, the birth name is listed in parentheses after the first mention of the pen name.

Bengali words are transliterated using both the Library of Congress system and the more informal, pronunciation-oriented system; Chinese words are transliterated using pinyin; Hindi words using the Library of Congress system; Japanese words using the modified Hepburn system used by *Kenkyusha's New Japanese-English Dictionary*; Korean words using a modified McCune-Reischauer system; Malayalam and Marathi words using the Library of Congress system; Thai words using the Royal Thai General

System of Transcription; and Urdu words using the BGN/PCGN Persian romanization systems.

In cases where persons with Asian names or their English-language translators list alternative transliterations of their names, I give both the standard and the alternative transliterations. Chinese, Japanese, Korean, Taiwanese, and Vietnamese names are given in their customary order, with family name preceding personal name or names, except for cases of Western-language publications in which name order is often reversed.

Introduction: Literature, Asia, Diasporas, and Pandemics of Gender Inequity and Gender-Based Violence

"All of you people listen and give me justice. . . . I was going to the city with a big, heavy basket full of bananas on my head to sell. When all of a sudden someone came up from behind and pounced on me. . . . When I came to, I realized that sexual violence [*balātkar*] had been committed against me" (Merrill 987).[1] So asserts the illiterate rural widow Paru Bapu Surve in the Marathi-language short story "Justice" ("Nyāy," न्याय, 1988), by the Indian Dalit feminist writer Urmila Pawar (Urmilā Pavāra, 1945–), when villagers demand the pregnant Paru reveal the identity of her unborn child's father. Impressed, Pawar's narrator, a Mumbai-based lawyer and absentee landlord, notes that "no educated woman taking the stand in *court* would have given testimony so clear and strong. As clear as Paru did that day in front of everyone" (987). After Paru effectively rebuts an elderly villager's subsequent claim that "on no account can we let that bastard child live," the narrator declares that "everyone was united in seeing so-called justice carried out against her. But Paru had taken justice into her own hands" (987).

Justice is reconfigured in Pawar's "Justice." The punishment called "justice" that Pawar describes in a 1998 interview as having inspired her short story becomes a rejection of punishment.[2] Paru's eloquence, agency, resistance, and resilience inspire the narrator, particularly given her subjugated social position.[3] Yet the reshaping of justice that takes place in "Justice" is only partial. It does not demand accountability. And it does not address other systemic gender inequities, much less the gender-based violence that Paru is likely to continue to face given the absence of structural changes that would reduce her vulnerability. Paru remains an impoverished farmer who will continue to travel alone to sell her produce in a society with little deterrence for rape.

Pawar's "Justice" resonates with many of the narratives discussed in *Gender Justice and Contemporary Asian Literatures*. This book illuminates how diverse writers from across East, South, and Southeast Asia and their diasporas in Asia and globally have engaged over the past 50 years with struggles for and denials of different types of gender justice amid pandemics of gender inequity and gender-based violence.[4] Each of the book's seven chapters closely analyzes three to five works of literature, from novels and short stories to memoirs and creative nonfiction, from narratives by literary celebrities translated into dozens of languages to those by writers little known outside their home communities. Engaging with a range of sources, the chapters of *Gender Justice* additionally place these works in wider cultural, social, and historical contexts and connect them to one another within and across chapters.

This book is one of few resources for students, teachers, and scholars who seek a broad understanding of gender, justice, and literature in Asia and its diasporas, particularly as these pertain to the oppression and empowerment of the majority of the world's female population and more than 25% of the population globally. *Gender Justice* is aimed at both specialists and nonspecialists, including students, teachers, and scholars of gender and justice with little background on Asia and its diasporas as well as students, teachers, and scholars of Asia and its diasporas who focus on a single nation or region or who have a limited background in gender, justice, literature, or all three. Just as important, the book's focus on gender justice across Asia and its diasporas propels gender studies, women's studies, ethnic studies, Asian studies, Asian American studies, Asian diaspora studies, comparative literature, and world literature in vital new directions.

Gender Justice

Gender in this book is understood as "the dynamic through which human beings are constructed as masculine or feminine subjects within a given cultural and historical framework, then made to occupy unequal social roles" (Stetz 92–93).[5] The term *gender justice* has since the late twentieth century generally been used to refer to issues of justice that have primarily but by no means exclusively concerned women, particularly gender inequity and gender-based violence. In recent years, the term has become more explicitly inclusive of transgender, gender nonconforming, and nonbinary individuals, in addition to cisgender women.[6] As summarized by San Diego

Pride, "Achieving gender justice would mean that people of all genders have a meaningful right to bodily autonomy, safety, health, and opportunity" ("Gender Justice"). Additionally, as articulated by the Third Wave Fund, gender justice does not stop with "women's liberation, reproductive justice, and queer and trans justice." Gender justice issues also "show up within immigration justice, education justice, racial justice, health and disability justice, and all efforts for justice and liberation" ("What"), including climate justice. Although most of the women featured in the narratives analyzed in this book are implicitly or explicitly identified as cisgender and straight, where relevant, *Gender Justice* speaks to queer coding and to depictions of the experiences of LGBTQIA+ individuals. Their numbers are much smaller, but per capita, queer individuals in Asia and its diasporas generally confront even greater inequity and violence than their cisgender and straight female counterparts, such as denunciations from gender-critical (i.e., trans-exclusionary radical) feminists—for instance, those participating in the South Korean online community WOMAD—that are homophobic, transphobic, and otherwise advocate anti-LGBTQIA+ positions.[7] I therefore intend to analyze narratives that prioritize Asian and Asian diaspora LGBTQIA+ experiences of gender justice in a future volume.[8]

Gender inequity and gender-based violence, deeply enmeshed in heteropatriarchal gender norms and patriarchal systems, are the world's most persistent and pervasive pandemics.[9] As Linda Scott asserts, "[H]umanity's treatment of females is one of the darkest parts of our history" (289). Indeed, women are the largest group treated inequitably because of gender. Instigated by intimate partners, family members, friends, neighbors, acquaintances, teachers, employers, colleagues, strangers, law enforcement, the military, governments, and societies more broadly, gender inequity and gender-based violence are structural, systemic, and endemic. Gender inequity and gender-based violence are also intersectional: ethnic, racial, Indigenous, religious, sexual, gender, and other minorities are at greatest risk, as are individuals and communities already disadvantaged by their education; occupation; class or caste; migration, immigration, or refugee status (including climate and war refugees); age; ability or disability; mental or physical health; location (urban versus rural); or other factors.[10] Moreover, gender inequity and gender-based violence are deeply enmeshed in imperial, neocolonial, and other transnational and global dynamics (Hune 9–10; Vang et al., "Hmong Women" viii). Societies around the world frequently silence victims and survivors, condoning and even openly promoting gender inequity and gender-based violence despite their proven adverse effects on the physical, mental, sexual, reproductive, and economic health of individuals, communities, and nations (García-Moreno and Riecher-Rössler; Homan; Knaul et al. 98). The gender pay gap alone reduces the global economy by approximately $160 trillion (Counts; see also Scott 3–27).

In many communities, women are subjected to physical, sexual, psychological, social, economic, and other forms of harm from before birth until after death (Watts and Zimmerman 1233; "Violence"). The World Bank's 2019 report *Gender-Based Violence* reveals that even before the responses to COVID-19 that intensified gender inequity and gender-based violence in many parts of the world, one in three women globally—more than 1 billion people—had experienced physical violence, sexual violence, or both because of their gender ("Gender-Based Violence"). Still greater numbers of women have been subjected to economic, emotional, mental, and other forms of bias, mistreatment, and abuse that constitute what Jessica Nordell terms "soul violence," assaults on an individual's choices, possibilities, and sense of self (7). For her part, Anita Hill describes gender-based violence as an "ongoing catastrophe" and the "literal and figurative foot on women's necks" (8). And she highlights the devastation it causes: "If all of our opportunities to be in the schools, workplaces, and homes of our choices can be defeated by an act of brutality, we are unlikely to have any real chance of sustaining social, economic, and political equality" (12). This is particularly true of women also marginalized because of their class, ability or disability, education, ethnicity, race, religion, sexuality, and other factors. Hill speaks here of "our" and "we," but as she and many others have long affirmed, there is no feminist universal; "women" are far from a stable, unified, homogeneous category and experience gender inequity and gender-based violence in many different ways (Brodsky 21; Mohanty).

The Vietnamese American writer Viet Thanh Nguyen declares "true justice" to be "creating a world of social, economic, cultural, and political opportunities that would allow all [the] voiceless to tell their stories and be heard, rather than be dependent on a writer or a representative of some kind" (20). Indeed, if justice is a "condition of right arrangement" (Mao 5), the "condition of rightness for each and all" (13), then gender justice envisions a world where no one would face inequity, much less violence, based on their actual or perceived gender or genders ("Gender Justice"). Given that global injustice is "shot through with gendered inequality," gender justice is becoming an increasingly significant component of discussions on global justice (Williams and Death 103). Notable in this context is the work of the feminist philosopher Alison Jaggar, whose "prologue to a theory of global gender justice" (23) recognizes large-scale gender disparities as both elements and manifestations of "transnational cycles of gendered vulnerability" (36). This understanding, Jaggar acknowledges, "discourages the idea that any simple strategy for global gender justice exists" (37). At the same time, assertions that patterns of gender disparity are "neither coincidental nor inevitable" and that cycles of gendered vulnerability are "created by human institutions and so are open to human intervention" leave space for creating different worlds (36), for becoming allies rather than adversaries.[11]

Why Literature?

Justice is often discussed in the abstract or as a matter of law, political history, protest movements, enfranchisement, and similar phenomena. Yet at its core, justice involves individuals and their experiences—experiences most directly accessed through stories. As Jacqueline Rose contends, literature shares experiences of violence "in ways that defy both the discourse of politicians and the defenses of thought" and "takes us deep into parts of the world crying out unambiguously for justice" (31, 33). In so doing, literature can create different worlds, those where survivors and victims alike retain dignity and make and remake traditions, perpetrators are held accountable, and systems are transformed.[12]

To be sure, for centuries, literatures from around the globe have reinforced heteronormative gender expectations and gender hierarchies, propagated prejudices and stigmas, and justified brutality. But many writers have challenged aesthetic and social expectations, relentlessly breaking silences, demanding accountability, and calling explicitly or implicitly for justice. Highlighting individual voices and experiences, many long disregarded, while exposing the ubiquity and ferocity of gender inequity and gender-based violence, the stories literature tells have long revealed the devastating short- and long-term physical, psychological, social, and economic impacts of gender injustice on individuals, families, and communities. Stories not only vividly depict, often through skillful deployment of literary techniques, the intensity of personal suffering but also create counternarratives, humanizing those facing injustice and those fighting for justice, spotlighting their dignity and agency amid broader familial, economic, social, cultural, and historical dynamics. Stories underscore the need to recognize and overhaul all forms of gender injustice. They are some of the loudest and most persistent voices in revealing the urgency of and possibilities for change. As such, they can help reduce and ultimately eradicate the inequities and the violence that so pervade our societies. Furthermore, literature can reinforce and even reveal to readers who have experienced similar violence that they are not alone and not to blame and confirm that what they are experiencing or have experienced is indefensible. Narratives likewise help readers put their own experiences and traumas into broader perspective. Teaching stories on gender inequity and gender-based violence has impressed on me their broad affective and emotional impact on readers, everyone from high school and college students to middle-aged professionals to retirees. At the same time, as Nguyen has passionately argued, "[l]iterature does not change the world until people get out of their chairs, go out into the world, and do something to transform the conditions of which the literature speaks" (20).[13]

Why Asia and Its Diasporas? Why Asian and Asian Diaspora Literatures?

East, South, and Southeast Asia, as well as their diasporas within Asia and around the world, together make up nearly 60% of the global population. Asia itself, the world's largest continent, is exceptionally diverse economically, historically, and culturally. The region is home to some of the world's wealthiest nations as well as to some of its most impoverished. Thousands of languages from a range of language families are spoken across an area that spans Pakistan in the West, Japan in the East, Mongolia and China in the North, and Indonesia in the South. Colonialism's legacy remains powerful; in the nineteenth and early twentieth centuries alone, France, Great Britain, the Netherlands, Portugal, Spain, the United States, and Japan all colonized parts of Asia. Manifestations of gender inequity and gender-based violence also differ greatly within Asian nations, not to mention across its subregions. Yet the overall severity and impact of such inequity and violence is irrefutable. The World Economic Forum's annual *Global Gender Gap Report* estimates that at the current pace it will take most of Asia anywhere from 149 years to nearly two centuries to close its gender gaps (6–7). To be sure, the report, which provides updated data on overall gender gaps as well as on gender gaps in educational attainment (generally the smallest), health and survival, economic participation and opportunity, and political empowerment (generally the largest), can be misleading. In particular, reducing gaps within a nation is distinct from reducing gaps among nations, and near parity within a nation should not distract attention from the inequities that a particular nation faces vis-à-vis other nations (Brinton). The report additionally obscures significant gaps among men and barely mentions gender and sexual minorities. At the same time, the statistics it provides on a range of gender gaps are important reference points.

Literatures from East, South, and Southeast Asia and their myriad global diasporas regularly speak to the multiple and diverse forms of gender inequity and gender-based violence experienced by women and gender and sexual minorities from before birth until after death. Yet scholarship on literature and gender-based violence remains largely concentrated on narratives from the United States, western Europe, and Canada. And the vast body of nonliterary scholarship on gender inequity and gender-based violence, feminisms, and women in Asia and its diasporas tends to center either on a particular region (i.e., East, South, or Southeast Asia) or, much more frequently, a particular nation.[14] Transcultural study of Asian literatures is still in its youth, and trans-Asian scholarship on literature and gender is even less developed. For their part, Asian studies and Asian diaspora studies, including Asian American studies, remain unnecessarily separated, frequently housed in different academic departments, book lists, and scholarly organizations. This book seeks to replace these tendencies with broader understandings of gender justice, Asia and its diasporas, and Asian and Asian diaspora literatures.

Methodologies and Sources

This book engages with a range of Asian and Asian diaspora literatures as individual works, in dialogue with one another, and in their specific historical, cultural, educational (formal and informal), material, legal, social, statistical, feminist, and activist contexts. Many of the writers whose works are featured in *Gender Justice* explicitly identify as feminist. Many do not. Yet most can be broadly thought of as feminist in their advocating for justice, placing "the critical examination of gender and its relationship to power at the center" (Stetz 92).[15] *Feminism* is a fraught term that many have explicitly rejected, such as Indira Gandhi, who in 1966 became the first and to date only female prime minister of India. Many post-independence (post-1947) Indian writers have rejected feminist politics, including the English-language writer Anita Desai, the Gujarati writer Saroj Pathak, the Hindi writers Mannu Bhandari and Krishna Sobti, the Kannada writer Triveni, the Tamil writer R. Chudamani, and the Urdu writer Ismat Chughtai (Mani 36). Similarly, Madhu Kishwar decries the ineffectiveness of self-proclaimed feminists to address "the basic issues crucial to the well-being of the overwhelming majority of Indian women" (269). She also observes that "the word *feminism* means nothing to most Indians, except a microscopic number of highly westernized, elite people. . . . Being labelled a feminist puts you in a tight box" (273). And she rightly calls attention to the culture of intolerance that characterizes many forms of feminism.

No single methodological approach or theoretical formulation could possibly accommodate the complexities of gender justice and contemporary Asian and Asian diaspora literatures. Instead, inspired by Victor Brombert, I have respected not only the inner coherence and texture of the works I discuss (2) but also their stochasticity. Furthermore, as Brombert asserts, "eschewing a dogmatic approach and stressing diversity and variation do not preclude a search for underlying patterns and common tendencies" (1). Nor should a search for patterns and tendencies erase diversity and variation; there is no "single authentic story" about any single individual, much less any single group (Shehabuddin 277).

Given the complexity of the phenomena discussed and the importance of understanding gender inequity and gender-based violence from a range of perspectives, as demonstrated in the bibliographies at the end of each chapter, *Gender Justice* draws from many different types of sources on gender inequity and gender-based violence: creative writing, film, memoirs and journalistic nonfiction, media reports, new media, publications by NGOs and other organizations, and academic scholarship in anthropology, gender studies, history, law, literature studies, medicine, philosophy, psychology, public health, sociology, and other fields. Integrating insights from a range of sources, from statistical reports to deeply researched and heavily footnoted academic publications to lyrical and aesthetically intricate creative discourses, enables *Gender Justice* to provide nuanced insights into portrayals of lived experiences across a vast swath of the world.

Gender Justice analyzes and places in broader context 28 narratives from 13 East, South, and Southeast Asian nations and their diasporas that focus on major forms of gender inequity and gender-based violence: pervasive inequities in familial and social expectations—especially as concerns relationships, caregiving, and employment—as well as reproductive, non-partner, family, and intimate partner violence. In addition, each of this book's seven chapters introduces further creative sources, primarily in the endnotes, from the same communities, other parts of Asia and its diasporas, and beyond in the hopes of inspiring continued exploration and translation.

The 28 narratives examined closely in *Gender Justice* were published between 1970 and 2019 by writers from many backgrounds and identities who spotlight the diverse experiences of nineteenth-, twentieth-, and twenty-first-century Asian women living in Asia and women who are part of Asian diasporas outside Asia. The women depicted all defy gender stereotypes, boundaries, and expectations, yet they differ in terms of age, class, desire and ability to have children or be in a sexual or other type of relationship, ability and disability, formal and informal education, ethnicity, health status, marital status, race, religion, sexuality, socioeconomic status, and other factors. They also are subjected to a range of inequities and violent acts, and they differ notably in their understandings and pursuit of justice.

Nine of the 28 novels, short stories, memoirs, and pieces of creative nonfiction highlighted in this book were originally written in English. Given the intended audience of *Gender Justice*, the non-English-language narratives featured in the book—originally written in Bengali, Chinese, Indonesian, Japanese, Khmer, Korean, Marathi, Thai, and Vietnamese—are all available in English-language translation. The same is true of many of the other sources discussed, such as works in Malayalam, Hindi, and Urdu. Most of these translations are readily purchased through online bookstores, including in digital format. Accessibility for classroom use was a key criterion in choosing on which works to focus. While facilitating the broad engagement of readers of *Gender Justice* with the primary texts discussed, this methodology—as is true in the study of world literature more broadly—necessarily omits many crucial voices that will need to be brought to the fore in future scholarship.[16]

Moreover, because most readers of *Gender Justice* will be relying largely if not solely on English-language translations, unlike in my other publications, analyses of texts are based on published English-language versions. Discrepancies between Asian-language source texts, published English-language translations, and, where relevant, published translations in languages other than English are highlighted in the endnotes. The choice to highlight such discrepancies provided employment opportunities for graduate and undergraduate students during the COVID-19 pandemic.[17] It also draws attention to these narratives as being actively transculturated and consumed across languages as well as to some of the challenges facing readers of literature in translation, particularly readers unfamiliar with the contexts discussed and readers of translated texts where the original version is inaccessible.[18] I hope that *Gender Justice* will stimulate scholarly and classroom discussions and inspire further teaching and research on gender, justice, and Asia and its diasporas as well as the publication of a greater diversity of Asian literatures in translation in order to further decolonize studies of comparative literature, world literature, Asia, gender, and feminisms.[19]

Structure

Chapter 1, "Confronting Tyrannies of Social Norms within and beyond Families," focuses on novels from South Korea, Japan, and Vietnam that advocate for gender justice by eliminating destructive gender norms in the home and in society. Chapter 2, "Struggling for Equity in Male-Dominated Professions," turns attention to writings from Japan, Pakistan, and Singapore that call for better enabling women to survive and even thrive in professions conventionally dominated by men that are embedded in societies with rigid gender expectations. Chapter 3, "Humanizing Migrant Reproductive Workers," engages with fiction from Cambodia, China, Indonesia, and Singapore that calls for justice for migrant sex workers, domestic workers, and caregivers. Chapter 4, "Capitulating to and Fighting against Reproductive Violence," spotlights narratives that take place in Japan, China, and India that discuss struggles for gender justice in the context of reproductive violence in Asia and its diasporas. In chapter 5, "Prosecuting Cultures of Shame, Silence, Rape, and Murder," attention turns to narratives that take place in Japan, the Philippines, South Korea, India, and their diasporas that engage with the pursuit of justice for women who have been raped, murdered, or both. For its part, chapter 6, "Perpetuating and Interrupting Cycles of Family Violence," highlights writings on intergenerational violence in Bangladesh, India, and China that reveal the devastating consequences of family violence, especially child and elder abuse. Chapter 7, "Intersecting Responsibilities for Intimate Partner Violence," focuses on narratives situated in Bangladesh, India, Korea, Taiwan, and Thailand that condemn the complicity of family, friends, neighbors, health professionals, and bystanders in perpetuating intimate partner violence and obstructing gender justice. As emphasized throughout, despite the brutality of their experiences, it is important that we not essentialize the women living in Asia and its diasporas that are portrayed in these narratives, seeing them only as victims of oppression. Instead, we must also recognize these women's agency, resistance, and resilience, their ability to hold societies accountable and shape and reshape tradition in pursuit of justice, broadly conceived, an idea inspired by Leena N. Her (24) and Shirley Hune (11).

The diverse women who are the focus of the narratives analyzed in this book hail from across East, South, and Southeast Asia and multiple Asian diasporas. But there are many more voices that need to be heard. In a book of necessarily limited length written for a broad audience, difficult choices had to be made, and there are lacunae that future scholarship will need to fill. The writers whose works are discussed here grapple with a broad range of contemporary gender-related struggles from numerous perspectives. Yet the number and types of challenges addressed in this book are also inescapably constrained, and there are many more aspects to gender justice that deserve our attention and that will need to be the focus of future scholarly endeavors by experts in a variety of fields. This includes not only narratives centering on gender justice for LGBTQIA+ individuals but also narratives that explore the intersections of gender- and race-based violence in Asian diasporic communities within and far beyond North America amid the COVID-19 pandemic and narratives focused on intersections of climate and gender justice, vital topics that deserve their own volumes.

Gender Justice is especially timely given the disproportionate burdens of care and economic impacts on women during the COVID-19 pandemic in addition to the increasing violence against women in Asia and globally—a "shadow pandemic" according to UN Women ("Facts"). This is by no means to suggest that all women have experienced COVID-19 in similar ways. As has been widely discussed, race, ethnicity, class, education, and other factors have as always made a tremendous difference, with those who are already vulnerable experiencing even greater abuse. Rather, it is to acknowledge the significant gender disparities that persist even within the most privileged families and communities. The pandemic's full impact on gender justice in Asia and around the world will not be known until later in the 2020s at the earliest. But Joni Seager's 2018 observations are even more pertinent today: gains in women's empowerment "are fragile, reversible, and always under pressures. . . . [A] remarkable number of governments . . . seem committed to turning back advances in women's autonomy" (8). While remaining informed about current and ever-evolving crises and the implications for what lies ahead, we cannot fully comprehend either the present or the future without grappling with the past.

Literatures from East, South, and Southeast Asia and their diasporas provide particularly important windows into gender inequity and gender-based violence across time, windows without which gender justice will remain an even more elusive goal. The diverse Asian and Asian diasporic perspectives analyzed in this book add context and depth to our learning, teaching, and research on gender, feminisms, comparative literature, and world literature as well as on Asia and its diasporas across many disciplines.

NOTES

1. The quotation is from Merrill's translation of Baisantry's Hindi version of "Justice" (Merrill; Pawar, "Nyay"). As in Deo's translation (Pawar, "Justice" 36, 37), the Hindi term *balātkar* generally is translated as "rape," although it can refer to any coercive act. Dalits remain one of India's most oppressed communities, and Dalit women are especially vulnerable to violence (Singh 12). Merrill discusses different versions of Pawar's story "Justice."

2. In the interview, Pawar describes learning about a pregnant widow who as punishment for not revealing the father of her child "had to bend and all the women would go behind her and kick her. . . . Her foetus was aborted. . . . They took justice into their own hands and beat this woman till she bled" (qtd. in Lakshmi 14). Pawar's memoir *The Weave of My Life* (*Aaydaan*, 2008) describes a similar scenario (131).

3. The focus on agency, resistance, and resilience is inspired by Hune (11). Thank you to Seton Uhlhorn for highlighting for me the importance of the reference to court proceedings, which are denied to Paru as a rural uneducated woman.

4. East Asia generally is understood as China, Japan, North and South Korea, Mongolia, and Taiwan; Southeast Asia as Brunei, Cambodia, Indonesia, Lao PDR, Malaysia, Myanmar, the Philippines, Singapore, Thailand, Timor-Leste, and Vietnam; and South Asia as Afghanistan, Bangladesh, Bhutan, India, the Maldives, Nepal, Pakistan, and Sri Lanka. East, South, and Southeast Asia are the most populous regions of the Asian continent, with 1.66 billion, 1.94 billion, and 676 million people, respectively. In contrast, West Asia (the Middle East) has 300 million, Central Asia (five former Soviet republics) 74 million, and North Asia (Siberia) 33 million people.

5. Eder provides a medical history of gender.

6. I am thankful to Durba Mitra for clarifying for me the changing uses of the term *gender justice*.

7. As of November 2023, Nepal and Taiwan are the only Asian nations to have legalized same-sex marriage. Same-sex relationships are not recognized in much of Asia and are criminalized in Afghanistan, Bangladesh, Brunei,

Malaysia, the Maldives, Myanmar, Pakistan, and Sri Lanka. A few nations recognize third genders.

8. Scholarship on narratives grounded in LGBTQIA+ experiences in Asia and its diasporas is increasing rapidly, although it generally remains focused on the discourse of a single nation or region. See, for instance, Chiang; Harada; Li; Kang; McLelland et al.; Perry; and scholarship such as Banerjee's "Identity at the Margins" on Deepa Mehta's highly controversial Indian Canadian film *Fire* (1996).

9. See Enloe, *Bananas* 24 and *Big Push* 21. See also Romito 1–3; Westmarland 1. The term *gender-based violence* is preferred to the heteronormative *male violence against women*, since the former includes violence committed by women, male-on-male violence, and violence perpetrated against the LGBTQIA+ community (Graaff 1–2, 8).

10. The Asian Pacific Institute on Gender-Based Violence lists many of these categories ("Lifetime Spiral"). See also Djamba and Kimuna's replication of the World Bank's "ecological model of gender-based violence" (xiv–xv). These categories are also relevant outside Asia: for instance, 80% of native Alaskan women are subjected to domestic violence, and as many as half are raped, but criminal charges rarely are brought against their abusers (Butcher 109).

11. Although Jaggar focuses on domestic work and sex work, her findings are illuminating well beyond these already expansive topics.

12. This wording is inspired by El Guabli's depiction of loss as generative and transformative (18) and Her's discussion of the Hmong American writer Burlee Vang's "Mrs. Saichue" (24–25).

13. An excellent example is the impact of the Korean writer Gong Ji-young's novel *Togani* (*The Crucible*, 2009) and its 2011 film adaptation, which exposed child sexual abuse at a state-run institution, on improving legal protections for individuals under state care.

14. Much has been written on literature by and about Asian women, but most of this scholarship focuses on the literature of a particular Asian nation or sometimes region (i.e., East, South, or Southeast Asia rather than Asia more broadly).

15. See also Jain on diverse feminisms, especially in relation to India (43–61); Mani on feminisms and Indian literature; and Levenstein on the limitations of feminism in the United States.

16. An excellent example of an emerging scholar working in this field is Amrita DasGupta, a PhD candidate at SOAS University of London whose research focuses on transnational migration, sex work, and climate crisis in the Sundarbans in South Asia and analyzes a range of cultural productions, including letters, painting, and dance (DasGupta).

17. I am grateful to students at Harvard University for identifying and analyzing these discrepancies and for providing literal translations, even from the Asian languages with which I regularly engage: Fangdai Chen (Chinese); Min Ji Choi

(Korean); Aniket De (Bengali); Alexandria Ho (Vietnamese); Cookie Kunarattanapruek (Thai); Adi Kusnodi (Indonesian); Akhil Thomas (Malayalam); Seton Uhlhorn (Hindi, Urdu); Bota Ussen (Japanese, with the exception of Murata Sayaka's *Convenience Store Woman* and Watanabe Jun'ichi's *Beyond the Blossoming Fields*).

18. Most texts were accessed in their original, Asian-language version. I identify those texts where the original could not be found.

19. I am inspired here, among other entities, by the UK-based nonprofit Tilted Axis Press, which aims to tilt "the axis of world literature from the center to the margins" by translating books with radical visions, such as those that "challenge the homogeneity demanded by white feminism," like the Nepali poet Sulochana Manandhar's 2014 collection *Night* (Ghimire). For more on "white feminism," see Zakaria.

WORKS CITED

Banerjee, Bidisha. "Identity at the Margins: Queer Diasporic Film and the Exploration of Same-Sex Desire in Deepa Mehta's *Fire*." *Studies in South Asian Film and Media*, vol. 2, no. 1, 2010, pp. 19–39.

Brinton, Mary. Personal communication with the author. 31 Jan. 2022.

Brodsky, Alexandra. *Sexual Justice*. Henry Holt, 2021.

Brombert, Victor. *In Praise of Antiheroes: Figures and Themes in Modern European Literature*. U of Chicago P, 1999.

Butcher, Amy. *Mothertrucker: Finding Joy on the Loneliest Road in America*. Little A, 2021.

Chiang, Howard, editor. *Queer Taiwanese Literature*. Cambria Press, 2021.

Counts, Laura. "Despite Ideals, People Don't Really Like Reducing Inequality, Study Finds." *Berkeley Haas*, 6 May 2022, newsroom.haas.berkeley.edu/research/study-shows-why-advantaged-people-resist-efforts-to-boost-equality.

DasGupta, Amrita. Personal communication with the author. 23 Feb. 2023.

Djamba, Yanyi K., and Sitawa R. Kimuna. Introduction. *Gender-Based Violence: Perspectives from Africa, the Middle East, and India*, edited by Djamba and Kimuna, Springer, 2015, pp. xi–xix.

Eder, Sandra. *How the Clinic Made Gender: The Medical History of a Transformative Idea*. U of Chicago P, 2022.

El Guabli, Brahim. *Moroccan Other-Archives: History and Citizenship after State Violence*. Fordham UP, 2023.

Enloe, Cynthia. *Bananas, Beaches, and Bases: Making Feminist Sense of International Politics*. U of California P, 2014.

———. *The Big Push: Exposing and Challenging the Persistence of Patriarchy*. U of California P, 2017.

"Facts and Figures: Ending Violence against Women." *UN Women*, Feb. 2022, www.unwomen.org/en/what-we-do/ending-violence-against-women/facts-and-figures.

García-Moreno, Claudia, and Anita Riecher-Rössler, editors. *Violence against Women and Mental Health*. Karger, 2013.

"Gender-Based Violence (Violence against Women and Girls)." *The World Bank*, 25 Sept. 2019, www.worldbank.org/en/topic/socialsustainability/brief/violence-against-women-and-girls.

"Gender Justice (Pillars of Justice)." *San Diego Pride*, 2010–23, sdpride.org/genderjustice/.

Ghimire, Sandesh. "In Search of Home—Reading Nepali Literature in Translation." *The Record*, 23 June 2019, www.recordnepal.com/in-search-of-home-reading-nepali-literature-in-translation.

Global Gender Gap Report 2023. World Economic Forum, 2023, www3.weforum.org/docs/WEF_GGGR_2023.pdf.

Gong Ji-young. *Togani*. Translated by Bruce and Ju-Chan Fulton, U of Hawai'i P, 2023.

Graaff, Karen. "The Implications of a Narrow Understanding of Gender-Based Violence." *Feminist Encounters: A Journal of Critical Studies in Culture and Politics*, vol. 5, no. 1, 5 Mar. 2021, pp. 1–12.

Harada, Kazue, editor. *Sexuality, Maternity, and (Re)Productive Futures: Women's Speculative Fiction in Contemporary Japan*. Brill, 2022.

Her, Leena N. "Rewriting Hmong Women in Western Texts." Vang et al., *Claiming*, pp. 3–27.

Hill, Anita. *Believing: Our Thirty-Year Journey to End Gender Violence*. Viking, 2021.

Homan, Patricia. "Structural Sexism and Health in the United States: A New Perspective on Health Inequality and the Gender System." *American Sociological Review*, vol. 84, no. 3, June 2019, pp. 486–516.

Hune, Shirley. "Our Histories." Introduction. *Our Voices, Our Histories: Asian American and Pacific Islander Women*, edited by Hune and Gail M. Nomura, New York UP, 2020, pp. 8–16.

Jaggar, Alison M. "Transnational Cycles of Gendered Vulnerability: A Prologue to a Theory of Global Gender Justice." *Gender and Global Justice*, edited by Jaggar, Polity Press, 2014, pp. 18–39.

Jain, Devaki. *The Journey of a Southern Feminist*. Sage Publications, 2018.

Kang, Wenqing. "Recent Scholarship on Queer East Asia: History and Present." *Harvard Journal of Asiatic Studies*, vol. 81, nos. 1–2, 2021, pp. 303–19.

Kishwar, Madhu. *Off the Beaten Track: Rethinking Gender Justice for Indian Women*. Oxford UP, 1999.

Knaul, Felicia Marie, et al. "Countering the Pandemic of Gender-Based Violence and Maltreatment of Young People: *The Lancet* Commission." *The Lancet*, vol. 395, 11 Jan. 2020, pp. 98–99.

Lakshmi, C. S. *Amhihi Ithihas Ghadawala: Urmila Pawar and the Making of History*. Sound and Picture Archives for Research on Women, 1998.

Levenstein, Lisa. *They Didn't See Us Coming: The Hidden History of Feminism in the Nineties*. Basic Books, 2020.

"Lifetime Spiral of Gender Violence." *Asian Pacific Institute on Gender-Based Violence*, 2010–22, www.api-gbv.org/resources/lifetime-spiral-gender-violence/.

Li Kotomi. *Solo Dance*. Translated by Arthur Reiji Morris, World Editions, 2022.

Mani, Preetha. "Feminine Desire Is Human Desire: Women Writing Feminism in Postindependence India." *Comparative Studies of South Asia, Africa, and the Middle East*, vol. 36, no. 1, May 2016, pp. 21–41.

Mao, Douglas. *Inventions of Nemesis: Utopia, Indignation, and Justice*. Princeton UP, 2020.

McLelland, Mark, et al. *Queer Voices from Japan: First-Person Narratives from Japan's Sexual Minorities*. Lexington Books, 2007.

Merrill, Christi. "'Justice' in Translation." *South Asia: Journal of South Asian Studies*, vol. 43, no. 5, Sept. 2020, pp. 970–87.

Mohanty, Chandra Talpade. "Under Western Eyes: Feminist Scholarship and Colonial Discourses." *Boundary 2*, vol. 12, no. 3 / vol. 13, no. 1, spring-autumn 1984, pp. 333–58.

Nguyen, Viet Thanh. Introduction. *The Displaced: Refugee Writers on Refugee Lives*, edited by Nguyen, Abrams Press, 2018, pp. 11–22.

Nordell, Jessica. *The End of Bias: A Beginning*. Henry Holt, 2021.

Pawar, Urmila. *Aaydaan*. Stree, 2008.

———. "Justice (Nyay)." *Motherwit*, by Pawar, translated by Veena Deo, Zubaan, 2013, pp. 24–39.

———. "Nyay." Translated by Kausalya Baisantry. *Hans*, vol. 5, no. 7, Feb. 1991, pp. 57–60.

———. *The Weave of My Life: A Dalit Woman's Memoirs*. Translated by Maya Pandit, Columbia UP, 2009.

Perry, Samuel, editor and translator. *A Century of Queer Korean Fiction*. Modern Language Association of America, 2023.

Romito, Patrizia. *A Deafening Silence: Hidden Violence against Women and Children*. Policy Press, 2008.

Rose, Jacqueline. *On Violence and On Violence against Women*. Farrar, Straus and Giroux, 2021.

Scott, Linda. *The Double X Economy: The Epic Potential of Women's Empowerment*. Farrar, Straus and Giroux, 2020.

Seager, Joni. *The Women's Atlas*. Penguin Books, 2018.

Shehabuddin, Elora. *Sisters in the Mirror: A History of Muslim Women and the Global Politics of Feminism*. U of California P, 2021.

Singh, Roja. *Spotted Goddesses: Dalit Women's Agency-Narratives on Caste and Gender Violence*. Lit Verlag, 2018.

Stetz, Margaret D. "Wartime Sexual Violence against Women: A Feminist Response." *Legacies of the Comfort Women of World War II*, edited by Stetz and Bonnie B. C. Oh, Routledge, 2001, pp. 91–100.

Togani. Directed by Hwang Dong-hyuk, Samgeori Pictures, 2011.

Vang, Chia Youyee, et al., editors. *Claiming Place: On the Agency of Hmong Women*. U of Minnesota P, 2016.

———. "Hmong Women, Gender, and Power." Introduction. Vang et al., *Claiming*, pp. vii–xxviii.

"Violence against Women." *World Health Organization*, 9 Mar. 2021, www.who.int/news-room/fact-sheets/detail/violence-against-women.

Watts, Charlotte, and Cathy Zimmerman. "Violence against Women: Global Scope and Magnitude." *The Lancet*, vol. 359, 6 Apr. 2002, pp. 1232–37.

Westmarland, Nicole. *Violence against Women: Criminological Perspectives on Men's Violence*. Routledge, 2015.

"What Is Gender Justice?" *Third Wave Fund*, www.thirdwavefund.org/gender-justice. Accessed 14 Dec. 2023.

Williams, Huw, and Carl Death. *Global Justice: The Basics*. Routledge, 2017.

Zakaria, Rafia. *Against White Feminism: Notes on Disruption*. W. W. Norton, 2021.

1. Confronting Tyrannies of Social Norms within and beyond Families

State ideologies, policies, and resource allocation regarding family vary widely across Asia, yet they mostly presume heterosexual marriage followed by procreation between a cisgender man and a cisgender woman. Mie Hiramoto and Cherise Shi Ling Teo's observations about injustices in Singapore apply generally across much of the region: "By prescribing members of an ideal family and their duties . . . the state normalizes the ideal family image. Simultaneously, it also normalizes the marginalization of a wide range of individuals who do not fit the norms. Homosexuals, singles, single parents, childless couples, divorcees, widowers and widows, are given reasons to be socially queered by society" (232). Moreover, being part of an "ideal family" is no guarantee of fulfillment, safety, security, or justice, either at home or in society. Because most nations are permeated by patriarchy and because patriarchal ideals suffuse informal and formal education, the heteronormative family is highly gendered: husbands generally are expected to be breadwinners, and wives generally are expected to do most of the child-rearing and housework (Enloe 16; Seager 11). In many communities, societies, and nations, husbands wield far more power and are granted far more liberties than their wives, who by the time they marry already have had to navigate years of gender oppression. This is true regardless of the wife's formal education, which increasingly is on par with if not greater than that of her husband, and regardless of whether she participates in the waged workforce, the demands of her career, and other responsibilities outside the home.[1] For many individuals, these expectations can be stifling, at the very least, if not detrimental or destructive to their economic, social, emotional, mental, and physical well-being. Particularly vulnerable are women who already are marginalized because of age, class, disability, education, ethnicity, geographic location (urban vs. rural), language, migration or refugee status, race, religion, sexuality, socioeconomic status, and related factors ("Gender").

This chapter focuses on three contemporary Asian novels that feature women who confront unjust social norms that reinforce heteronormative images of the ideal family: *Kim Jiyoung, Born 1982* (*82-nyŏnsaeng Kim Chiyŏng*, 82년생 김지영, 2016), by the South Korean writer Cho Namjoo (Cho Namju, 1978–); *Convenience Store Woman* (*Konbini ningen*, コンビニ人間, lit. *Convenience Store Human*, 2016), by the Japanese writer Murata Sayaka (1979–); and *An Insignificant Family* (*Gia đình bé mọn*, 2005), by the Vietnamese writer Dạ Ngân (1952–). These narratives feature three very different types of women whose stories are rarely told—a mid-30s college-educated upper-middle-class South Korean wife subjected to gender oppression from early childhood who has a mental breakdown after leaving a fulfilling career to become a stay-at-home mother; a mid-30s college-educated working-class Japanese convenience store clerk who refuses marriage, children, and regular employment, preferring instead to devote her life and her body to her work despite the censure of family and friends; and an impoverished Vietnamese writer in her mid-50s who came of age during Vietnam's gruesome civil war and, despite being disowned by her family, divorced her husband, with whom she had two children, to pursue more fulfilling yet no less fraught relationships. At the same time, as is true of many writings from across Asia and globally, *Kim Jiyoung*, *Convenience Store Woman*, and *An Insignificant Family* all provide deeper insight into how conventional social norms regarding family relentlessly impinge on health and well-being. Cho's, Murata's, and Dạ Ngân's novels advocate for increasing gender justice by expanding if not scrapping entirely conceptions of what is appropriate and normal.

Overwhelmed by Exploitative Social Norms: Cho Namjoo's *Kim Jiyoung, Born 1982* (2016)

More than 76% of South Korean women between the ages of 25 and 34 have attained a tertiary educational qualification, the highest proportion among Organization for Economic Cooperation and Development (OECD) and partner nations, and a higher proportion than South Korean men ("Korea"). Yet long-standing beliefs that men make better employees and deserve more for their labor, and that housework and childcare are primarily women's responsibilities, mean that South Korean women who enter the workforce frequently face tremendous disparities. This is the case both on the job and at home, giving women little relief from the gender-based discrimination, oppression, and violence to which they have been subjected from early childhood by both their families and South Korean society. Moreover, South Korea has one of the world's most quickly aging societies, making low-paid and unpaid eldercare another significant and disproportionate burden on South Korean women (Jayoung Yoon, "Counting"; Seok), as is true in so much of the world, including China, the setting of Zhou Daxin's *Longevity Park* (*Tianhei de hen man*, 天黑的很慢, lit. *Getting Dark/Old Slowly*, 2018), analyzed in chapter 3.[2]

In general, just as they can pursue tertiary education in higher numbers than earlier generations, South Korean women today have more employment opportunities than did their mothers and grandmothers. But the barriers to full economic participation remain daunting. The World Economic Forum ranks South Korea a low 105 of 146 nations in its 2023 *Global Gender Gap Report* and 104 of 146 in economic participation and opportunity, with 55% of South Korean women participating in the paid workforce compared with 73.66% of men (*Global Gender Gap Report 2023* 11, 17, 225).[3] Women in South Korea occupy just 14.6% of senior positions and just 8.7% of board seats (Choe; *Global Gender Gap Report 2023* 225–26). Furthermore, South Korea has by far the largest gender wage gap in the OECD, at 31.06% (*Global Gender Gap Report 2023* 226).[4] Social expectations and a dearth of childcare options result in many female employees leaving the paid workforce after becoming pregnant or giving birth, if not after getting married (Cho, *Kim Jiyoung* 133). Once their children attend day care, women struggle to secure similarly remunerative yet more flexible employment (J. Lee 214, 221).[5]

Cho's highly controversial and bestselling *Kim Jiyoung, Born 1982*, which has been widely translated in Asia and globally, tells the story of one of these women, the "exceptionally average" Kim Jiyoung: "Jiyoung" was the most popular female first name and "Kim" the most common family name in 1980s South Korea (Alter; Hoyong Jung 211). This short novel opens with a brief chapter titled "Autumn, 2015," which introduces Jiyoung as a 33-year-old woman who married Jung Daehyun in 2012, resigned from her job shortly before giving birth in the summer of 2014, spent a year as sole caregiver for her daughter Jung Jiwon, and developed a serious mental health condition not long after enrolling Jiwon in half-day childcare. The third-person narrator then flashes back with one chapter each on Jiyoung's childhood (1982–94), adolescence (1995–2000), early adulthood (2001–11), and marriage (2012–15), depicting every stage as suffused with gender injustice—in the home (both natal and marital), at school, in the workplace, and in society more broadly. In the novel's final chapter, "2016," the narrator discloses that he is Jiyoung's psychiatrist.

As in *One Left* (*Han myŏng*, 한명, lit. *One Person*, 2016), by Cho's fellow South Korean writer Kim Soom (Kim Sum, 1974–), discussed in chapter 5, the narrator of *Kim Jiyoung* cites numerous external sources, both in the body of the text and in footnotes. These news reports, government publications, official statistics, scholarly articles, and other studies explicitly connect Jiyoung's experiences with gender oppression to the experiences of the majority of middle-class South Korean women. The narrator also addresses aspects of Jiyoung's and many other women's experiences that are deliberately elided from both scholarly and public discourse and even from conversations among friends. The focus on Jiyoung enables *Kim Jiyoung*, as is true of most narratives analyzed in *Gender Justice*, to humanize individuals experiencing gender inequity and gender-based violence, countering the dehumanization or at least depersonalization of scholarly and media accounts, and to draw attention to the nuances of their suffering and their agency. At the same time, the literary strategy of having Jiyoung's psychiatrist tell her story rather than an anonymous third-person narrator, much less Jiyoung herself, points to Jiyoung's continued silencing. This aesthetic choice, and especially the narrator's extensive use of free indirect speech rather than direct quotations or even indirect discourse, draws attention to just how frequently women are denied opportunities to tell their own stories. More specifically, it highlights how patients' stories continue to be filtered through their (male) physicians, who, as is the case in *Kim Jiyoung*, not only are unsure how to diagnose their patients but also are far from fully appreciating the injustice of their experiences, much less using their power to instigate needed structural change.

Kim Jiyoung was read as "a cultural call to arms" (Alter), both celebrated and condemned for its dry narration and minimalist yet stark exposure, in the words of Cho, of "the everyday and common but nonetheless undeserved experience of women around me, about the despair, exhaustion and fear that we feel for no reason other than that we're women" (qtd. in Alter). Translating the experiences of the women around her into a readily consumable novel—chronological, straightforward language, relatable characters—that addresses taboo topics that many experience but cannot discuss (e.g., the difficulties of childbirth and child-rearing, including postpartum depression; the complicity of family in exacerbating gender injustice; impacts of gender oppression on mental health and social factors exacerbating mental illness) has enabled Cho both to reach much wider audiences than the sources she cites and to bring attention to these sources and similar studies.

The narrator of *Kim Jiyoung* speaks of violence against females as beginning before birth, with sex-selective abortions of third children common in South Korea in the 1980s and 1990s. Jiyoung's family is no exception, her mother having aborted a female fetus several years before giving birth to Jiyoung's younger brother. Jiyoung's earliest memories are of her grandmother valuing her toddler brother more than Jiyoung and her older sister, and of her younger brother receiving the best of everything. In elementary school, among other examples of mistreatment, Jiyoung was verbally harassed and physically attacked by her male deskmate. Yet when she asked to be assigned another partner, her teacher attempted to convince her that boys are "meaner to the girls they like" and that she should become friends with her tormentor (Cho, *Kim Jiyoung* 31). Jiyoung's older sister told her to "ignore him," given that boys are "immature," while her mother "chided Jiyoung for crying and complaining over a classmate who was just messing around because he wanted to play" (28).

With adolescence and high school come new challenges, as young women enter a world "filled with perverts" and stow away "repulsive, frightening experiences with males deep in their hearts without even realizing it" (Cho, *Kim Jiyoung* 51–52). They also are blamed for their own harassment: Jiyoung's father, for instance, berates her for being stalked by a male classmate while returning from cram school late one night. As the narrator notes, Jiyoung had grown up "being told to be cautious. . . . That it's your job to avoid dangerous places, times of day and people. It's your fault for not noticing and not avoiding" (56). Traumatized, Jiyoung "quit the cram school. . . . She stopped smiling at people. . . . She was afraid of all men, and she screamed sometimes when she ran into her younger brother in the stairwell" (56–57). Jiyoung's one comfort after the stalking incident came from the reassurance of the woman whose quick thinking had foiled her attacker. When Jiyoung and the woman reconnected, she shared with Jiyoung that it was not her fault, that there "were far too many crazy men in the world" and that "the problem was with them, not with the women" (56). With Jiyoung crying and unable to respond, the woman adds, "There's far more great guys out there" (57). The sentences "*Not my fault. There's far more great guys out there*" reverberate within Jiyoung, the narrator noting that without them Jiyoung "would have lived in fear for even longer" (57). At the same time, the fact that "great guys" outnumber "crazy men" does little to challenge the broader structures of systemic oppression that permeate Jiyoung's life and the lives of so many women of her generation.[6]

To be sure, despite the fact that girls face gender-based discrimination, oppression, and violence throughout their youth, "gone were the days when parents thought girls didn't have to get good grades or receive the same education as boys. . . . This was a time of widespread social support for women's ambitions" (Cho, *Kim Jiyoung* 60). After all, the narrator points out, in 1999, the South Korean government introduced legislation against gender discrimination, and in 2001 it formed the Ministry of Gender Equality and Family (Yŏsŏng kajokbu; lit. Ministry of Women and Family). Having had to give up her own dream of becoming a teacher to finance her brothers' education, Jiyoung's mother was determined that her daughters face no such burden, and she reassured Jiyoung that the family would cover her university expenses.[7]

Yet, the narrator acknowledges, in one of his many generalizations about Jiyoung's experiences, "[i]n certain pivotal moments in women's lives, the 'woman' stigma reared its head to obscure their vision, stay their hands, and hold them back" (Cho, *Kim Jiyoung* 60). One such moment is the transition from college to the workforce. With graduation on the horizon, Jiyoung's friend Hyejin warned her about the barriers she would face on the job market. The narrator cites a newspaper article that reported that in 2005, the year Jiyoung graduated from college, "only 29.6 percent of new employees at 100 companies were women" (82–83). Another survey revealed that 88% of companies "would rather hire male to female candidates with equivalent qualifications," and none "would hire women over men" (83). As Hyejin described, "The process was kept so carefully under the radar that it was difficult to ascertain exactly who was recommended to which company for what reason, and if the college recommended only male students or if the company asked specifically for men" (83).

Jiyoung struggled even to land an interview. And then, at her first, she was asked what she would do if a client began fondling her. She responded calmly that she "would find a natural way to leave the room" but later, home alone, she furiously shouted at the mirror, "I would break his fucking arm! . . . Your question is sexual harassment!" (Cho, *Kim Jiyoung* 89, 90). Subsequent job interviews were no better: potential employers commented on Jiyoung's physical appearance, stared at her lecherously, and touched her gratuitously. Once employed at a marketing agency, Jiyoung immediately noticed the gender divide, with higher positions held disproportionately by men, and she discovered that men in her company were paid more from the outset. Both phenomena contribute, the narrator explains, to

South Korea's significant wage gap, the largest among OECD nations (112). Moreover, as Jiyoung learned from her former colleague Hyesu, the summer after Jiyoung left the agency, a security guard installed a camera in the restroom and uploaded pictures to a pornography website; a male section manager at their agency discovered the compromising pictures and shared them with male colleagues. The director of the agency would not even apologize to the women, concerned that so doing would both ruin the company's reputation and impair the abusers' futures. Female employees paradoxically recognized that while "offenders were in fear of losing a small part of their privilege, the victims were running the risk of losing everything" (145). Not surprisingly, the toll on their mental health was significant. As Hyesu reports, "Most women in the office are on meds or getting therapy. Jungeun overdosed on sleeping pills and had to get her stomach pumped" (143).

The stigma attached to being a woman rears its head just as aggressively in marriage. Even after South Korea abolished its *hoju* system, the family registration protocol where all family members were registered under the patriarch, very few families chose to register their children under the mother's name. As Jiyoung recognized, in one of her many direct condemnations of oppressive social structures, "The world had changed a great deal, but the little rules, contracts, and customs had not, which meant the world hadn't *actually* changed at all" (Cho, *Kim Jiyoung* 119). This is particularly true regarding childcare. With the pregnant Jiyoung's due date drawing near, she and her husband Daehyun "concluded that one of them had to be a stay-at-home parent, and that one person, of course, was Jiyoung" (130). Not only was Daehyun's salary higher and his position more stable, "it was more common for husbands to work and wives to raise the children and run the home" (130). Again contextualizing Jiyoung's experiences, the narrator is quick to observe that in 2014, around the time Jiyoung resigned from her job, "one in five married women in [South] Korea quit their job because of marriage, pregnancy, childbirth and childcare" (133).

After giving birth to her daughter, Jiyoung became aware of additional injustices faced by women. She heard belatedly from her mother how difficult it was to raise three children without any assistance from her husband, Jiyoung's father. Jiyoung wondered why no one, even new mothers, speaks candidly about motherhood, instead depicting babies as immutably "pretty and cute" and mothers as unwaveringly "beautiful and noble" (Cho, *Kim Jiyoung* 138).[8] Moreover, Jiyoung recognized that "her career potential and areas of interest were being limited just because she had a baby" (152). Mothers are also ridiculed simply for taking a few minutes for themselves: one afternoon, with her daughter asleep in her stroller, Jiyoung was enjoying a cup of cheap coffee from a new café when she heard a nearby group of office workers calling her a "mom-roach" ("mamch'ung"; 맘충) and accusing her of "bumming around" (Cho, *Kim Jiyoung* 153; Cho, *82-nyŏnsaeng* 164).[9] This seems to have been the last straw. That night she opened up to her husband: "I suffered deathly pain having our child. My routine, my career, my dreams, my entire life, my self—I gave it all up to raise our child. And I've become vermin. What do I do now?" (154). Daehyun attempted to comfort her, but he could not appreciate the depth of her despair, and soon after Jiyoung had a mental breakdown.

In the novel's final chapter, Jiyoung's psychiatrist, after revealing that he is the narrator of the preceding chapters, comments briefly on his patient and then speaks of the struggles of his own wife, a former tenured professor of ophthalmology who gave up her career to care for their son after he began acting out and one of his teachers "prescribed 'stay-at-home mommy'" (Cho, *Kim Jiyoung* 159). The narrator's wife, once a math prodigy who in medical school was a more accomplished student than the narrator, now buries herself in elementary school math workbooks. The narrator also speaks of the departure of Suyeon, a therapist in his medical practice who is a "great employee": not only is she popular with patients, she also has "a neat and snappy way of dressing, and a quick wit and charm." Just as important to the narrator, "she even remembers how I take my coffee—which coffee shop, how many shots of espresso—and brings it in on the way to work" (162).

Kim Jiyoung highlights how despite their university degrees and professional accomplishments, when in the office, South Korean women are still judged on their appearance and are still responsible for running errands. And they are still expected to sacrifice everything for their children; Suyeon has a high-risk pregnancy and has decided to "'temporarily' give up her job" (Cho, *Kim Jiyoung* 162). So, the narrator concludes *Kim Jiyoung*, "[e]ven the best female employees can cause many problems if they don't have the childcare issue taken care of. I'll have to make sure her replacement is unmarried" (163). Oppressive gender expectations and injustices persist. Women do have more professional opportunities than in the past (i.e., the narrator-psychiatrist is not averse to hiring female therapists per se). But rather than address the need for more comprehensive maternity leave and childcare, including having fathers shoulder greater responsibility, Jiyoung's psychiatrist resolves to hire only single women.[10] The experiences of his wife, his patient Jiyoung, and his coworker have "enlightened" this psychiatrist "as to what it means to live as a woman, especially as a mother, in [South] Korea" (157). But far from defying gender norms and pushing for justice, making it possible for women to succeed both at home and in the paid workforce, at least in his own office, he instead resolves to further reinforce gender disparities (157).

The Gangnam Station incident—the murder, on 17 May 2016, of a woman in her 20s near Seoul's Gangnam subway station by a man in his 30s who was angry at having been "ignored by women" (J. Kim 38)—predated *Kim Jiyoung* by five months. Although the authorities initially labeled the Gangnam incident a "random killing" (*mutjima sarin*) and ascribed the murder to the perpetrator's mental illness, activists demanded that it be called a femicide (38). Online and off-line, through everything from thousands of Post-it notes stuck to Gangnam Station's Exit 10 to gatherings across Seoul, activists protested violence against women. They likewise decried the "enormous gap between the dominant rhetoric of gender equality . . . and the reality of life as a woman in South Korea" (55). As Jinsook Kim has argued, this activism, which connected "everyday discrimination" with "more extreme forms of misogynistic violence" (40), led to "the collective articulation of feminist voices and practices challenging misogyny in South Korea" (55).

Challenges to misogyny were further catalyzed by Cho's *Kim Jiyoung*, which quickly rose to the forefront of South Korea's "ever-heated debate on gender politics" (C. Lee), provided impetus for South Korea's Me Too movement, and resonated with Japanese women (Hawon Jung, *Flowers* 136), even as Korea's Me Too movement has been quite distinct from Japan's, discussed further in chapter 5.[11] *Kim Jiyoung* was likewise popular among male political leaders, and copies were gifted to the South Korean president Moon Jae-in by a fellow politician as well as to the entire National Assembly by a member who urged his colleagues to create a world "where Kim Jiyoungs born in 1992 don't have to be in despair" (C. Lee). But Cho and her novel also faced significant backlash: former male fans burned photos and albums of the K-pop star Irene (Bae Joo-hyun) after she spoke about reading the book, and they bullied other female celebrities who shared how the novel resonated with their own experiences (Sebastian).[12] The attack on *Kim Jiyoung* is part of South Korea's intensifying anti-feminist backlash, which has "vilified prominent women" and their supporters and called for the extermination of all feminists (Choe). Protestors have also condemned quotas for women and called for abolishing South Korea's Ministry of Gender

Equality and Family, arguing that South Korean men, not women, are the true victims of gender discrimination.[13] Gender issues likewise played a significant role in the March 2022 presidential election, with Yoon Suk Yeol inching ahead in part because of his strong anti-feminist rhetoric. To be sure, Kim Jiyoungs born in 2022 are unlikely to be as exploited as those born in 1982, but the final lines of *Kim Jiyoung* ring ominously, giving a very different sense of the future from the novel's 2019 film adaptation. In the latter, not only does Jiyoung have a powerful voice that disrupts the chronological narrative with flashbacks, and not only does she strike back at the man who calls her a "mom-roach."[14] The film, which depicts Jiyoung's husband as more actively engaged in childcare, also ends with Jiyoung sitting down to write her own story, *Kim Jiyoung, Born 1982*.

Evading Prescriptive Social Norms: Murata Sayaka's *Convenience Store Woman* (2016)

Published the same year as Cho's *Kim Jiyoung*, the Japanese writer Murata Sayaka's Akutagawa Prize–winning *Convenience Store Woman* is also a short and accessible runaway bestseller that has been translated across Asia and globally.[15] Yet whereas Jiyoung is presented as a seemingly ordinary woman in her 30s who adheres to social norms, Furukura Keiko, the 36-year-old protagonist of Murata's novel and a clerk (*ten'in*) at a convenience store, has never been considered normal. Thwarting prescriptive social expectations and the hounding of family, friends, and strangers, she continues to refuse relationships, not to mention marriage, children, and a more stable career. She also tells her own story. Keiko's engaged first-person style, in contrast with the relatively detached discourse of Jiyoung's psychiatrist, gives the reader more direct access to Keiko the individual. Even as she highlights her separation from so-called normal society, sharing her thoughts and feelings about a range of experiences underscores her humanity and, by extension, the humanity of clerks and other essential workers who are largely invisible and whose stories often go unheard. Literature also enables *Convenience Store Woman* to make a strong case for the normality or at least appropriateness of less conventional life trajectories, countering scholarly, media, political, and other discourse criticizing the choices of those who remain unmarried and those who are childfree (i.e., who deliberately choose not to have children), despite the global population having more than quadrupled over the last century and climate crises becoming more extreme.

It has been several decades since single women in Japan over age 25 were routinely called "Christmas cakes" (*Kurisumasu kēki*). This pejorative refers to the ubiquitous Japanese sponge cakes with whipped cream and strawberries that are a staple of the holidays and difficult to sell after 25 December because they are no longer moist, fresh, or needed (Brinton, "Christmas Cakes" 80; Yamaguchi 50).[16] Not only do Japanese increasingly postpone marriage until well into their thirties, more also are likely to remain single throughout their lives (Hertog 94). In 2015, nearly 25% of Japanese men and more than 14% of Japanese women aged 50 and over had never married, up from 1.7% and 3.33%, respectively, in 1970 (94). Birthrates, too, have fallen significantly in Japan since the mid–twentieth century, from more than 3.5 children per woman in 1950 to about 1.4 in the first two decades of the 2000s, one of the lowest in the world (Brinton, "Family" 180–81).[17]

Yet entrenched social expectations persist, with the "typical" family composed of "two married heterosexual parents and one or more biological children" (Brinton, "Family" 171).[18] Even as discourse on "positive singlehood" (*ohitorisama*) remains robust, considerable hand-wringing continues "over young women rejecting marriage and motherhood" and over "young men unable or unwilling to engage in carnal pursuits" (Kano 29, 132).[19] Expectations regarding employment also persist: men are still expected to have regular full-time employment with benefits, earning enough to support wives and children; unmarried women are still expected to work full-time unless they are caring for elders or other family members; most married women are still expected to contribute to family finances while also devoting themselves to motherhood, juggling reproductive and productive labor, the latter frequently in the form of jobs with little opportunity for advancement (Hertog 95; Kano 132, 179).[20] Japan's model of "male breadwinner / female carer" remains intact (Brinton, "Japan's Approach"). Japan is ranked 125th of 146 nations in the World Economic Forum's *Global Gender Gap Report 2023*, 123rd in economic participation and opportunity, and 138th in political empowerment (11, 17–18). Japanese women earn much less than Japanese men, and the number of women working part-time is more than twice that of men (218). Japan's labor force participation rate of highly educated women is the lowest among postindustrial societies (Brinton, "Japan's Approach").

As suggested by the derogatory terms "parasite single" (*parasaito shinguru*, an unmarried person who lives with their parents into their 30s without contributing meaningfully to the household) and "herbivorous male" (*sōshokukei danshi*, a man uninterested in relationships or marriage and without full-time employment), those who do not adhere to social expectations regarding marriage, children, and employment are deemed abnormal.[21] In some cases, individuals choose to live off others even though they are capable of supporting themselves. Many more are casualties of broader socioeconomic and employment conditions in Japan: while nearly 87% of Japanese men and 73% of women are in the labor force, 22.2% of men and 50.8% of women are employed part-time, not necessarily by choice (*Global Gender Gap Report 2021* 37).[22] Still others who are targeted for not conforming to social norms actually are contributing meaningfully to society, albeit in unconventional ways; find their work fulfilling; and are content with their lives. In other words, for them, society needs to jettison its unjust, rigid, and unreasonable expectations.

The narrator of *Convenience Store Woman* is a prime example of this phenomenon. Keiko works at the Hiiromachi Station Smile Mart in Tokyo, having thrived in the same position since the store's opening 18 years before, when she was 18 and just starting college (Murata, *Convenience Store Woman* 12).[23] To be sure, there is no Hiiromachi Station among Tokyo's hundreds of train and subway stations and no Smile Mart among Tokyo's nearly ubiquitous and indispensable 24/7 convenience stores.[24] In contrast, the biased reactions to Keiko's choices and the psychological pressure Keiko's family, friends, and coworkers place on her to conform to social expectations regarding marriage and employment are all too real. Yet ultimately, unlike Kim Jiyoung, who is overwhelmed by exploitative expectations, Keiko skillfully evades prescriptive social norms, embracing her singlehood and her job at Smile Mart, even as she recognizes that she will not be able to perform such physically demanding work indefinitely.

Also unlike *Kim Jiyoung*, most of *Convenience Store Woman* takes place in the present. In general, flashbacks are brief and focus largely on how Keiko defies expectations from an early age. She shares that while she was born into a "normal family" and raised in a "normal suburban residential area" (Murata, *Convenience Store Woman* 6), with her sister Mami a "normal child" (11), she has always been considered a "rather strange child" (6) and in need of being "cured" (12).[25] It is not until employee training that she learns "how to accomplish a normal facial expression and manner of speech" (15). It is only as a convenience store clerk, Keiko writes, that she can be "a cog in society," a metaphor for "a normal person" (21).[26] And, unlike Kim Jiyoung, she thrives in her new position. Finding in the store "a dependable, normal world that keeps turning" (30), Keiko assiduously follows the employee instruction manual and performs all her tasks to the highest standards. Keiko makes clear that she has no interest in being promoted to management, reflecting both Japan's dearth of female managers and her own preference for lower-prestige work—quite unlike that of Ayesha in Saba Imtiaz's *Karachi, You're Killing Me!* (2014), discussed in chapter 2. Keiko even volunteers for extra shifts over the New Year's holidays, enabling other staff members to spend time with their families. She is the embodiment of the essential worker: "I'm not particularly brilliant . . . but I'm second to none in terms of never being late or taking days off. I just come in every day without fail, and because of that I'm accepted as a well-functioning part ["buhin"; 部品] of the store" (*Convenience Store Woman* 43; *Konbini ningen* 47).

Yet Keiko recognizes that outside Smile Mart is another "normal world" that "eliminates foreign objects" (Murata, *Convenience Store Woman* 80). To be sure, "foreign objects" are not exclusively women. Japanese men must also adhere to strict criteria that are becoming more difficult to meet. Keiko's coworker Shiraha, who also sees himself as a "foreign object," protests, "I don't make trouble for anyone, but they all seem to think nothing of raping me just because I'm in the minority" (86–87).[27] Shiraha initially declares that "we men have it much harder than women" (89). This is because men must "get a job, and if you've got a job, it's earn more money, and if you earn more money, it's get married and have offspring. Society is continually judging us" (89). Yet in the end, men have better options. As Shiraha asserts:

> You're still in a dead-end job at your age, and nobody's going to marry an old maid like you now. You're like secondhand goods. Even if you are a virgin, you're grubby. You're like a Stone Age woman past child-bearing age who can't get married and is left to just hang around the village, of no use to anyone, just a burden. I'm a man, so I can still make a comeback, but there's no hope for you, is there, Furukura. (90–91)[28]

Soon thereafter, Shiraha proclaims, "Without a career or a husband, you're of no value to society, and people like you get expurgated from the village" (106). Using the simile of the Stone Age, Shiraha speaks frequently about how little society has changed across history, with men expected to hunt (i.e., provide), women to give birth, and anyone who does not fit or at least try to fit these roles "meddled with, coerced, and ultimately banished from the village" (90).[29] This is especially true in the aftermath of Japan's March 2011 triple disaster, with the "remasculinization of Japanese men" a "central agenda" (Koikari 19).

Keiko similarly believes that "unless I'm cured, normal people will expurgate me" (Murata, *Convenience Store Woman* 81).[30] Whether Keiko is happy is irrelevant to her family, friends, and coworkers. All that matters is that she adheres or at least tries to adhere to society's script. For instance, Keiko knows that "it was considered weird for someone of my age to not have either a proper job or be married." So, to appear less unusual, she has told her friends that she has certain health issues "that make it more convenient for me to have a part-time job" (35). And she has told her coworkers that caring for her parents precludes her taking a more demanding position (35). When Keiko admits to her friends that she has never dated, they assume she is gay or asexual and that life must be difficult for her, even though Keiko claims, "I was indifferent to the whole thing and had never really given it any thought," in contrast with Natsuko, the first-person narrator of *Breasts and Eggs* (*Natsu monogatari*, 夏物語, lit. *Natsu's Tale, Summer's Tale*, 2019), by the Japanese writer Kawakami Mieko (1976–), discussed in chapter 4. As Keiko recognizes, condemning labels, however inclusive they may seem to be, "They didn't want to think it through that far. . . . They wanted to settle the matter this way because that was the easiest option for them" (37).

Most striking are the reactions of her family, friends, and coworkers when Shiraha becomes her roommate. Having hounded Keiko relentlessly about her failure to get married or find regular employment, they are ecstatic that she is now living with a man, instantly assume she is in a relationship, and invent a narrative ("monogatari"; Murata, *Konbini ningen* 113) about the two that "had absolutely nothing to do with me or Shiraha" (Murata, *Convenience Store Woman* 112). No one in Keiko's life recognizes that hers is a home share of convenience that almost immediately becomes untenable: Shiraha sets up camp in Keiko's bathtub and contributes nothing to the household, his family comes after him for unpaid bills, and he verbally harasses her. Echoing the businessmen who accuse Kim Jiyoung of being a "mom-roach," Shiraha declares, "I always did want revenge, on women who are allowed to become parasites just because they're women. I always thought to myself that I'd be a parasite one day. That'd show them. And I'm going to be a parasite on you, Furukura, whatever it takes" (123). Soon thereafter, he asserts, "You're so lucky you met me, Furukura. If you'd gone on like before you'd have ended up dying alone and destitute" (140). Keiko recognizes that her sister Mami is "far happier thinking [Keiko] is normal, even if she has a lot of problems, than she is having an abnormal sister for whom everything is fine. For her, normality—however messy—is far more comprehensible" (133). The same is true of Keiko's coworkers at

Smile Mart, who despite Keiko's devotion to the store are thrilled that she, at Shiraha's urging, is resigning to pursue more conventional employment and is thereby "taking on the form of a person that their brains all imagined as normal" (144).

In the end, however, Keiko refuses to conform and instead seeks justice for herself. En route to an interview for a more socially acceptable position, she feels the sounds of a nearby convenience store stream into her, informing her what it needs (Murata, *Convenience Store Woman* 156–57). Not only personifying the store but also believing that "more than a person, I'm a convenience store worker," Keiko determines that returning to life as a store clerk is more important than pleasing her family, friends, and society, much less Shiraha, whom she is now supporting financially (161). She asserts that even if everyone persecutes her and she dies alone, as Shiraha threatens will happen, she needs to be true to herself.[31] *Convenience Store Woman* ends with Keiko describing the cells of her body as once again resonating with the music emanating from the store, echoing her many aesthetic descriptions of the soundscapes of convenience stores and their special meaning for every aspect of her being, which she continues to see as separate from broader society.

Keiko's figurative language by no means romanticizes the convenience store, where every act is scripted and from which "foreign objects" are expelled, just as they are from the world outside. Nor does *Convenience Store Woman* glamorize Keiko's occupation. Keiko describes her body as belonging to the store. Her job at Smile Mart depends not only on her determination and reliability but also on her physical strength; when the latter is depleted, she knows she will become "a worn-out part ["buhin"], ready to be replaced, no longer of any use to the convenience store" (Murata, *Convenience Store Woman* 83; Murata, *Konbini ningen* 86). But the novel, which distinguishes Shiraha's freeloading from Keiko's providing, does make a strong case for enabling individuals to find and create spaces in which they can thrive and for accepting as part of the social fabric people with diverse aspirations. Murata has commented that one reason she wrote *Convenience Store Woman* was "to illustrate how odd the people who believe they are ordinary or normal are. . . . They are the so-called normal people, but when you switch the direction of the camera, it is they who appear strange or odd" (qtd. in Rich). Strange and odd, at least in the context of the novel, not only because they attempt to impose their standards on a person who is content with her life and who, like many individuals, does not want to be in a relationship, marry, or have children. Just as important, the "so-called normal people" are far more dependent than they recognize on individuals such as Keiko for the functioning of their so-called normal lives, of which shopping at convenience stores is such an integral part. Murata's narrative gives voice to the stories of those who all too often are rendered invisible.[32]

Decades of Struggling against Social Norms: Dạ Ngân's *An Insignificant Family* (2005)

Cho's *Kim Jiyoung* and Murata's *Convenience Store Woman* feature women, Jiyoung and Keiko, born in South Korea in 1982 and in Japan in 1980, respectively, whose societies underwent significant transformations between the 1980s and the 2010s. Yet they did not experience tumult and whiplash akin to those living in mid- to late-twentieth-century Vietnam, the setting of the Vietnamese writer Dạ Ngân's popular and prizewinning, yet much less circulated, *Insignificant Family*. This lengthy, vivid novel suffused with poetic language is set primarily in the 1980s, with numerous flashbacks to the 1960s and 1970s; its final chapter is set in 2002. *Insignificant Family* focuses on Nguyen Thi Mỹ Tiệp (Tiệp; b. 1950/51), a writer and former guerrilla based in part on Dạ Ngân herself, who spends decades struggling against her family's, community's, and nation's stigmas and prohibitions against divorce, extramarital affairs, and remarriage.[33] The aesthetic devices and stylistic techniques of *Insignificant Family*—particularly its striking imagery and unfiltered discourse—accentuate the high price Tiệp pays for pursuing a life very different from what her family and society deem important, a price far greater than what has been and is likely to be exacted from Keiko in *Convenience Store Woman* as she moves into her 30s and 40s. As Wayne Karlin summarizes, Tiệp is "the antithesis of the stereotype of the pure-minded revolutionary prevalent in war and post-war, pre-*doi moi* [market reforms], Vietnamese literature, or the Confucian ideal of the submissive woman" (v). In short, Tiệp is the type of person whose story is rarely told.[34]

Insignificant Family situates Tiệp and her extended family within the broader landscape of mid- to late-twentieth-century Vietnam and presumes knowledge of Vietnamese history as well as conventional Vietnamese attitudes toward women. Colonized by France in the 1880s, Vietnam was occupied by Japan from September 1940 to August 1945; declared independence from France in September 1945; fought for independence from France until 1954, when the Geneva Accords temporarily divided it at the seventeenth parallel; and endured civil war from 1955 to 1975, during which time millions were killed.[35] The northern communist

Democratic Republic of Vietnam was aided by communist nations and by the largely guerrilla National Liberation Front (Viet Minh cadres based in the South), while the southern anti-communist Republic of Vietnam was aided by anti-communist nations.[36] After northern victory and the establishment in 1976 of the Socialist Republic of Vietnam, controlled by the Communist Party of Vietnam, the newly unified country fought a war with Cambodia from 1978 to 1989. Vietnam's market reforms (known as *Đổi Mới*, or "Renovation"), initiated in 1986, helped the nation transition from a centrally planned top-down command economy to a socialist-oriented state-directed market economy (Tran, "Complex Transformation" 227). In the decades that followed, Vietnam gradually reestablished formal diplomatic relations with the nations from which it had been politically and economically isolated and became more tightly integrated into the global economy (Benjamin et al. 26). Although in 1988 it was one of the world's most impoverished nations, Vietnam became a middle-income country by the early 2010s ("Vietnam: Achieving"). At the same time, inequality has persisted along rural-urban, ethnic, and gender lines (Ramachandran and Scott 695).

Historically, women in Vietnam were governed by two seemingly contradictory expectations. The first was that they would take up arms against the nation's invaders as their forebears had done, beginning with the legendary Trung Sisters, who rebelled against Han dynasty Chinese from 43 to 40 BCE. The second was that they would follow Chinese Confucian prescriptions, especially the Three Obediences and Four Virtues (*Tam tòng, tứ đức*), which demanded that women obey their fathers, then their husbands (chosen by their parents), and then, if widowed, their eldest sons; that they demonstrate a humble character, gentle speech, and proper appearance; and that they diligently perform domestic tasks (Lessard 107, 122). Mostly denied an education, women were expected to live with their husband's family after marriage and generally were not permitted to divorce (107, 109).[37] Conditions changed in the early twentieth century, when both French colonizers and Vietnamese intellectuals (anti-French and Francophile alike) called for the education of Vietnamese girls and young women (110–14). The Indochinese Communist Party, founded in 1930, insisted on women's equality, including the right to divorce, and the Constitution of 1946 not only gave women the right to vote (118, 120) but also declared that "women have the same political, economic, cultural, social, and family rights as men. For equal work, they have equal pay" (Ungar 294).

Under wartime socialism, women's economic, political, and social roles expanded dramatically (Werner 170–72; Ungar 293–95). Women were urged "to take charge of agricultural and industrial production, and all other work activities left vacant by men," and "to support soldiers at the front and to take up arms when necessary" (Chiricosta 136). Yet disparities persisted, and women were also told "to manage all family affairs" (136). Women continued to do nearly all the domestic labor (e.g., childcare, cooking, housework) and spent more time contributing to the family economy (e.g., gardening, tending livestock). Men, for their part, played a larger role in the collective economy of the village (Werner 185–86). Opportunities for women were notably restricted after the reunification of Vietnam in 1975; women's participation in lower-level jobs continued, while the number of women in higher-level positions dropped considerably (Ungar 295–96, 300).

The diversification of economic sectors under the market reforms initiated in 1986, and especially industrialization and privatization, created unprecedented employment opportunities for women (Earl; Hong et al. 170). Yet the return of the household to an autonomous economic unit reinforced conventional beliefs concerning the expected place of women and men at home and in society (Hong et al. 171). For instance, the Vietnamese government has promoted conventional gender roles as vital to the nation, establishing policies that exhort women "to participate fully in economic, social, and political activities alongside men, whilst still being expected to continue to fulfill their traditional role of maintaining harmony in the family" (173). As Khuat Thu Hong and colleagues argue, "[D]eep down at the cultural core, gender inequality remains practically intact" (167). Indeed, women are still expected not only to marry men and to have children with their husbands but also to remain married. Although divorce rates in Vietnam increased significantly after the 1986 market reforms, particularly in urban areas (Tran, "Complex Transformation" 226), divorce is highly stigmatized both in Vietnam and in the Vietnamese diaspora, and Vietnam's divorce rate remains one of the lowest in the world (Tran, "Divorce Prevalence"). Remarriage after divorce and cohabitation without remarriage also remain uncommon, at 15% and 10%, respectively (Tran, "Complex Transformation" 226).

Raised in a small village in southern Vietnam, Tiệp, the protagonist of *Insignificant Family*, joined the National Liberation Front of South Vietnam as a teenager, following the death of her father in the notorious southern Vietnamese Côn Đảo prison. Like Kim Jiyoung, Tiệp adheres to the social norm that women have a husband and children. She marries Tuyên, a fellow guerrilla whom she met during the war, and with him has a daughter, Thu Thi, and then a son, Vĩnh Chuyên. Tiệp also abides by the social expectation of balancing a career and raising children, working for the Writers' Union in the southern Vietnamese town of Định Bảo. But unlike Kim Jiyoung, whose marriage remains relatively stable, Tiệp cannot tolerate her loveless relationship with Tuyên. So, despite her family's and society's strong condemnations and the extreme challenges she knows she will face, not unlike those of Ogino Ginko, discussed in chapter 2, she files for divorce.[38] Embracing her sexuality, she pursues an affair with a celebrated journalist, who soon abandons her. Tiệp's next relationship is with Nguyễn Việt Đính (Đính), a married writer and father of three children from central Vietnam living in the northern city of Hanoi. Tiệp and Đính must endure a highly censured 20-year mostly long-distance affair before they can live together and finally marry.

In the afterword to the French translation of *Insignificant Family*, Charlotte Dang describes the novel's lively, colorful, and artistically sensual writing; its descriptions that appeal to multiple senses—sight, sound, and smell; and its lyrical comparisons and images. Dang addresses the musicality and melodious orality of the narrative, accentuated by the tones of the Vietnamese language, as well as the abundant descriptions of the Vietnamese countryside's distinctive flora and fauna (343–48). The narrator's skill with language also enables her to provide grippingly thorough and graphic depictions of the corruption and poverty of postwar Vietnam and the crushing consequences of intransigent social norms surrounding divorce and remarriage: unrelenting denunciation from family, community, and nation, together with devastating internalized stigma (self-stigma), that combined make life exceptionally treacherous but do not ultimately extinguish agency.

From the beginning, *Insignificant Family* foregrounds the distance between Tiệp and her family, especially her female relatives, highlighting, as do many of the narratives in *Gender Justice*, the role women play in perpetuating gender injustice. As the narrator observes:

> The women of her family, who knew only too well how to exploit their control, cared only for hierarchy and order, for the four traditional feminine attributes of industry, appearance, speech, and behavior, and above all for peace and comfort. To them, [Tiệp's] job as a cadre was to bring glory to the family by advancing her position, and their job as peasants was to be industrious and solicitously attend the family altar. Tiệp's newspaper articles they could grasp, but this thing called literature . . . had no redeeming value. . . . [I]t was nothing, utterly unimportant. (Dạ, *Insignificant Family* 8)[39]

Even more deplorable to her family than her pursuit of literature is Tiệp's wanting, at age 28, to divorce Tuyên, her husband of eight years. The novel opens in the fall of 1981, with Tiệp home for her father's annual memorial, a ceremony she could not attend the previous year because she "doesn't dare show that sorry, adulterous face of hers" (5).[40] Once they have Tiệp in their sights, the women of the family lecture her on the importance of honor, and more specifically sacrifice: "The fact that she was struggling to be free of Tuyên meant that she did not have the virtue of sacrifice. Which was why she had to be pummeled again and again; she had threatened the strand that bound them together, a strand plaited from multiple sacrifices made by multiple people over the last half century, beginning before she was born" (14).[41]

Although the family violence Tiệp experiences is not as extreme as the family violence exposed by the narratives discussed in chapter 6, Tiệp's older brother Trường and her Aunt Ràng are ruthless. Trường declares that if Tiệp divorces Tuyên, her children will "have a father but no mother" (Dạ, *Insignificant Family* 42). When Tiệp demands "justice for herself" (42), Trường threatens her, reminding her that if the family does not agree to the divorce, neither will the courts (43). And Tiệp's Aunt Ràng, herself a widow and the younger sister of Tiệp's deceased father, declares, "When you kill your reputation, you kill yourself and kill the good name of your entire family. Then later, if Tuyên decides he'd like to do you in, who'll dare to stop him? He's got a gun, you know. . . . No one would blame him if he shot you" (49).[42] Aunt Ràng also warns Tiệp that if she comes "crawling back with double the dishonor, all that will be left is for you to do yourself in" (53). At one point Tiệp does attempt to reconcile with Tuyên, but letting him have his way with her results in a miscarriage and traumatic surgical procedure:

> Her hands grabbed at the stainless steel bars of the birthing table as the blows ripped into her like a hoe into dirt: prolonged, echoing, biting, mutilating. . . . These people were ripping her in two, as one rips a frog in two before eating it. . . . Why were those hoes still boring into her, excavating her, pushing her down further and further, until she was standing on the final step of a stairway that led to hell. (74)

Here, as in many parts of Dạ Ngân's novel, the Vietnamese source text is even more graphic than its English translation.[43]

Two years later, pursuing a relationship with Đính, whom she met shortly before her miscarriage, Tiệp recognizes that even though the northern city of Hanoi is "far from her provincial Pharisees who were so eager [to use laws] to throw stones, there was a real risk of knives and scissors and even acid thrown in her face by a jealous wife" (Dạ, *Insignificant Family* 124).[44] Tiệp recoils when Đính's mother suggests as a compromise an "informal arrangement" rather than divorce and then remarriage for Đính: "I have my honor, for myself and for my children, for my whole family. . . . The way things are these days, if it isn't official it doesn't count for squat. Đính and I would still be outcasts, targets of vilification and rumor. How could I bear it?" (160).

Tiệp's predictions are all too accurate. Even though her supervisor at the Writers' Union supports her relationship with Đính, he is unable to prevent either charges of adultery from being brought against Tiệp or Tiệp's relatives from requesting from the party a complete dissolution of all family ties.[45] The assembled judge and jury do admit that there is not enough evidence of adultery to prosecute her. At the same time, they warn that "the Party will deal with you by other means" (Dạ, *Insignificant Family* 180). They hold fast to their promise, doing their best going forward to "bury Tiệp in obscurity by banning this scabies-ridden black sheep from all meetings" (190), the narrator's colorful metaphor spotlighting how thoroughly everyone has dehumanized Tiệp. At the disciplinary hearing, they also draw attention to Tiệp's isolation, indulging in hyperbole: "never has anyone in this province, nay, in our entire nation, never in our times has a person been so utterly rejected by their family. Never!" (180). Recognizing the collusion among Đính's wife, Aunt Ràng, and Tuyên, Tiệp feels

> as though she had just been lifted down from the gallows only to find that the court had slapped her with an additional charge. A charge which caused her more suffering and mortification than any other. Let them say she had committed debauchery, or adultery, or husband theft, or usurped another woman's happiness. . . . Bereft of family, no Vietnamese could possibly be at peace. (181)

Unfortunately for Tiệp, the years that follow—as she continues her affair with the still-married Đính—bring not only the grief of losing her family, described as "slow death by poison" (226), but also the relentless disapproval of everyone around her:

> Everyone demanded that piece of paper [the marriage license]: the Party demanded it; her children demanded it; her family demanded it; her friends couldn't understand why she had visited the north twice

> now and still didn't have it. . . . Without that piece of paper, it was impossible to present oneself as a respectable person anywhere under the sun of their homeland. (217–18)[46]

Moreover, Tiệp continues to be plagued by poverty. As she protests in 1990 to her uncle Ba, a high-ranking official, "[W]hile my ex-husband has remarried, been promoted, and assigned a new house of the highest rank, I have had to raise our children all these years in a room in my office that has no running water" (251).[47]

It is only in the mid-1990s that Đính obtains a divorce, nine years after his separation from his wife and three years after the death of his mother. By then, Tiệp's family has mellowed, Aunt Ràng urging Đính to treat Tiệp with respect: "My niece is worth more than gold or pearls to us, and she's been through enough misery. Don't add to that by forcing on her the shame of being a mistress, something less than" (Dạ, *Insignificant Family* 265). Tiệp sighs with relief that "the final knot has been untied. . . . [F]rom now on events would unfold, one after the other, just as after a typhoon the cleanup begins and a new life is built" (265).[48] A new life is built, but not without continued hardship. Given that Đính's household registration is in the North, Tiệp is forced to move to Hanoi, far from her family, especially her grown children, and she recognizes that "to live with the man she loved, she would have to forever suffer the mournful condemnation of her maternal conscience" (269).[49] The more she travels between North and South, a trip that had once taken several days by train but is now a quick flight, the more she recognizes "that when a man remarries he gains a second family, whereas when a woman remarries she leaves behind only failure and ruin" (276).

Tiệp had spent her young adulthood "trapped within a blockade of war widows; a widowed aunt, widowed mother, widowed sisters" (Dạ, *Insignificant Family* 11). She was one of the few women in her family who were not widowed during Vietnam's mid-twentieth-century conflicts. With the loss of their husbands, many widows in Vietnam in the late 1970s and 1980s also lost hope for a better life: while men could live in cities with increasingly modern conveniences, widows were "stuck in an orchard full of poisonous snakes and millipedes, bomb and artillery craters, and leftover mines which no one could clean up because no one knew where they lay" (46). In the immediate postwar period, Tiệp had believed that "no misfortune could possibly compare to the misfortune of widowhood" (12). Yet she had also questioned whether it was in fact "selfish and unprincipled of her to simply recognize that she was not happy in her marriage . . . and that she had the right to make a new peacetime life for herself in the hopes of fulfillment" (13).[50] And she had decided to follow her heart.

Yet doing so is no panacea; Tiệp is plagued by self-doubt, if not self-loathing. Learning how terrified her daughter Thu Thi had been to hear her mother (Tiệp) asking her father (Tuyên) for a divorce, Tiệp felt "the true extent of her vileness. . . . She hadn't known how to suppress her emotions like so many other women in similar circumstances, how to wait for the right time. It was a black mark on her conscience that did not fade over time" (Dạ, *Insignificant Family* 37). *Insignificant Family* concludes in 2002 with the circle of Tiệp's life overlapping with that of her daughter Thu Thi. Thu Thi's husband has deserted her for another woman, and Thu Thi calls on her mother for support, causing Tiệp to wonder whether this is "yet another price she [Tiệp] had to pay for her 'unseemly ambition'" (281). Tiệp is convinced that her daughter's university bears some of the blame for Thu Thi's predicament: Thu Thi and her husband were each just one credit shy of graduation, having neglected to study "military practice," so they were denied their diplomas and are now struggling to make ends meet (280).[51] Even so, Tiệp feels ultimate responsibility for her daughter's fate, and the novel concludes with her anticipating a dark future: "This was her shadow, her tragedy, her inadequacy. This was her guilt, which she always and ever carried, as long as the path of motherhood still stretched out before her" (282). Tiệp has internalized the tremendous stigmas and prohibitions against divorce, extramarital affairs, and remarriage that have been pummeled into her for decades by her judgmental family and censorious society, and there seems to be no escape, for her or for her daughter.[52] The powerful language and graphic imagery of *Insignificant Family* highlight how destructive even the most "insignificant" family can be, particularly when enmeshed in a society with uncompromising gender norms. This novel aesthetically humanizes a woman who, seen as less than insignificant, is utterly dehumanized by all around her.

Unjust gender norms surrounding marriage show little sign of releasing their grip. More Vietnamese women are postponing marriage, and in general, only the poorest, most desperate families force their daughters into marriage as child brides, and only the most destitute women marry regardless of the personal cost.[53] In addition, women with family caregiving responsibilities or who provide economically for their family (e.g., raising siblings, replacing brothers in agriculture, supporting elderly parents) are generally excused from marriage (Bélanger and Hồng 104–05). Even so, not only is divorce highly stigmatized, marriage and children remain "the most highly desirable life paths for women in Việt Nam" (109), despite high rates of physical, sexual, emotional, and economic intimate partner violence ("Nearly").[54] As the driver in the Vietnamese writer Phan Triều Hải's short story "Forever on the Road" ("Đi mãi trên đường," 2011) reluctantly recognizes, even though he has accomplished his "life-long ambition" ("ước mơ") of sending his daughter to school in Saigon (Ho Chi Minh City), she will still "end up with the expectation to become a [wife and] mother" (Phan, "Forever" 235; Phan, "Đi mãi").[55] Gender norms surrounding marriage and children are especially challenging for women who, unlike Dạ Ngân's Tiệp, have no desire to marry or have children in the first place. One of these women is Din, the narrator of the Vietnamese writer Đỗ Bích Thúy's short story "Sage on the Mountain" ("Ngải Đắng ở Trên Núi," 2000). A member of the Tay ethnic minority village raised in in Vietnam's northern mountains, Din "rebelled" against her family, leaving home to pursue a career "in a foreign land" (120).[56] When her sister-in-law asks whether she will ever marry, Din brushes her off, echoing earlier Japanese notions of women as "Christmas cakes" who become undesirable after age 25: "These days no one wants to marry a twenty-six-year-old. . . . I'm an old maid already" (121). Yet in truth, Din, whose mother is desperate for her to marry, has deliberately remained single; a primary reason for leaving home had been fear that she would "fall into the expectations of being a mother or a sister-in-law" (124), the fate of most of her peers.[57]

The South Korean writer Cho Namjoo's *Kim Jiyoung*, the Japanese writer Murata Sayaka's *Convenience Store Woman*, and the Vietnamese writer Dạ Ngân's *Insignificant Family* are three of many Asian and Asian diaspora narratives that feature women confronting tyrannies of social norms and struggling for justice within and beyond family. These narratives reveal the devastating impact of rigid gender assumptions and expectations, both on those such as Jiyoung who conform, however reluctantly, and on those such as Keiko and Tiệp who stridently reject such ideals. The narrative techniques and aesthetic choices of these novels enable them to humanize individuals dehumanized by their families, their societies, or both and to tell stories that are frequently silenced.

Although by no means among the most marginalized in their societies, Jiyoung, Keiko, and especially Tiệp suffer significant trauma. As more individuals across Asia reject heterosexual marriage followed by procreation between a cisgender man and a cisgender woman, governments, communities, and families alike must embrace beliefs, practices, institutions, and structures that support the needs and ensure the well-being of more diverse populations, including, among many groups, women who are fighting for equity in the professional world, discussed in the following chapter, and migrant women who engage in paid reproductive labor, examined in chapter 3.

NOTES

1. Globally, gender differences in educational attainment are relatively small, with 117 of 146 nations having closed at least 95% of the gap, and 61 having closed at least 99.5% (*Global Gender Gap Report 2023* 17). In contrast, the gender gap in economic participation and opportunity remains significant (17–18).

2. See also Thornber, *Global Healing* and "Japanese Literature"; the South Korean writer Kim Hye-jin's *Concerning My Daughter* (*Ttal e taehayŏ*, 2017); and the Japanese writer Itō Hiromi's poetic autofiction *The Thorn Puller* (*Toge-nuki: Shin Sugamo Jizō engi*, lit. *Thorn Puller: New Tales of the Sugamo Jizō*, 2007).

3. In 2008, South Korean women's employment rate was even lower, at 50.5%, but a significant increase from 1963, when it stood at 37% (Jayoung Yoon, "Gender Norms" 113)

4. In the 1980s, women in South Korea earned only 40% of what men earned (Lee and Vignoles).

5. More than half of South Korean children under age five attend day care (J. Lee 221). Seung-Ah Hong discusses the gendered politics of work-life balance in South Korea.

6. The polarized response to Kim Jiyoung, addressed later in this chapter, is particularly ironic given the number of "great guys" in the novel; systems and structures are to blame much more than individuals. (Thank you to Min Ji Choi for this observation.) The phrase "great guys" is originally written as "good guys" (좋은 남자), and "crazy men" reads more literally as "strange" or "weird" men (이상한 남자; Cho, *82-nyŏnsaeng* 69).

7. Not all Jiyoung's classmates are so fortunate.

8. As the narrator describes, when Jiyoung was pregnant, the fad for natural birth was thriving in South Korea; women were expected to give birth with minimal medical intervention. Jiyoung notes the irony that people who do not think twice at popping a painkiller "demand that women giving birth should gladly endure the pain, exhaustion, and mortal fear" (Cho, *Kim Jiyoung* 139). This passage echoes Jiyoung's sister's earlier lament that there "isn't a single pill to treat menstrual cramps" because "the world wants our uterus to be drug-free. Like sacred grounds in a virgin forest" (51).

9. Men had long ridiculed Jiyoung: a fellow student had referred to her as "chewing gum someone spat out" (Cho, *Kim Jiyoung* 80), and a coworker had called her "bean paste woman," which the narrator identifies as "a popular

[South] Korean portmanteau word among a host of other misogynistic new terms" (102).

10. Single motherhood is highly stigmatized in South Korea. Birth rates are also among the lowest in the world, having dropped from 4.5 children per woman in the 1970s to 1.19 in 2013 (Ahn 1), shortly before Jiyoung gave birth. Young women today are on both a "birth strike" and a "marriage strike," frustrated with society's treatment of women as "baby-making machines" and "impossible expectations of mothers"; at 0.79 children per woman today, South Korea has the lowest fertility of any nation (Hawon Jung, "Women").

11. The South Korean prosecutor Sŏ Chihyŏn catapulted South Korea's Me Too movement on 28 January 2018, when she spoke publicly about being sexually harassed by the former prosecutor and director of policy planning at the Ministry of Justice An T'ae-kŭn. Sŏ published an account of her experiences on 30 January 2018, explicitly identifying with Cho's character Kim Jiyoung, despite their age difference (H. Lee 216, 218). *Kankoku, feminizumu, Nihon* (*Korea, Feminism, Japan*, 2019), edited by Saitō Mariko, Cho's Japanese-language translator, lists *Kim Jiyoung* as one of the five South Korean novels most directly related to Me Too. See also Taba for more on intersections between Korean and Japanese feminism.

12. Male celebrities who were enthusiastic about *Kim Jiyoung* generally did not face backlash.

13. See also "Anti-Feminism Backlash"; Chaigne. Some radical feminists, including in Korea, target both men and LGBTQIA+ individuals, who are already vulnerable to injustice given their minority status (John Yoon).

14. In addition, her psychiatrist is a woman, reflecting the growing number of women psychiatrists. While in 1975 women made up just 1.6% of psychiatrists in South Korea, in 2006 they made up 18% of psychiatrists and 39% of psychiatry residents (Kim and Kim 558).

15. The Akutagawa Prize is one of Japan's most prestigious literary prizes. Murata, a prolific writer who has won multiple awards, worked as a convenience store clerk in Tokyo for nearly 20 years. Translations of *Convenience Store Woman* were also bestsellers, including in Thailand (Wiriyaenawat). Other twenty-first-century Japanese novels on single women in their 30s grappling with similar concerns include Kawakami Hiromi's *Strange Weather in Tokyo* (*Sensei no kaban*, lit. *Teacher's Bag*, 2001) and Shibasaki Tomoka's *Spring Garden* (*Haru no niwa*, 2014): see Thornbury. See also Tanabe Seiko's short story "Sekenshirazu" ("The Innocent," 1977).

16. Consider also China's "leftover women" (*shengnü*). This term is part of China's propaganda campaign to shame urban professional women over age 27 who are highly educated, attractive, and unmarried (Fincher, *Betraying* 130). See also Fincher, *Leftover Women*.

17. Although most married couples continue to have children, the number of married couples having only one child has risen sharply (Brinton, "Family" 182–83). As discussed in chapter 4, having children as a single woman or

otherwise outside heterosexual marriage is highly stigmatized in Japan. Japan's low birth rate and high life expectancy have made it what is commonly termed a "super-aged society," where more than 21% of the population is over age 65 (Tahara 1102). See chapter 3 for narratives on the impact of aging populations on caregiving.

18. Berry and Yonemoto provide historical perspectives on the Japanese family.

19. The sociologist Ueno Chizuko, one of Japan's most prominent scholars of feminism, coined the term *ohitorisama*, or "positive singlehood," recognizing that most people die alone, even if they have (or had) a life partner and children (Kano 132–33). Leung discusses the impact of Ueno in China, where her works are bestsellers. Alpert provides insight into matchmaking in contemporary Japan.

20. Kano analyzes Japanese debates on motherhood and work from the early twentieth through the early twenty-first century (104–39). One of the first was the "motherhood protection debate" (*bosei hogo ronsō*): the poet Yosano Akiko, best known for the sexually daring tanka collection *Tangled Hair* (*Midaregami*, 1901), argued that only financially independent women should become mothers, while the writer Hiratsuka Raichō insisted the state must protect mothers. Li gives additional resources on Japanese women's lived experiences.

21. Although the term *sōshokukei danshi*, or "herbivorous male," coined in 2006, initially applauded men who departed from the stereotype of Japan's "brash and bossy 'carnivores' chasing after money and women" (Kano 178), it soon began to refer to "weak men trapped in irregular labor" (179). Also of note are the terms "freeter" (*furītā*), an individual without full-time employment who instead works part-time, low-wage jobs; and "loser dogs" (*makeinu*) and "demon hags" (*onibaba*), women who remain single and without children (Kano 131, 177–78; Yamaguchi 41).

22. Japan's share of temporary jobs and other forms of nonregular employment rose from 17% in 1988 to 38.5% in 2019. These positions are characterized by lower pay, fewer benefits, and less stability (Heinrich and Imai 80). Nonregular employees are half as likely to marry as are regular employees (Dales and Taga 363).

23. The Japanese source text describes Keiko's job as an "arubaito" (Murata, *Konbini ningen* 27), which usually refers to a part-time job but can also be a low-level hourly wage job without benefits, regardless of the number of hours worked.

24. Japan is home to more than 56,000 convenience stores, where customers can purchase a range of food items, daily necessities, and reading material. Customers can also book tickets, pay bills, and receive packages, among other services (Whitelaw 69). Increasing numbers of convenience store clerks are retirees or international students.

25. Here and elsewhere in the English translation, the Japanese "futsū" is translated as "normal" (Murata, *Konbini ningen* 11), when it more literally means "ordinary."

26. In the Japanese source text, Keiko describes herself as becoming a "cogwheel" ("haguruma"; 歯車) rather than simply a "cog" (Murata, *Konbini ningen* 27).

27. Keiko is taken aback by Shiraha's use of the word *rape*, particularly given how close his own behavior has come to that of sexual assault.

28. The English version translates "Jōmon jidai" (縄文時代; Murata, *Konbini ningen* 88) as "Stone Age," but the two are not equivalent. The beginning of the Jōmon period is pegged to the date of Japan's oldest pottery (14,000–10,000 BCE) and the end of which ranges from 900 BCE to 200 BCE (Ebrey and Walthall 2; Matsumoto et al. 437). In contrast, the Stone Age dates back several million years and ended several thousand years BCE.

29. The Japanese source text reads more literally as "eliminated from the village" (ムラから排除されます; Murata, *Konbini ningen* 107).

30. Here, too, the Japanese source text reads, more literally, as "eliminate" (排除; Murata, *Konbini ningen* 84).

31. Of course, having children is no guarantee of lifetime companionship. Many narratives address this phenomenon, including the Malaysian Chinese-language writer Ho Sok Fong's "Summer Tornado" ("Xiatian de xuanfeng," 2014), in which the protagonist, Su Qin, recognizes that even with children, it is likely that "when she died, she would be alone, she would die a lonely old woman" (85).

32. The Indian writer Anita Nair's Akhilandeswari (Akhila), an income-tax clerk and the 45-year-old protagonist of *Ladies Coupé* (2001), is a kindred spirit to Murata's Keiko. Described by her sister as a "misfit" as a woman (Nair 172), Akhila became the "man of the family" (i.e., the breadwinner) at age 19, when her father died (81). Years later, hearing the inspiring stories of other women, Akhila determines that she at long last will live independently and enjoy her sexuality (284–85).

33. A prolific writer, Dạ Ngân was born Le Hong Nga in southern Vietnam, near the Mekong Delta. She served for nine years in the National Liberation Front of South Vietnam before joining the Vietnamese Writers' Union. She has claimed that *Insignificant Family* "is at least 80% true" (Christiansen).

34. Cf. the stories—films and written narratives—examined by Duong.

35. The French Indochinese Federation (Vietnam and Cambodia) was formally declared in 1887, with Laos added in 1893. After France was defeated in 1954, a temporary demarcation line was created at the seventeenth parallel, pending reunification elections that never occurred; the communist Viet Minh under Hồ Chí Minh was given control of the North, while Ngô Đình Diệm was the president of the South, a noncommunist jurisdiction.

36. The 1955–75 war is also known as the Second Indochina War, the American War, and the Vietnam War; the National Liberation Front of South Vietnam is known pejoratively as the Vietcong.

37. Vietnamese historians call attention to the greater respect Vietnamese have given their heroic women and to the greater freedoms Vietnamese women enjoyed compared with their Chinese counterparts (Lessard 108–09). Even so, in "The Condition of Women" ("Thân Phận Đàn Bà"), a poem ascribed to the

late-eighteenth- and early-nineteenth-century Hồ Xuân Hương, one of early Vietnam's most prominent poets, but likely a "modern imitation" in the poet's voice (Balaban 124 un), the narrator declares, "Rushing around all helter-skelter. // Husband and child, what obligations!" (Hồ Xuân Hương 73).

38. Thinking about why "desperately unhappy women continued to stay on in their marriages," Maria Seetoh, the protagonist of the Singaporean writer Catherine Lim's *Miss Seetoh in the World* (2011), determines that "[s]uddenly she would have to face and justify her decision, not only to her husband but the entire support system of relatives, friends, colleagues, fellow church members. . . . Even the much steeled woman would quail before the hideous prospect of facing the shock and disapproval, disappointment and sorrow of such a force" (143).

39. The phrase "above all" does not appear in the Vietnamese text, which does not prioritize "peace and comfort" above the other qualities listed. Nguyen's English-language translation takes many liberties with its source text. Changes relevant to *Gender Justice* are noted later in this chapter. Dang's French translation, *Une bien modeste famille*, adheres more closely to its Vietnamese source.

40. The Vietnamese version of *Insignificant Family* does not mention the word "adulterous." The phrase that appears—"không dám vác cái mặt về" (Dạ, *Gia đình bé mọn* 16)—is commonly used to describe situations where an individual is too ashamed to return home.

41. At the same time, Tiệp recognizes that to her family, honor in fact "meant nothing more than saving face. And saving face meant flaunting the good while keeping the bad well hidden" (Dạ, *Insignificant Family* 31). The Vietnamese source text includes additional details on the sacrifices made by previous generations.

42. The Vietnamese source text reads more directly: "the public wouldn't condemn him even if he killed you" ("mình rồi thì thằng Tuyên nó có muốn giết con cũng hổng ai dám cản"; Dạ, *Gia đình bé mọn* 98).

43. The narrator likewise speaks more vividly about Tiệp's abortions in the Vietnamese source text, discussed in chapter 4.

44. The English translation adds a phrase not included in the Vietnamese: "and even acid thrown in her face by a jealous wife" (Dạ, *Insignificant Family* 124).

45. At the time, extramarital sex was a punishable crime (Nguyen et al. 1065). See also Mitra, who examines the ideas of deviant female sexuality that British authorities and Indian intellectuals used to control modern Indian society. As Mitra notes, her findings are relevant well beyond India.

46. She is unable even to reserve a motel room with Đính.

47. In the Vietnamese source text, Tiệp highlights her position as Vietnam's first female writer to challenge the unequal treatment of herself and her ex-husband.

48. There do not seem to be equivalent passages in the Vietnamese source text for these two passages from page 265 in the English translation.

49. Before the 1986 reforms, Vietnam's *hộ khẩu* (household registration) system was linked directly to employment, food, housing, land, health care, and other benefits and was almost impossible to transfer. Some restrictions relaxed with the 1986 reforms, but it was not until after 2008 that most faded away (Siu and Unger 346–47).

50. The Vietnamese source text uses the word "heartless" ("vô tâm"; Dạ, *Gia đình bé mọn* 24) rather than "unprincipled."

51. In 2002 only 9.8% of Vietnamese obtained a tertiary education, compared with 28.64% today ("School Enrollment").

52. K. Saraswathyamma's Malayalam-language short story "Female Intellect (Women Have a Mind Too)" ("Peṇbuddhi," 1948) likewise features a woman, Vijayalakshmi, who asserts that her daughter's experiences in Kerala (southwestern India) will mimic hers: "Tradition, circumstances, societal customs, and nature's secrets have gotten together and the woman's brain has to surrender before all these" (28). The Malayalam reads more literally: "Will not the [female] intellect be crushed under the traditions, circumstances, societal customs, secrets of the universe and their conspired forces?" (Saraswathyamma, "Penbuddhi" 23:00–23:15). Vijayalakshmi had initially enjoyed married life but quickly finds it stultifying, recognizing that for women, "being too intelligent is a curse" (Saraswathyamma, "Female Intellect" 27). Similarly, Malathy, the narrator of Sara Thomas's Malayalam-language short story "A Rest House for Travelers" (1998), comments that although the protagonist had been an excellent, energetic student before she married, "[s]he had gone through many dark corridors under the dominance and disregard of her husband. In that darkness she had lost her 'self'" (160). The source text for this translation was not discoverable.

53. Child marriage, defined as marriage under age 18, is on the rise in Vietnam, particularly among the poorest families and ethnic minorities (Trinh and Zhang 1620). Some impoverished Vietnamese women marry much older men from wealthier parts of Asia who often are abusive. Lee et al., for instance, focus on marriage migration to South Korea.

54. A 2020 report revealed that nearly two-thirds of Vietnamese women are subjected to intimate partner violence ("Nearly").

55. As in South Korea and Japan, single motherhood, especially single motherhood by choice, remains highly stigmatized in Vietnam (Benuyenah and Tran). The Vietnamese source text reads "dream" ("ước mơ"), followed by a sentence detailing how assiduously the driver has worked to send his daughter to school (Phan, "Đi mãi").

56. The narrator does not specify whether she leaves Vietnam or moves to a different part of the country.

57. The anguish Din's mother experiences is not unusual in Vietnam, given the continued social cost of having an unmarried daughter, even as attitudes and behaviors toward single women are gradually changing (Bélanger and Hồng).

WORKS CITED

Ahn, Kyunghoon. *A Study of Determinants of the Birthrate Change in South Korea*. 2015. Martin School of Public Policy and Administration, U of Kentucky, MPA/MPP capstone project.

Alpert, Erika R. *The Relationship People: Mediating Love and Marriage in Twenty-First Century Japan*. Lexington Books, 2022.

Alter, Alexandra. "The Heroine of This Korean Best Seller Is Extremely Ordinary." *The New York Times*, 8 Apr. 2020, www.nytimes.com/2020/04/08/books/cho-nam-joo-kim-jiyoung-born-1982.html.

"Anti-Feminism Backlash on the Rise in South Korea." *France 24*, 8 Dec. 2021, www.france24.com/en/live-news/20210812-anti-feminism-backlash-on-the-rise-in-south-korea.

Balaban, John, translator. *Spring Essence: The Poetry of Hồ Xuân Hương*. Copper Canyon Press, 2000.

Bélanger, Danièle, and Khuất Thu Hồng. "Too Late to Marry: Failure, Fate or Fortune? Female Singlehood in Rural North Việt Nam." *Gender, Household, State: Doi Moi in Viet Nam*, edited by Jayne Werner and Bélanger, Cornell UP, 2018, pp. 89–110.

Benjamin, Dwayne, et al. "Growth with Equity: Income Inequality in Vietnam, 2002–14." *Journal of Economic Inequality*, vol. 15, no. 1, Feb. 2017, pp. 25–46.

Benuyenah, Vic, and Phuong Bich Tran. "Postpartum Psychological Pressure on Single Mothers: An Interpretative Phenomenological Analysis." *Journal of Humanities and Applied Social Sciences*, vol. 3, no. 3, June 2021, pp. 199–216.

Berry, Mary Elizabeth, and Marcia Yonemoto, editors. *What Is a Family? Answers from Early Modern Japan*. U of California P, 2019.

Brinton, Mary. "Christmas Cakes and Wedding Cakes: The Social Organization of Japanese Women's Life Course." *Japanese Social Organization*, edited by Takie Sugiyama Lebra, U of Hawai'i P, 1992, pp. 79–107.

———. "Family and Demographic Issues in Japan." Takeda and Williams, pp. 171–90.

———. "Japan's Approach to Work-Family Balance: Policies without Teeth." Indiana U, 26 Jan. 2022.

Chaigne, Thaïs. "The South Korean Men Waging a Vulgar and Violent War against Feminists." *The France 24 Observers*, 9 Sept. 2021, observers.france24.com/en/asia-pacific/20210914-the-south-korean-men-waging-a-vulgar-and-violent-war-against-feminists.

Chandersekaran, Achamma C., translator. *Daughters of Kerala: Twenty-Five Short Stories by Award-Winning Authors*. Hats Off Books, 2004.

Chiricosta, Alessandra. "Following the Trail of the Fairy-Bird: The Search for a Uniquely Vietnamese Women's Movement." *Women's Movements in Asia: Feminisms and Transnational Activism*, edited by Mina Roces and Louise Edwards, Routledge, 2010, pp. 124–43.

Choe Sang Hun. "The New Political Cry in South Korea: 'Out with Man Haters.'" *The New York Times*, 1 Jan. 2022, www.nytimes.com/2022/01/01/world/asia/south-korea-men-anti-feminists.html.

Cho Namjoo. *82-nyŏnsaeng Kim Chiyŏng*. Minumsa, 2016.

———. *Kim Jiyoung, Born 1982*. Translated by Jamie Chang, Liveright Publishing, 2016.

Christiansen, Paul. "Meet the Author of the Most Important Vietnamese Novel You've Never Read." *Saigoneer*, 18 June 2018, saigoneer.com/vietnam-literature/13629-meet-the-author-of-the-most-important-vietnamese-novel-you-ve-never-read.

Dales, Laura, and Futoshi Taga. "Femininity and Masculinity." Takeda and Williams, pp. 361–68.

Dang, Charlotte. Postface. *Une bien modeste famille*, by Dạ Ngân, translated by Dang, Éditions Intervalles, 2014, pp. 341–49.

Dạ Ngân. *Une bien modeste famille*. Translated by Charlotte Dang, Éditions Intervalles, 2014.

———. *Gia đình bé mọn*. NXB Thanh niên, 2010, archive.org/details/giadinhbemon/mode/2up.

———. *An Insignificant Family*. Translated by Rosemary Nguyen, adapted by Wayne Karlin, Curbstone Books, 2009.

Đỗ Bích Thúy. "Sage on the Mountain." Translated by Nguyễn Hùng and Charles Waugh. Waugh et al., pp. 119–29.

Duong, Lan P. *Treacherous Subjects: Gender, Culture, and Trans-Vietnamese Feminism*. Temple UP, 2012.

Earl, Catherine. "Freedom to Choose? Marriage and Professional Work among Urban Middle-Class Women in Ho Chi Minh City, Vietnam." *Women of Asia: Globalization, Development, and Gender Equity*, edited by Mehrangiz Najafizadeh and Linda L. Lindsey, Routledge, 2019, pp. 236–47.

Ebrey, Patricia, and Anne Walthall. *East Asia: A Cultural, Social, and Political History*. 3rd ed., Wadsworth Cengage, 2014.

Enloe, Cynthia. *The Big Push*. U of California P, 2017.

Fincher, Leta Hong. *Betraying Big Brother: The Feminist Awakening in China*. Verso, 2018.

———. *Leftover Women: The Resurgence of Gender Inequality in China*. Zed Books, 2014.

Fong, Ho Sok. "Summer Tornado." *Lake Like a Mirror*, translated by Natascha Bruce, Two Lines Press, 2020, pp. 75–86.

"Gender and Health." *World Health Organization*, 2023, www.who.int/health-topics/gender.

Global Gender Gap Report 2021. World Economic Forum, 2021, www3.weforum.org/docs/WEF_GGGR_2021.pdf.

Global Gender Gap Report 2023. World Economic Forum, 2023, www3.weforum.org/docs/WEF_GGGR_2023.pdf.

Heinrich, Steffen, and Jun Imai. "Work and Employment: Inside, Outside, and Beyond the Lifetime Employment Model." Takeda and Williams, pp. 80–101.

Hertog, Ekaterina. "Attitudes to Marriage and Childbearing." *The Routledge Companion to Gender and Japanese Culture*, edited by Jennifer Coates et al., Routledge, 2021, pp. 92–105.

Hiramoto, Mie, and Cherise Shi Ling Teo. "Heteronormative Love Makes a House a Home: Multimodal Analysis of Luxury Housing Ads in Singapore." *Journal of Language and Sexuality*, vol. 4, no. 2, Oct. 2015, pp. 223–53.

Hong, Khuat Thu, et al. "'To Be Good at Public and Domestic Work, I Need Three Heads and Six Hands': The Dilemma of Vietnamese 'Modern' Women." *Asian Women and Intimate Work*, edited by Ochiai Emiko and Aoyama Kaoru, Brill, 2012, pp. 167–88.

Hong, Seung-Ah. "Gendered Politics of Work-Life Balance in South Korea." *Routledge Handbook of East Asian Gender Studies*, edited by Jieyu Liu and Junko Yamashita, Routledge, 2020, pp. 185–96.

Hồ Xuân Hương. "The Condition of Women." *Spring Essence: The Poetry of Hồ Xuân Hương*, translated by John Balaban, Copper Canyon Press, 2000, pp. 72–73.

Itō Hiromi. *The Thorn Puller*. Translated by Jeffrey Angles, Stone Bridge Press, 2022.

Jung, Hawon. *Flowers of Fire: The Inside Story of South Korea's Feminist Movement and What It Means for Women's Rights Worldwide*. BenBella Books, 2023.

———. "Women in South Korea Are on Strike against Being 'Baby-Making Machines.'" *The New York Times*, 27 Jan. 2023, www.nytimes.com/2023/01/27/opinion/south-korea-fertility-rate-feminism.html.

Jung, Hoyong. "*Kim Ji-young, Born 1982* Revisited." *Journal of Asian Sociology*, vol. 50, no. 1, Mar. 2021, pp. 203–46.

Kano, Ayako. *Japanese Feminist Debates: A Century of Contention on Sex, Love, and Labor*. U of Hawai'i P, 2016.

Karlin, Wayne. Introduction. *An Insignificant Family*, by Dạ Ngân, translated by Rosemary Nguyen, adapted by Karlin, Curbstone Books, 2009, pp. v–x.

Kim, Ha Kyoung, and Soo In Kim. "The Significance of the Increase of Women Psychiatrists in Korea." *Psychiatria et neurologia Japonica*, vol. 110, no. 7, 2008, pp. 558–62.

Kim Hye-jin. *Concerning My Daughter.* Translated by Jamie Chang, Restless Books, 2022.

Kim, Jinsook. "Sticky Activism: The Gangnam Station Murder Case and New Feminist Practices against Misogyny and Femicide." *Journal of Cinema and Media Studies*, vol. 60, no. 4, summer 2021, pp. 37–60.

Kim Jiyoung, Born 1982. Directed by Kim Do-young, Spring Wind Film, 2019.

Koikari, Mire. *Gender, Culture, and Disaster in Post-3.11 Japan.* Bloomsbury, 2020.

"Korea: Overview of the Education System (EAG 2023)." *OECD*, gpseducation .oecd.org/CountryProfile?primaryCountry=KOR&treshold=10&topic=EO. Accessed 21 Dec. 2023.

Lee, Claire. "Feminist Novel Becomes Center of Controversy in South Korea." *The Korea Herald*, 27 Mar. 2018, www.koreaherald.com/view.php?ud= 20180327000799.

Lee, Hye-Ryoung. "From the Front Line of Contemporary South Korean Feminist Criticism." *Azalea*, vol. 14, no. 14, Jan. 2021, pp. 215–40.

Lee Hyunok et al. "Adapting to Marriage Markets: International Marriage Migration from Vietnam to South Korea." *Journal of Comparative Family Studies*, vol. 47, no. 2, Apr. 2016, pp. 267–88.

Lee, Joohee. "South Korea: Work, Care and the Wollstonecraft Dilemma." *Women, Work, and Care in the Asia-Pacific*, edited by Marian Baird et al., Routledge, 2017, pp. 214–29.

Lee, Sangwoo, and Anna Vignoles. "Does College Level the Playing Field? Socioeconomic Gaps in the Earnings of Similar Graduates: Evidence from South Korea." *Higher Education*, 13 Aug. 2021, link.springer.com/article/ 10.1007/s10734-021-00745-0.

Lessard, Micheline R. "Women's Suffrage in Việt Nam." *Women's Suffrage in Asia: Gender, Nationalism, and Democracy*, edited by Louise Edwards and Mina Roces, Routledge, 2004, pp. 106–26.

Leung, Kanis. "As China Censors Homegrown Feminism, a Feminist Scholar from Japan Is on Its Bestseller Lists." *AP News*, 29 Sept. 2023, apnews.com/ article/china-japanese-feminist-scholar-chizuko-ueno-3a7ef7a9e8d5a8ed 87314fac69ba768d.

Li, Danke. "Teaching the History of Women in China and Japan: Challenges and Sources." *ASIA Network Exchange*, vol. 21, no. 2, spring 2014, pp. 63–73.

Lim, Catherine. *Miss Seetoh in the World.* Marshall Cavendish, 2011.

Matsumoto, Naoko, et al. "Subsistence, Sedentism, and Social Complexity among Jomon Hunter-Gatherers of the Japanese Archipelago." *Handbook of East and Southeast Asian Archaeology*, edited by Junko Habu et al., Springer, 2017, pp. 437–50.

Mitra, Durba. *Indian Sex Life: Sexuality and the Colonial Origins of Modern Social Thought*. Princeton UP, 2020.

Murata Sayaka. *Convenience Store Woman*. Translated by Ginny Tapley Takemori, Grove Press, 2018.

———. *Konbini ningen*. Bungei shunjū, 2020.

Nair, Anita. *Ladies Coupé*. St. Martin's Press, 2001.

"Nearly Two in Three Married Women Face Violence from Husbands: Study." *Việt Nam News*, 15 July 2020, vietnamnews.vn/society/749593/nearly-two-in-three-married-women-face-violence-from-husbands-study.html.

Nguyen, Huong, et al. "Extramarital Sex among Vietnamese Married Men: Results of a Survey in Urban and Rural Areas of Northern and Southern Vietnam." *The Journal of Sex Research*, vol. 53, no. 9, Nov. 2016, pp. 1065–81.

Phan Triều Hải. "Đi mãi trên đường." *Kilopad*, 18 May 2014, kilopad.com/truyen-ngan-c197/di-mai-tren-duong-b10038.

———. "Forever on the Road." Translated by Charles Waugh. Waugh et al., pp. 231–40.

Ramachandran, Leela, and Steffanie Scott. "Single-Player Universities in the South: The Role of University Actors in Development in Vietnam's North Central Coast Region." *Regional Studies*, vol. 43, no. 5, June 2009, pp. 693–706.

Rich, Motoko. "For Japanese Novelist Sayaka Murata, Odd Is the New Normal." *The New York Times*, 11 June 2018, www.nytimes.com/2018/06/11/books/japanese-novelist-sayaka-murata-convenience-store-woman.html.

Saitō Mariko, editor. *Kankoku, feminizumu, Nihon*. Kawade shobō shinsha, 2019.

Saraswathyamma, K. "Female Intellect (Women Have a Mind Too)." Chandersekaran, pp. 21–28.

———. "Penbuddhi." Audiobook ed., DC Books, 2015.

"School Enrollment, Tertiary (% Gross)–Viet Nam." *The World Bank*, 2023, data.worldbank.org/indicator/SE.TER.ENRR?locations=VN.

Seager, Joni. *The Women's Atlas*. Penguin Books, 2018.

Sebastian, Meryl. "'Kim Ji-young, Born 1982,' Korea's #MeToo Book, Is Now a Hit Movie." *HuffPost India*, 23 Nov. 2019, www.huffpost.com/archive/in/entry/korea-metoo-kim-ji-young-born-1982_in_5dbfb859e4b0615b8a9550d6.

Seok, Jae Eun. "Public Long-Term Care Insurance for the Elderly in Korea: Design, Characteristics, and Tasks." *Social Work in Public Health*, vol. 25, no. 2, Feb. 2010, pp. 185–209.

Siu, Kaxton, and Jonathan Unger. "Work and Family Life among Migrant Factory Workers in China and Vietnam." *Journal of Contemporary Asia*, vol. 50, no. 3, May 2020, pp. 341–60.

Taba Bukkusu, editor. *Kankoku feminizumu to watakushitachi: Han'guk p'eminijŭm kwa uri*. Taba bukkusu, 2019.

Tahara, Yoshio. "Cardiopulmonary Resuscitation in a Super-Aging Society." *Circulation Journal*, vol. 80, no. 5, Apr. 2016, pp. 1102–03.

Takeda, Hiroko, and Mark Williams, editors. *Routledge Handbook of Contemporary Japan*. Routledge, 2021.

Tanabe Seiko. "Sekenshirazu." *Sekenshirazu*, by Tanabe, Kodansha, 1982, pp. 29–54.

Thomas, Sara. "A Rest House for Travelers." Chandersekaran, pp. 151–66.

Thornber, Karen Laura. *Global Healing: Literature, Advocacy, Care*. Brill, 2020.

———. "Japanese Literature in the Medical and Health Humanities Curriculum: Ariyoshi Sawako's *The Twilight Years*." *Teaching Postwar Japanese Fiction*, edited by Alex Bates, Modern Language Association of America, 2023, pp. 311–21.

Thornbury, Barbara. "The Thirty-Something 'Tokyo Daughters' of Kawakami Hiromi's *Strange Weather in Tokyo*, Shibasaki Tomoka's *Spring Garden*, and Murata Sayaka's *Convenience Store Woman*." *U.S.-Japan Women's Journal*, no. 57, Apr. 2020, pp. 57–74.

Tran Thi Minh Thi. "Complex Transformation of Divorce in Vietnam under the Forces of Modernization and Individualism." *International Journal of Asian Studies*, vol. 18, no. 2, July 2021, pp. 225–45.

———. "Divorce Prevalence under the Forces of Individualism and Collectivism in 'Shortcut' Modernity in Vietnam." *Weaving Women's Spheres in Vietnam: The Agency of Women in Family, Religion, and Community*, edited by Kato Atsufumi, Brill, 2016, pp. 81–115.

Trinh, Trong-Anh, and Quanda Zhang. "Adverse Shocks, Household Expenditure and Child Marriage: Evidence from India and Vietnam." *Empirical Economics*, vol. 61, no. 3, July 2020, pp. 1617–39.

Ungar, Esta. "Re-Gendering Vietnam: From Militant to Market Socialism." *Women in Asia: Tradition, Modernity, and Globalisation*, edited by Louise Edwards and Mina Roces, Allen and Unwin, 2000, pp. 291–317.

"Vietnam: Achieving Success as a Middle-Income Country." *The World Bank*, 12 Apr. 2013, www.worldbank.org/en/results/2013/04/12/vietnam-achieving-success-as-a-middle-income-country.

Waugh, Charles, et al., editors. *Wild Mustard: New Voices from Vietnam*. Translated by Hung Nguyen et al., Curbstone Books, 2017.

Werner, Jayne. "Women, Socialism, and the Economy of Wartime North Vietnam, 1960–1975." *Studies in Comparative Communism*, vol. 14, nos. 2–3, summer-autumn 1981, pp. 165–90.

Whitelaw, Gavin. "*Konbini*-Nation: The Rise of the Convenience Store in Post-industrial Japan." *Consuming Life in Post-Bubble Japan: A Transdisciplinary Perspective*, edited by Katarzyna Cwiertka and Ewa Machotka, Amsterdam UP, 2018, pp. 69–88.

Wiriyaenawat, Piyanuch. "A Study of the Thai Translation and Cultural Reception of *Convenience Store Woman* by Sayaka Murata." *The Journal of Japanese Language Literature Studies*, vol. 11, no. 1, Dec. 2020, pp. 135–51.

Yamaguchi, Kiyoko. "Going Back to Traditional Ethics? The Importance of Marriage for Female College Graduates in Japan from 1995." *Gender and Family in East Asia*, edited by Siumi Maria Tam et al., Routledge, 2016, pp. 36–53.

Yoon, Jayoung. "Counting Care Work in Social Policy: Valuing Unpaid Child- and Eldercare in Korea." *Feminist Economics*, vol. 20, no. 2, Apr. 2014, pp. 65–89.

———. "Gender Norms, Housework, and Class: A Study of Korean Time Use Survey." *Asian Journal of Women's Studies*, vol. 16, no. 3, 2010, pp. 112–38.

Yoon, John. "South Korea Inches toward Same-Sex Equality, but Broader Bill Is Stalled." *The New York Times*, 22 Feb. 2023, www.nytimes.com/2023/02/22/world/asia/south-korea-lgbtq-law.html.

2. Struggling for Equity in Male-Dominated Professions

Globally, gender parity in labor force participation stands at only 64% (*Global Gender Gap Report 2023* 7). To be sure, the proportion of female leaders and skilled professionals continues to grow in many parts of the world, and progress is being made toward wage equality. But the wage gap, defined as the ratio of women's salaries to those of men in similar positions, is approximately 37%, while the income gap is approximately 51% (*Global Gender Gap Report 2021* 14). In addition, women remain significantly underrepresented in leadership positions, including in politics, with only 12 of 146 nations having bridged at least half of their political empowerment gender gap (*Global Gender Gap Report 2023* 18).[1] No Asian nation has gender parity in its parliament; women parliamentarians average just 20% (Joshi 2). Notable challenges for gender parity in economic participation and opportunity exist going forward, not just because of the greater impact of the COVID-19 pandemic on women's participation in the workforce. Even more important, six of the eight tracked "jobs of tomorrow" clusters are male-dominated, jobs conventionally held by women are more likely to be automated, and occupational segregation remains significant, making women less likely than men to change careers (*Global Gender Gap Report 2021* 5–6, 63–64).[2]

Moreover, the relationship between gender diversity and organizational performance is closely tied to broader social and institutional contexts. When gender diversity is normatively accepted in an industry or a society, gender-diverse teams outshine their more homogeneous counterparts. In contrast, gender-diverse groups are not as productive or profitable as their more homogeneous counterparts in industries and societies where gender diversity is not valued or even tolerated (Zhang).[3] Increasing gender diversity in environments hostile to such dynamics can thus create self-fulfilling prophecies. But they need not do so—individual leaders can create conditions where women feel psychologically safe speaking up, contributing fully, and thereby improving the performance of their group and industry (Turban et al.).

Some Asian nations rank high in parity of economic participation and opportunity: Laos is fifth in the world, with 85.1%, while Thailand, the Philippines, and Singapore have all closed at least 75% of their gender gaps. Many parts of Asia have more significant disparities in this subindex, including South Korea and Japan, which rank 114th and 123rd, respectively (*Global Gender Gap Report 2023* 17). As discussed in chapter 1, Cho Namjoo's novel *Kim Jiyoung* in particular highlights the potentially severe impacts of this opportunity gap on women's mental health. Inequities are even starker in Bangladesh, India, and Pakistan, which rank 139th, 142nd, and 143rd of 146 nations, respectively; overall, South Asia has closed only 37.2% of its economic participation and opportunity gender gap (*Global Gender Gap Report 2023* 17, 24).

Late-twentieth- and early-twenty-first-century literatures from across Asia and its diasporas have grappled with the injustices women in the paid workforce suffer in societies with rigid gender expectations. This includes less privileged women in typically female positions, the focus of chapter 3. It also includes women in professions conventionally dominated by men, the core of the present chapter, which analyzes *Beyond the Blossoming Fields* (*Hanauzumi*, 花埋み, lit. *Flower Burial*, 1970), by the Japanese writer Watanabe Jun'ichi (1933–2014); *Karachi, You're Killing Me!* (2014), by the Pakistani writer Saba Imtiaz (1985–); and "The Gunpowder Trail" (1999), by the Singaporean writer Claire Tham (1967–). Whereas Watanabe's historical novel highlights the formidable structural, social, and personal barriers Ogino Ginko (1851–1913) confronted as she strived to become Japan's first female physician licensed in Western medicine, Imtiaz's satirical novel underscores the struggles, determination, and ultimately triumph of a young Pakistani journalist. *Beyond the Blossoming Fields* and *Karachi, You're Killing Me!* are very different novels with very different protagonists and aesthetic sensibilities. At the same time, both highlight not only the tremendous courage of women breaking into and through male-dominated professions but also the significant role played by virtual strangers in ameliorating seemingly insurmountable barriers and seeking justice.

In contrast, Tham's parodic "Gunpowder Trail" depicts a once thriving female investment banker striking back at her industry after she was fired for refusing to continue her affair with her boss, then blacklisted without being given the opportunity to move to a different firm. This short story highlights the vulnerability of even the most gifted, dedicated, and productive women in industries where their mere presence triggers resentment and hostility. Watanabe's, Imtiaz's, and Tham's narratives take place from the late nineteenth to the early twenty-first century, in Japan, Pakistan, and Singapore. Telling stories seldom shared while addressing broader national and global challenges, they reveal that the injustices facing women in male-dominated professions are strikingly and soberingly consistent, even for exceptionally skilled and determined individuals.[4]

Moderating Medicine: Watanabe Jun'ichi's *Beyond the Blossoming Fields* (1970)

Women have been practicing medicine since ancient times and, regardless of culture, generally have been expected to care for the ill as part of their domestic obligations. Yet when women attempted to apply their medical skills in the public forum, they encountered, in the words of Lilian Furst, "an almost ubiquitous opposition which varied only in its intensity, overt pretexts, and underlying motivation" (1).[5] This has certainly been the case in Japan, which has a long lineage of *joi* (lit. "female doctors"), young women who assisted with births, dressed wounds, and performed acupuncture from the Nara period (710–84) to the Muromachi period (1336–1573). Although female doctors then virtually disappeared from the historical record, they continued as a "hidden force in medicine" in Japan until the introduction of Western medicine in the late nineteenth century (Nakamura, "Ogino Ginko's Vision" 6). One of the first Japanese women to practice Western medicine in Japan was Kusumoto Ine (1827–1903), daughter of the prominent German physician and botanist Philipp Franz von Siebold and his Japanese concubine Kusumoto Taki. Ine trained in general medicine and obstetrics with the Siebold network in Nagasaki and over time established a flourishing medical practice, albeit without a license (Nakamura, "Working" 197–98, 202, 206). As Ellen Nakamura has argued, referring to Ine's ability to take advantage of both her father's fame and the lack of medical regulation before the Meiji period (1868–1912), Ine's genealogy trumped her gender (209).[6]

In contrast, gender was a formidable barrier for Ogino Ginko, who in 1885 became the first woman licensed to practice Western medicine in Japan.[7] Ogino was married as a teenager to an older man who infected her with gonorrhea, an especially stigmatized chronic condition. Subjected to relentless harassment by her in-laws, she divorced and returned home to her parents. Constantly humiliated by her physicians at Tokyo's Juntendō

Hospital, all of whom were men, she recognized how different her experience as a patient likely would have been had she had a female physician. Despite her family's strident protests, Ogino joined the inaugural class of Tokyo Women's Normal School (est. 1875, now Ochanomizu University) and then, with the assistance of the influential physician Ishiguro Tadanori, was admitted to Kōjuin Medical College as its first female student. After graduating in 1882, Ogino fought for three years to be permitted to take the medical practitioner's examination. Although the pressure of preparing for the examination caused her gonorrhea to relapse, she passed on her first attempt and established the Ogino Gynecology Clinic in Yushima, Tokyo, where she made her name first as a physician and then increasingly as a feminist activist. A decade later she followed her new husband to Hokkaido, where she continued practicing medicine. In 1906, not long after he passed away, she returned to Tokyo, where she saw patients until her own death in 1913 (Nakamura, "Ogino Ginko's Vision").[8]

The Japanese novelist and former orthopedic surgeon Watanabe Jun'ichi's best-selling *Beyond the Blossoming Fields* is the fictionalized biography of Ogino Ginko and a social history of Meiji Japan. The omniscient third-person narrator creatively interweaves stories, episodes, and details from Ogino's life. These include her thoughts and feelings, some imagined and some documented. The narrator also includes more objective commentary and information from sources cited at the novel's conclusion on the familial and bureaucratic obstacles as well as the daily harassment and even violence facing women seeking an education and especially medical training in late-nineteenth-century Japan.[9] This deft narrative strategy—which differs notably from that of the Indonesian writer Ratna Khaerudina's "Susi" ("Potret Susi," lit. "Portrait of Susi," 2010), discussed in chapter 3, and resonates with but is distinctive from that of Cho's *Kim Jiyoung*, a novel that also frequently and explicitly contextualizes the experiences of its protagonist—enables Watanabe's *Beyond the Blossoming Fields* not only to contextualize but also to humanize a formidable historical figure who even in her early years had been dismissive of the struggles of women less privileged than herself.

Unlike Ine's family, which actively facilitated her medical studies, Ginko's family disowns her. Echoing Tiệp's experiences when she seeks a divorce in Dạ Ngân's *Insignificant Family*, discussed in chapter 1, Ginko's mother, Kayo, declares:

> Think of how the villagers would laugh if they ever heard that you planned to go to Tokyo to study and become a doctor. They'll point

> their fingers at you, and talk about "that madwoman." . . . Once you leave here, no one will ever have anything to do with you again. You'll never be able to come back. . . . Women have their own place, and they should stay there. Society would fall apart otherwise. Stop this nonsense, and resign yourself to staying here. (Watanabe, *Beyond* 57–58)

As happens frequently in *Beyond the Blossoming Fields*, the narrator follows contentious dialogue with compelling descriptions of Ginko's inner thoughts, an aesthetic strategy that personalizes her struggles: "Gin [Ginko] was not willing to give in. Her mother did not know the extent of the shame she had endured. . . . Up to now Gin had taken at face value everything her mother said and obeyed her unquestioningly, but no longer. *My mother and I are as different as night and day.* This discovery left Gin feeling more alone than ever" (58). Here as elsewhere in the narrative, italics graphically accentuate Ginko's struggles.

The president of Kōjuin Medical College grudgingly agrees to accept Ginko, but he makes no accommodations for her. And so, "from day one, Ginko was in for nothing but rude shocks" (Watanabe, *Beyond* 102). Her classmates mercilessly harass her, believing "her mere presence besmirched the reputation of the school" (103). They assert that "our honorable profession is being degraded to the work of women and children. . . . We have been demoted to the level of women" (104). Whenever they see Ginko, they "pound their desks and stomp their feet," and they hiss at her, "Woman, go home" (105). They torment her in the school's one bathroom.[10] And they pull back from gang-raping her only when they learn she has gonorrhea (109). Ginko has even less recourse than Imtiaz's Ayesha, or the Japanese journalist Itō Shiori, discussed in chapter 5, and unlike these women and Paru in Pawar's "Justice," discussed in the introduction, Ginko blames herself: "It had been her decision to study with men, which could be viewed as a dangerous undertaking from the start, and she could not say that it had not been a mistake to take that isolated path in the evening. . . . Any attempt she made to punish the thugs would merely damage her own name" (109). Contextualizing Ginko's experiences, the narrator describes Ginko's fears as "well founded. . . . Struggling all alone among these men twenty years [before the founding of Tokyo Women's Medical School, Japan's first medical school for women, est. 1900], the odds were unquestionably stacked against her" (110).[11] At the same time, as Ginko repeatedly reminds herself, the humiliation to which she is subjected in medical school does not compare to the degradation she endured as a gonorrhea patient in Juntendō Hospital (103, 111). The narrator speaks expressively here and elsewhere of Ginko's terror, using figurative language to impress on readers the depth and pervasiveness of her trauma: "Like sand caught in her teeth, the repulsiveness of the men was something she wanted to spit out back at them, but she had to keep it locked inside. . . . Against the background [of the hospital] any other trouble she had experienced seemed light and ordinary, like a glass bead with its colours faded and paled into insignificance" (111).

Beyond the Blossoming Fields additionally describes Ginko's lengthy battle to sit for the medical licensing examination, something most of her former (male) medical school classmates take for granted. As the narrator comments, "The fact that it was blatant discrimination based solely on her gender was intolerable [to Ginko]. Would women ever be treated equally to men? There was no indication that such a day would ever arrive" (Watanabe, *Beyond* 151). Thanks again to Ishiguro's intervention, permission eventually is granted for Ginko to take the examination, and in March 1885, at age 34, Ginko becomes the first female doctor to be licensed by the Japanese government. Once "derided as an eccentric and a woman who did not know her place," Ginko is suddenly a celebrity (167). Many still believe women "could never make suitable doctors," but the demand for skilled physicians is so high that Ginko's obstetrics and gynecology clinic quickly overflows with both women and men desperate for a range of care (170). Ironically, although Ginko treats some of her patients with compassion, her personal experiences with sexually transmitted infection, harassment, and other trauma make her overconfident with patients who have had similar experiences. Her financially privileged upbringing shields her from the lived realities of her patients, which when left unacknowledged and unaddressed renders her care ineffective if not harmful.[12]

The historical Ogino's three-part "The Past and Future Prospects of Women Doctors in Japan" ("Honpō joi no yurai oyobi sono zento," 本邦女医の由来およびその前途, 1893), published nearly a decade after Ogino established her clinic, argues for increasing the number of women doctors in Japan.[13] Even as Ogino moved more toward Christianity and activism, her achievements in medicine enabled other Japanese women to become licensed physicians. Yet women remained a small minority of physicians in Japan for much of the twentieth century, and even today, only 20% of Japanese physicians are women, lowest among OECD (Organization for Economic Cooperation and Development) nations, where the average is 46% (Dyer).[14] Particularly notorious is the case of Tokyo Medical University, one of Japan's most prestigious medical schools. In 2011, this institution began deliberately lowering the examination scores of its female applicants to reduce the proportion of women enrolling, from a high of 38% in 2010 to a low of 18% in 2018, when the scheme was discovered. Ultimately, 10 of Japan's 81 medical schools were found to have rigged women's exams. Conditions have improved slightly: the 2021 acceptance rate for women surpassed that of men in 36 medical schools, and women passed the national medical school exam at a somewhat higher rate than men in 2021; in 2022, the number of female high school seniors hoping to become physicians grew 13% ("More"; "Women"). Yet partly because of the hostile working environment, 86% of Japanese women who graduate from medical school stop working full-time within a decade of earning their MD (Yamaguchi 37).[15]

Conditions in medicine resemble those in other professions. A third of Japan's major companies have no female executives, and women occupy only 12.9% of senior positions ("33%"; *Global Gender Gap Report 2023* 217).[16] Japan is far from meeting the targets of former Japanese prime minister Abé Shinzō's 2013 Womenomics initiative, which aimed to increase the percentage of women in senior and leadership positions and to boost childcare options and benefits (Lambert 348).[17] Pointing to studies that reveal Japanese women as happier overall than men, Gill Steel argues that rather than protest inequalities and injustices, "most [Japanese] women have generally crafted individual solutions to structural problems" (17).[18] This is certainly the case for the protagonist of Murata Sayaka's *Convenience Store Woman*, discussed in chapter 1. And, as Watanabe's *Beyond the Blossoming Fields* emphasizes through its vigorous narrative and aesthetic choices and particularly through its humanization of a key figure in Japan's medical history, solutions for individuals can in time create possibilities for marginalized groups. Over decades, Japanese women have made inroads into a broader range of professions. Yet for most, justice is frequently thwarted and stubbornly distant.

Making It in Media: Saba Imtiaz's *Karachi, You're Killing Me!* (2014)

Set more than a century later and written in a very different style from the fictionalized biography of the Japanese physician Ogino Ginko, Imtiaz's epistolary Pakistani novel *Karachi, You're Killing Me!*, about a female journalist determined to become a prominent reporter, nevertheless resonates powerfully with its predecessor.[19] As is true of studies on gender disparity in medicine, studies on the gender disparities in media have proliferated since the 1970s, drawing attention to the underrepresentation of women as news producers and both the underrepresentation and the misrepresentation of women as news subjects (Ross et al. 824).[20] Inspired by the February 1994 Bangkok conference Women Empowering Communication, in which more than 400 women from more than 80 nations participated, the Canadian NGO Media Watch coordinated the first three iterations of the Global Media Monitoring Project (1995, 2000, 2005). Since 2010, these quinquennial reports have been coordinated by the World Association for Christian Communication (825). Today, the Global Media Monitoring Project is the world's "longest running research and advocacy initiative that seeks to advance gender equality in and through the news media" ("About Us").

Although not without its shortcomings, the project provides a longitudinal view of the severe gender disparities in print, radio, television, and now digital media. As Sarah Macharia, the editor of the 2020 report, summarizes, findings "reveal a mixed picture of progress, stagnation, and regression. While some glass ceilings are clearly being edged upwards, others are setting in on certain important news media gender equality indicators" (5). Globally, only 24% of news subjects are female; male voices prevail even in stories on gender-based violence (Lee 1). In Asia, the figure is even lower: only 21% of news subjects in print, radio, and television are female, the lowest percentage anywhere outside the Middle East (Macharia 21). Conditions are especially lopsided in Pakistan, where women make up just 7% of reporters and 17% of subjects and sources in print, radio, and television news; in Internet news, Pakistani women make up only 25% of reporters and 15% of subjects and sources (81, 120). These numbers resonate with those of the World Economic Forum's 2023 *Global Gender Gap Report*, which ranks Pakistan 142nd of 146 nations overall, 138th in educational attainment, and 143rd in economic participation and opportunity. Just 24.5% of women are in the labor force, and women hold a mere 5.7% of senior, managerial, and legislative positions; women's average income is only 25% of men's average income (*Global Gender Gap Report 2023* 11, 17, 18, 293).[21]

Both a journalist and a creative writer, Imtiaz has been vocal about the injustices facing women in Pakistan and their impact on every part of a woman's body, being, and life. As she remonstrates in a July 2021 blog post on her personal website:

> Nothing is free or safe [for women]. Every act is up for being taken for something else. (I wrote out a list of acts here that men think are for

> them, things like standing on the balcony, breathing in the air outside, and then I realized I could just spend all day writing out acts). . . . The incessant policing, moral, social . . . I spend my life living with my heart in my throat, clenched jaw, a frozen expression, a body so tense it never knows when it will ever calm down. ("What")[22]

Ayesha Khan, the 28-year-old first-person narrator of *Karachi*, is less concerned than Imtiaz about her safety, not to mention the safety of women in general, even as rape remains a very real concern. Yet Ayesha's despair as an intrepid female reporter for the city of Karachi's *Daily News* is no less palpable. To be sure, Imtiaz's novel does not offer solutions for the systemic misogyny to which women of all classes and education levels in Pakistan are subjected by both locals and outsiders. At the same time, even more than *Beyond the Blossoming Fields*, and in sharp contrast with Cho's *Kim Jiyoung*, *Karachi* reveals the transformative role individual colleagues can play in tempering structural sexism and in the struggle for justice.

Karachi consists of 25 chronological diary entries spanning Friday, 31 December 2011 to Tuesday, 11 May 2012; two-thirds of the novel takes place in April and May 2012. Not only is the diary an inherently personal genre, the entries are in the present tense, keeping pace with Ayesha's experiences, conversations, thoughts, and feelings in real time. Imtiaz's narrative strategies are notably different from the third-person novels that engage with much longer periods of Ginko's, Tiệp's, and even Kim Jiyoung's lives and that interweave external perspectives with individual stories across decades. *Karachi* gives the impression of unmediated insight into a short yet transformative period of Ayesha's life and career. As a fearless journalist who in her reporting for the *Daily News* covers everything from bombings and gang violence to fashion shows and bakeries, Ayesha shares directly the personal impact of gender injustice, humanizing the person behind the byline.

From the beginning, Ayesha describes herself as "miserable" and as "hating" her life (Imtiaz, *Karachi* 11, 30). Karachi, Pakistan's largest, most cosmopolitan, and most secular city, is depicted as a "wasteland . . . where it's easier to hire an assassin than meet an attractive, intelligent, normal single man" (15). Ayesha relates many instances where she is patronized, harassed, and even assaulted because of her gender; the narrative's short time span highlights the frequency of these attacks. For instance, early in *Karachi* a policeman asks Ayesha why a "nice girl" like her is smoking, even though, Ayesha notes, "every other man on the site is also smoking" (21). The following day, Ayesha arrives at dinner soaking wet "because a group of 20-something boys [with a police escort] were throwing water balloons at every girl walking on the road from their car" (30). Ayesha likewise comments that her boyfriend, Hasan, with whom she soon parts ways, is "perplexed" by her career and intolerant of her irregular hours and the risks she takes (34).

Life as a female journalist is brutal. Despite having graduated from both college and business school in a nation where just 12% of women attend college (*Global Gender Gap Report 2023* 293)—not to mention her enviable talents and exceptional work ethic—Ayesha is treated as "a glorified intern" (Imtiaz, *Karachi* 17). She watches male colleagues who rely on her for their stories being offered prestigious positions by both national and international news organizations and becomes increasingly frustrated with the flattening of her own trajectory. Unlike Keiko, in *Convenience Store Woman*, Ayesha speaks repeatedly of longing to grow her own career.

The fallout from her interview with Abbu Khan, a former Guantánamo detainee, is particularly egregious. Learning that Khan is back in Karachi, Ayesha recognizes instantly that interviewing him could vault her into prominence. When her boss, Kamran, tells her that they could "send a guy" instead, despite Ayesha's connection with Khan's son, Ayesha snaps back: "This is not something a guy can do better. I've covered everything that most of your male reporters have said no to" (Imtiaz, *Karachi* 139). Kamran ultimately agrees to the interview, but not before asking Ayesha to order him takeout, highlighting her continued inferior standing at the paper. Then, pressured by Pakistani intelligence, Kamran refuses to run her story. Ayesha quickly finds a work-around and arranges to have the interview published by a prominent news website in the United Kingdom (155). But her article is scooped by CNN's James Maxwell (Jamie), a (fictional) character with whom Ayesha has just started a relationship, and the UK editor retracts his offer to Ayesha. The irony with Jamie is that he, unlike some of Ayesha's other boyfriends, had very much encouraged her career (132, 134).[23] Ayesha is inconsolable. Referring to the colonization of the Indian subcontinent from the seventeenth through the twentieth centuries, she remarks, "I am such a cliché: white man comes to Pakistan, befriends local, steals her due right. It's like the bloody East India Company all over again" (176).

Ayesha enjoys greater support from family members, friends, and colleagues than do many of the protagonists featured in *Gender Justice*, including the fellow journalist Itō Shiori, discussed in chapter 5. In the short period shared in *Karachi*, the NBC bureau chief Andrea Altman (another fictional character, seemingly based loosely on Andrea Mitchell) particularly stands out. Although having met Ayesha just a few days before, Andrea connects her with an editor at *Al Jazeera* looking for someone from Pakistan to contribute to its website. The promise of succeeding as a freelancer gives Ayesha the self-assurance to resign from the *Daily News* when Kamran refuses to give her a raise. Ayesha proclaims, "Fuck Kamran and fuck this job. I have a potential Al Jazeera story, a bunch of great ideas, and hundreds of contacts. . . . I'll be fine" (Imtiaz, *Karachi* 194–95). And after *Al Jazeera* brings her on board, her confidence reaches new heights, capital letters, here as elsewhere, accentuating her passion and determination: "I AM NOT AN ABJECT FAILURE! I AM A BRILLIANT REPORTER AND I AM GOING TO BE RICH AND FAMOUS AND WIN A PULITZER. . . . For once, I feel proud of the work I've done. . . . It's finally happening. I am actually doing the kind of stories I've wanted to do for so long" (219–20). In addition to connecting Ayesha with *Al Jazeera*, Andrea introduces Ayesha to a contact at the BBC, forwards her other opportunities, and offers to write letters of recommendation. She also exposes Jamie's misconduct, prompting CNN to fire him.

Andrea downplays the impact she has had on Ayesha's career. But what takes little effort for her makes all the difference for Ayesha. Ayesha exuberantly declares, "In this moment, I could erect a shrine to her and offer a pint of my blood to her every single day to express my gratitude. . . . The knot of tension in my stomach that's been omnipresent since the day CNN scooped me is gone, and even my achy muscles feel more relaxed. There's a jolt of energy coursing through me" (Imtiaz, *Karachi* 259). Whereas Imtiaz, as previously cited, speaks of "a body so tense it never knows when it will ever calm down," Ayesha can finally begin to unwind, however temporarily. To be sure, Andrea does not create a position for Ayesha at NBC, suggesting either the limits of her own agency, or, less likely, her own biases. And it requires a non-Pakistani to liberate Ayesha from another non-Pakistani's malfeasance and a ruthless Pakistani boss, despite Ayesha's vast network of Pakistani family, friends, and colleagues, underscoring persistent postcolonial power differentials. Yet ultimately, Imtiaz's *Karachi* highlights the potentially significant impact that even small acts can have when it comes to pursuing justice.

In the foreword to the *Sixth Global Media Monitoring Project*, the UN under-secretary-general and executive director of UN Women Phumzile Mlambo-Ngcuka decries:

> When women are on average 46 percent of health specialists in reality but appeared as such in just 27 percent of coronavirus stories,

> inaccurate gender stereotypes are reinforced. At a time when a "shadow pandemic" of violence against women and girls raged around the world, the fact that only 6 out of 100 stories were related to sexual harassment, rape, and sexual assault against women risks normalizing gender-based violence.

Mlambo-Ngcuka highlights the frequently untapped power of media to "push against simplistic stereotypical gender roles" and "create the more accurate, inclusive and empowering representation we need as the world rebuilds." Doing so necessitates diversifying the media to include more female journalists and other marginalized voices; reducing significant gaps in salary, work assignments, decision-making power, and promotion; and empowering all reporters to prioritize a broader range of women's experiences (De Vuyst 1). Although, as in other professions conventionally dominated by men, change in media is frequently glacial (Macharia 5), Ayesha's diary entries reveal how rapidly change can sometimes take place and justice sometimes be served. In so doing, Imtiaz's novel *Karachi* undercuts stereotypes surrounding Pakistani women and female journalists alike.[24]

Breaking Banking: Claire Tham's "The Gunpowder Trail" (1999)

Even more than medicine and journalism, investment banking in many parts of the world remains dominated by men, who hold most of the highly compensated senior positions, while women occupy most of the lower-ranked administrative posts (Dabla-Norris and Kochhar 9; Margot).[25] Women who do penetrate the senior ranks are rarely treated equally to men in equivalent positions: they are frequently paid less, passed over for promotions, and expected to adhere to rigid gender norms. They also risk isolation, if not condemnation, from family, other women, and their broader society, given the long hours and particular skills such positions require. The Singaporean writer and lawyer Claire Tham's prizewinning "Gunpowder Trail," the opening story of Tham's eponymous collection, focuses on one such woman and her daughter: 36-year-old Lina and her 16-year-old daughter, Wen Shan.[26] Lina adeptly oversees the private banking unit of an American investment bank in Singapore that has just been taken over by a German commercial banking giant. Despite having strongly considered having an abortion, she gave birth to Wen Shan while in college in the United States; unlike many of the women discussed in chapter 4, she had the choice. Yet Lina has no desire to mother Wen Shan;

"Where was it written," the narrator asks, "that you had to love your child?" (Tham 238). Lina's physician had attributed Lina's malaise after Wen Shan's birth to postpartum depression, misdiagnosing her. Unlike Kim Jiyoung, who had no family to help care for her daughter, and Tiệp, who was desperate to retain custody of her children, Lina eagerly turned Wen Shan over to her grandparents, Lina's parents. The three lived together until Lina's parents were killed in a car crash when Wen Shan was twelve, at which point she moved in with her mother.

"Gunpowder Trail" adeptly alternates between five sections titled "Lina," narrated in the third-person limited omniscient, and five sections titled "Wen Shan," narrated in the first person by Wen Shan. Wen Shan devotes most of her narrative to writing about her mother, including describing herself through her mother's eyes. In contrast, the third-person narrator of the "Lina" sections says little about Wen Shan. This aesthetic strategy makes palpable the uneven dynamics of Lina's relationship with her daughter. It additionally spares the story from addressing the fate of the migrant domestic workers who service many Singaporean households, where they often encounter significant abuse, as discussed in chapter 3. "Gunpowder Trail" is even more condensed than *Karachi*, taking place across an approximately 20-hour period, from 6:30 a.m. to past midnight on the day Lina disappears, and relying on extensive flashbacks to tell more of Lina's and secondarily Wen Shan's stories. Both narrators (i.e., Wen Shan and the narrator of the "Lina" sections) use very direct language with limited dialogue, preferring to summarize rather than cite.

Tham's short story can be read as a parody of an exceptionally driven and high-achieving professional woman. Although Watanabe's and Imtiaz's protagonists are also impressively ambitious, they are very different from Lina, who is described as a coldhearted individual who cycles rapidly through married men, has little time for family, and ultimately disappears, absconding with 50 million dollars from the accounts of her private banking clients. At the same time, as *Beyond the Blossoming Fields* does for Japan and *Karachi* does for Pakistan, "Gunpowder Trail" reveals the significant gender biases Lina has had to confront just by existing as a woman in Singapore, and especially as one with high career aspirations.[27] "Gunpowder Trail" also exposes the considerable obstacles that professionally successful women continue to face, portraying Lina less as a villain than as an individual unjustly deprived of meaningful connections and legitimate options.

From the beginning, Lina is depicted not as someone who juggles roles (banker, mother, and daughter) but instead as someone who has "waged a battle for years over the ill-fitting roles . . . [of] compliant daughter, dutiful mother" (Tham 226).[28] The chasm between Lina and her parents resembles that between Lina and her daughter, who describes herself as "bookish, withdrawn, badly-dressed, uninterested in money, everything my mother was not. . . . We had nothing to say to each other" (244). Although having wanted to flee for a while, Lina had never done so, "because of a tiresome, intermittent sense of responsibility—to her parents, to her daughter—that came and went like the flu and never allowed her to recover sufficiently to take flight" (257). It is only when she believes her daughter can care for herself that Lina escapes, leaving Wen Shan with 10 million dollars in a Cayman Islands account, as well as, in the words of Wen Shan, a metaphoric "ball and chain" that would "dog my life" (256).

For Lina, relationships with other women are even more difficult than those with her parents and daughter. As Wen Shan observes:

> My mother was not interested in women, just as she was not interested in housework, cooking, children, or anything remotely domestic. For their part, women instinctively disliked my mother. I saw them stiffen when she walked into a room. . . . There might have been a time when my mother had made a token attempt to disarm the women. . . . But, rebuffed once too often, she must have rapidly got bored and accepted her outsider status. It was different with men; it always had been. (Tham 243)

Not surprisingly, given that "Gunpowder Trail" refers repeatedly to Lina's ability to captivate men, Wen Shan declares that her own "natural instinct" is "to side with the women" (243). At the same time, Wen Shan's description of her mother's isolation from other women reveals Lina as the one rebuffed and instinctively disliked. Similarly, Wen Shan observes that at her grandparents' wake, their relatives instinctively "gave [Lina] an extremely wide berth, as though she might be contagious, or bad luck" (242). Paradoxically, Lina's incapacitating "flu" of responsibility renders her "contagious" to her family.

In only one role, the narrator declares, had Lina "ever felt completely at home: her job as an investment banker" (Tham 226). And Lina had excelled in that position, as Wen Shan perceptively confirms, her figurative language accentuating her mother's success:

> Her rise had been meteoric. . . . Her investments were shrewd, her instincts unfailing. She could talk shop for hours with the money men;

> it was one of the reasons women disliked her. Deals fueled her life; taking her numerous calls at home, hearing the roar of dealing rooms in the background, the electronic urgency of billions being traded. . . . I thought of her as being at the centre of some vast, spider's financial web, a queen arachnid to which all the subject arachnids brought their daily offerings. (255)

Nevertheless, Lina was unjustly passed over for a promotion, the bank instead bringing in an Australian, Peter Holbrooke, as her boss. And, not surprisingly, the narrator reports, she "resented his entry, ascribing it, correctly, to the jobs-for-the-boys principle that still prevailed, ever so subtly, at the bank" (245). Although Peter is described as "essentially [Lina's] male counterpart" in personality (245), he is not as accomplished professionally (246). Peter and Lina are drawn to each other, but their passionate affair quickly turns sour as Peter becomes possessive, then abusive, like the male partners discussed in chapter 7. Peter degrades Lina with claims, echoing Shiraha in *Convenience Store Woman*, that "time's running out" and that when Lina turns fifty she will be "a pathetic, raddled figure, propping up bars, scaring off all the men within a fifty-yard radius" (250). Soon after, Lina is fired for refusing to resume the affair with Peter. Seeking revenge, she defrauds their clients and implicates Peter, who is taken into police custody while she flees the country.

Lina is easy to condemn. At the same time, she believed she had no future in Singapore, "[a] country where she'd always felt out-of-kilter: too driven, too unsentimental, too sexual, too much of everything" (Tham 257).[29] Here, in the final "Lina" section, the narrator speaks explicitly of Lina as just "too much" for Singapore. The only spaces for her had been at the bank and with charismatic men. With the former no longer available and the latter no longer appealing, Lina believes that she has no options. That Lina, despite her talent, is not hired by another bank and that her story is told through a third-person narrator, particularly one who cites her only infrequently, give prominence to her silencing. This is in sharp contrast with her daughter, Wen Shan, who expertly narrates her own story and particularly that of her mother with a sophistication that belies her age. Even as "The Gunpowder Trail" highlights the injustices Lina has faced because of her gender and ambition, the narrative structure of Tham's story suggests some potential for a more just future, particularly given Wen Shan's hope of becoming a writer.[30]

Nearly 25 years after the publication of "The Gunpowder Trail," Singapore was one of only five nations to reach 80% wage parity (*Global Gender Gap Report 2023* 321).[31] Yet there is still a long way to go. Many of the gender dynamics described in Tham's "The Gunpowder Trail" remain stubbornly persistent in Singapore and across Asia and the world. The entrenchment of rigid gender expectations; the relative dearth of women in senior positions, especially in lucrative and powerful professions; and the notable pay gaps at most levels of employment demonstrate the continued vulnerability of women, no matter how wealthy or professionally successful, to being professionally and personally disenfranchised.

Medicine, media, and investment banking are just three of countless male-dominated professions in which women have made important inroads over the last decades but in which they remain highly marginalized, if not always in terms of numbers then often in terms of expectations and experiences. The narrative strategies and aesthetics of *Beyond the Blossoming Fields*, *Karachi*, and "Gunpowder Trail" draw further attention to the barriers and injustices confronting Ginko, Ayesha, and Lina. Particularly impactful are the considerable sociohistorical contextualization in Watanabe's novel, the first-person narration over a brief time span in Imtiaz's novel, and the third-person narration with scant dialogue yet graphic language in Tham's short story. At the same time, all three narratives highlight the agency of their protagonists: Ginko makes a tremendous impact on Japanese medicine, Ayesha succeeds in her quest for greater recognition, and Lina liberates herself from an untenable career and inhospitable environment while still providing for her daughter. The ending of Ginko's story is known; the futures of Ayesha and Lina are less certain, as Ayesha faces decades of fighting the patriarchy in Pakistan and Lina decades of evading law enforcement. Although they are very different works that feature very different protagonists situated in East, South, and Southeast Asia from the nineteenth through the twenty-first century, Watanabe's, Imtiaz's, and Tham's narratives all engage with some of the steepest gender barriers facing women who struggle for justice in male-dominated professions, even as they enjoy varying degrees of career success and personal fulfillment. Frequently even more traumatizing are the experiences of women in conventionally female and far less privileged professions, especially migrant domestic workers, nurses, and others in caregiving professions, explored in chapter 3.

NOTES

1. The political empowerment subindex reveals the widest gender gap, at only 22.5% closed (*Global Gender Gap Report 2023* 16). As explained in the World Economic Forum's *Global Gender Gap Report 2023*, "The Global Gender Gap Index measures scores on a 0 to 100 scale and scores can be interpreted as the distance covered toward parity (i.e., the percentage of the gender gap that has been closed)" (5).

2. For instance, women are just 14% of the workforce in cloud computing, 20% in engineering, and 32% in data and AI, figures that have either decreased or only very slightly increased during the past few years (*Global Gender Gap Report 2021* 61).

3. Zhang studied 1,069 leading firms across 35 countries and 24 industries. *Normative acceptance* refers to "a widespread cultural belief that gender diversity is important" and is distinguished from *regulatory acceptance* (Turban et al.).

4. See also the Indonesian writer Titis Basino's "A Decision" ("Suatu Keputusan," 1963). Another promising comparison is with the Chinese writer He Jiahong's *Hanging Devils: Hong Jun Investigates* (*Xue zhi zui*, lit. *Crime of Blood*, 1994), on women in law enforcement (Thornber, "Comparison" 203–07), and narratives on Asian women's participation in public affairs and political leadership, such as *My Fight for a New Taiwan: One Woman's Journey from Prison to Power* (2014), by Lu Hsiu-lien (Annette Lu, Taiwan's first female vice president), and the former Indian prime minister Indira Gandhi's *My Truth* (1980). Earlier narratives likewise depict the struggles of women breaking into male-dominated professions. See, for instance, Yukiko Tanaka's *To Live and to Write: Selections by Japanese Women Writers, 1913–1938*. Films such as China's *Tiyu huanghou* (*Queen of Sports*, 1934), on a female sprinter, "supported Chinese nationalist visions of a fit female citizenry" (Gao 208). This film provides an important contrast with the Hindi-language Indian film *Dangal* (*Wrestling Competition*, 2016), based on the Phogat sisters, India's first female wrestlers to compete on the global stage. Whereas *Wrestling Competition* devotes considerable attention to the sisters breaking significant gender barriers, *Queen of Sports* creates "the athletic movie star as an important archetype for Chinese film" (210).

5. Notably, between 1901 and 2021, only 12 of the 224 Nobel awardees in medicine or physiology were women; Senz connects the dearth of female scientists to fewer medical treatments for women. Zimmer summarizes biases against women in science (19–29), while Trimble and Weintraub's volume shares powerful autobiographical essays by female astronomers on countering gender injustice.

6. Japan's 1874 *Regulations on Medical Practice* (*Isei*) for the first time required all medical doctors to be licensed. Given that the only approved form of training

was in Western medicine, those who had trained in Chinese medicine, then the great majority of doctors, were granted temporary licenses and permitted to continue practicing until they were gradually replaced by those trained in Western medicine (Nakamura, "Ogino Ginko's Vision" 5). Unlike the men with whom she had practiced, Ine notably applied in 1884 for a license as a previously practicing "old midwife" rather than as a physician or "new midwife" (Nakamura, "Working" 200). Ine has captivated the imagination of dramatists, manga artists, and novelists such as Yoshimura Akira, whose highly romanticized *Von Siebold's Daughter* (*Fuon Shiiboruto no musume*, 1978) has long been the most popular version of her life (Nakamura, "Kusumoto Ine" 249).

7. Other prominent early Japanese female physicians trained in Western medicine were Yoshioka Yayoi, who in 1900 founded Japan's first medical school for women, and her student Takeuchi Shigeyo. Some nineteenth-century Japanese women sought medical training in the United States; until recently, the contributions of these and other female health professionals have been overlooked in scholarly discourse (Fujimoto and Nakamura).

8. Ogino died just two years after Hiratsuka Raichō founded *Seitō* (*Bluestocking*), Japan's first journal "to openly defy existing norms for women's behavior," including the ideal of women as "good wife, wise mother" (*ryōsai kenbo*; Bullock et al. 2).

9. Here I focus primarily on the difficulties Ginko encountered because of her gender. For more on her efforts, hampered by the traumas she experienced, to save women and humanize medical care, see Thornber, *Global Healing* 341–62. For more on narratives that highlight the experiences of female physicians, see also Thornber, *Global Healing* 328–85. *Brotherless Night* (2023), by the American writer of Ilankai Tamil (Sri Lankan) descent V. V. Ganeshananthan, speaks to the tremendous challenges facing a young woman longing to become a physician during wartime. Watanabe is best known for the novel *A Lost Paradise* (*Shitsurakuen*, 1997), adapted into multiple media and widely translated.

10. School violence and sexual harassment are frequent topics in contemporary Asian literatures, including the Japanese writer Akiyoshi Rikako's *The Dark Maidens* (*Ankoku joshi*, 2013), the Chinese (Hong Kong) writer Chan Ho-Kei's *Second Sister* (*Wangneiren*, 2017), and the Indonesian writer Djenar Maesa Ayu's "Painting a Window" ("Melukis Jendela," 2001).

11. Tokyo Women's Medical School attracted women from across East Asia, part of the larger movement of Chinese, Korean, and Taiwanese students to Japan following Japanese victory in the first Sino-Japanese War (1894–95; Thornber, *Empire* 1–27). Before 1900, the Saisei Gakusha (est. 1876) was the only medical school in Japan to accept women (Nakamura, "Ogino Ginko's Vision" 9). Tocco summarizes women's education in Tokugawa (1600–1868) and Meiji Japan, while Molony discusses women's rights and education in Meiji Japan.

12. For more on this phenomenon, see Thornber, *Global Healing* 343–62.

13. Nakamura summarizes this essay in "Ogino Ginko's Vision."

14. Women remain a distinct minority in higher education in Japan: they account for only 30% of faculty members (and just 16% of faculty members at the University of Tokyo, one of the nation's most prestigious universities), compared to the OECD average of 45% ("Japan"; "University").

15. For more on Japanese medicine's glass ceiling, see Nomura and Gohchi 1613, 1615; Nomura et al. 651. Female physicians face similar barriers globally, particularly in terms of compensation and opportunities for advancement. As Dr. Suzanne Koven observes, "The amount of sexism and sexual harassment in medicine is astonishing" ("Letter" [2023]); over the past decades "shockingly little has changed for women in medicine" ("Letter" [2021]). See also Mangurian et al. and *The State of Women in Academic Medicine* on the barriers women in the United States face in attaining leadership positions in medicine.

16. For additional statistics on conditions for women in Japan, see chapter 1.

17. The idea of Womenomics was first articulated by Kathy Matsui and colleagues at Goldman Sachs in 1999. Matsui et al. discuss areas for improvement, while Lambert examines the cultural, institutional, and structural barriers limiting women's opportunities in Japan.

18. Gong and Yang examine a similar phenomenon in Chinese Internet fiction (85). As narratives such as the Japanese writer Kirino Natsuo's *What Remains* (*Zangyakuki*, lit. *Record of Brutality*, 2004) make clear, circumstances prevent many women from crafting such solutions (Scrolavezza).

19. *Karachi* was adapted into the Hindi-language film *Noor: Mumbai, You're Killing Me* (2017), featuring a female journalist eager for her big break, scooped by a male journalist, yet in the end attaining prominence.

20. Women are even scarcer in media leadership positions; it was not until 2011 that *The New York Times* hired its first female executive editor, Jill Abramson.

21. Only 41.6% of Pakistani girls attend high school (*Global Gender Gap Report 2023* 293).

22. For instance, Pakistan's prime minister has explicitly linked rape to women's "vulgarity" and women's behaviors, including their choice of clothing (Masood). Imtiaz has written on a range of topics for prominent media outlets. Fluent in five languages, she has reported from across the Middle East (Imtiaz, "About").

23. Cf. the Bangladeshi British writer Tahmima Anam's *The Startup Wife* (2021).

24. Cf. the portrayal of female journalists in much popular culture (Painter and Ferrucci).

25. See Wilkinson for more on the gender gap in investment banking in 2007. For conditions in 2018, see Margot; Dabla-Norris and Kochhar. Ha et al. establish the prevalence rates of the three primary psychosocial illnesses: depression (38%), anxiety (70%), and stress (32%) among bank employees in Singapore (169). Kang outlines the gender wage gap in multiple industries in Singapore,

while Roth discusses processes of sex segregation on Wall Street, revealing repeating structural patterns (204).

26. "Gunpowder Trail" won the 1999 National Arts Council Golden Point Short Story Award, one of Singapore's most prestigious creative writing competitions. It was adapted into a bilingual (English and Malay) theatrical production in 2011. Tham is also known for *The Inlet* (2013), a novel based loosely on the drowning of a Chinese migrant to Singapore who worked as a hostess. For more on the experiences of migrant workers, see chapter 3. Jamie Fiore Higgins's *Bully Market: My Story of Money and Misogyny at Goldman Sachs* (2022) describes a similarly abusive corporate culture in the United States.

27. Although Lina is a Singaporean woman employed by an American and then German bank in Singapore, "Gunpowder Trail" depicts her gender as much more of an obstacle in the workplace than her ethnicity.

28. Lina's parents adore Lina and Wen Shan, but they dislike Lina's boyfriends, especially Lester, a Black man, to whom they are openly hostile.

29. Even Lina's height is a problem: as Wen Shan states, at five-eight Lina was "a giantess as far as Asians were concerned" (Tham 240).

30. On the other hand, making it as a female writer in Singapore has been no easy task. See, for instance, the Singaporean author Catherine Lim's *Miss Seetoh in the World*. This novel satirizes gender dynamics in 1980s and 1990s Singapore through the story of Maria Seetoh, a teacher who longs for "a bed, a room, a house, a life of her own" (Lim 449). As Angelia Poon observes, writing is Maria's one way of escaping "the oppressiveness of a highly gendered, male-centered society which dictates that a woman always needs to be with a man" (232).

31. Between 2006 and 2023, Singapore's overall score increased from 0.655 to 0.739, where 1.0 represents parity (*Global Gender Gap Report 2006* 9; *Global Gender Gap Report 2023* 11).

WORKS CITED

"About Us." *Who Makes the News?*, 2021, whomakesthenews.org/about-us/.

Akiyoshi Rikako. *The Dark Maidens*. Translated by Kristi Fernandez, Vertical, 2018.

Anam, Tahmima. *The Startup Wife*. Scribner, 2022.

Ayu, Djenar Maesa. "Painting a Window." *They Say I'm a Monkey*, by Ayu, translated by Michael Nieto Garcia, Metafor Press, 2005, pp. 27–36.

Basino, Titis. "A Decision." *Women's Voices: An Anthology of Short Stories by Indonesian Writers*, translated by Pamela Allen, Longman, 1995, pp. 81–87.

Bullock, Julia C., et al. Introduction. *Rethinking Japanese Feminisms*, edited by Bullock et al., U of Hawai'i P, 2018, pp. 1–14.

Chan Ho-Kei. *Second Sister*. Translated by Jeremy Tiang, Black Cat, 2020.

Dabla-Norris, Era, and Kalpana Kochhar. "Closing the Gender Gap." *Finance and Development*, Mar. 2019, pp. 6–11.

Dangal. Directed by Nitesh Tiwari, Aamir Khan Productions, 2016.

De Vuyst, Sara. *Hacking Gender and Technology in Journalism*. Routledge, 2020.

Dyer, Owen. "Tokyo Medical School Investigates Claims That It Rigged Exam Results to Turn Women Away." *The British Medical Journal*, vol. 362, 6 Aug. 2018, www.bmj.com/content/362/bmj.k3416.

Fujimoto, Hiro, and Ellen Nakamura. "Women and Medicine in the Japanese Empire." Workshop, 26 Feb. 2022, online.

Furst, Lilian R. Introduction. *Women Healers and Physicians: Climbing a Long Hill*, edited by Furst, UP of Kentucky, 1997, pp. 1–9.

Gandhi, Indira. *My Truth*. Vision Books, 1981.

Ganeshananthan, V. V. *Brotherless Night*. Random House, 2023.

Gao, Yunxiang. *Sporting Gender: Women Athletes and Celebrity-Making during China's National Crisis, 1931–1945*. U of British Columbia P, 2013.

Global Gender Gap Report 2006. World Economic Forum, 2006, www3.weforum.org/docs/WEF_GGGR_2006.pdf.

Global Gender Gap Report 2021. World Economic Forum, 2021, www3.weforum.org/docs/WEF_GGGR_2021.pdf.

Global Gender Gap Report 2023. World Economic Forum, 2023, www3.weforum.org/docs/WEF_GGGR_2023.pdf.

Gong, Haomin, and Xin Yang. *Reconfiguring Class, Gender, Ethnicity, and Ethics in Chinese Internet Culture*. Routledge, 2017.

Ha, Huong, et al. "Psychosocial Well-Being of Employees in the Banking Sector in Singapore." *International Journal of Environment, Workplace, and Employment*, vol. 5, no. 2, 2019, pp. 169–92.

He Jiahong. *Hanging Devils: Hong Jun Investigates*. Viking, 2016.

Higgins, Jamie Fiore. *Bully Market: My Story of Money and Misogyny at Goldman Sachs*. Simon and Schuster, 2022.

Imtiaz, Saba. "About." *Saba Imtiaz*, sabaimtiaz.com/about. Accessed 15 Dec. 2023.

———. *Karachi, You're Killing Me!* Random House India, 2014.

———. "What Is It Like?" *Saba Imtiaz*, 24 July 2021, sabaimtiaz.com/blog/2021/7/21/what-is-it-like.

"Japan Ranked Last in Women Staff in Tertiary Education in 2020: OECD." *Japan Times*, 10 Oct. 2022, www.japantimes.co.jp/news/2022/10/10/national/universities-female-staff/.

Joshi, Devin K. "Substantive Representation of Women by Parliamentarians in Asia: A Comparative Study of Ten Countries." *Substantive Representation of Women in Asian Parliaments*, edited by Joshi and Christian Echle, Routledge, 2022, pp. 1–23.

Kang, Duckju. "How Bad Is the Gender Wage Gap in Singapore?" *ValueChampion Singapore*, 8 Aug. 2017, www.valuechampion.sg/2017/08/how-bad-gender-wage-gap-singapore.

Koven, Suzanne. "Letter to a Young Female Physician." 13 Oct. 2021, Harvard Medical School. Lecture.

———. "Letter to a Young Female Physician." 5 Dec. 2023, Harvard University. Lecture.

Lambert, Priscilla. "Gender Equality in Japan." *Routledge Handbook of Contemporary Japan*, edited by Hiroko Takeda and Mark Williams, Routledge, 2021, pp. 348–60.

Lee, Philip. Preface. Macharia, pp. 1–2.

Lim, Catherine. *Miss Seetoh in the World*. Marshall Cavendish, 2011.

Lu Hsiu-lien. *My Fight for a New Taiwan: One Woman's Journey from Prison to Power*. U of Washington P, 2014.

Macharia, Sarah, editor. *Sixth Global Media Monitoring Project: Who Makes the News*. Creative Commons, 2020.

Mangurian, Christina, et al. "What's Holding Women in Medicine Back from Leadership." *Harvard Business Review*, 19 June 2018, hbr.org/2018/06/whats-holding-women-in-medicine-back-from-leadership.

Margot, Patrick. "U.S. Lenders Reveal Big Gender Pay Gaps in Britain." *The Wall Street Journal*, 27 Mar. 2018, www.wsj.com/articles/credit-suisse-reveals-u-k-gender-pay-gap-1522137793.

Masood, Salman. "Pakistan's Prime Minister Links Rape to 'Vulgarity' and How Women Dress." *The New York Times*, 8 Apr. 2021, www.nytimes.com/2021/04/08/world/asia/pakistan-rape.html.

Matsui, Kathy, et al. "Womenomics 4.0: Time to Walk the Talk." *Goldman Sachs, Portfolio Strategy Research*, 30 May 2014, www.goldmansachs.com/intelligence/pages/womenomics4.0.html.

Mlambo-Ngcuka, Phumzile. Foreword. Macharia, p. 3.

Molony, Barbara. "The Quest for Women's Rights in Turn-of-the-Century Japan." Molony and Uno, pp. 463–92.

Molony, Barbara, and Kathleen Uno, editors. *Gendering Modern Japanese History*. Harvard UP, 2005.

"More Female University Exam Takers in Japan Favoring Science over Liberal Arts amid COVID Crisis." *Japan Times*, 14 Jan. 2022, mainichi.jp/english/articles/20230113/p2a/00m/0na/025000c.

Nakamura, Ellen. "Kusumoto Ine (1827–1903): A Feminist Reappraisal." *Japanese Studies*, vol. 40, no. 3, Sept. 2020, pp. 249–66.

———. "Ogino Ginko's Vision 'The Past and Future of Women Doctors in Japan' (1893)." *U.S.-Japan Women's Journal*, no. 34, Jan. 2008, pp. 3–18.

———. "Working the Siebold Network: Kusumoto Ine and Western Learning in Nineteenth-Century Japan." *Japanese Studies*, vol. 28, no. 2, Jan. 2008, pp. 197–211.

Nomura, Kyoko, and Kengo Gohchi. "Impact of Gender-Based Career Obstacles on the Working Status of Women Physicians in Japan." *Social Science and Medicine*, vol. 75, Nov. 2012, pp. 1612–16.

Nomura, Kyoko, et al. "Gender Differences in Clinical Confidence: A Nationwide Survey of Resident Physicians in Japan." *Academic Medicine*, vol. 85, no. 4, Apr. 2010, pp. 647–53.

Noor: Mumbai, You're Killing Me. Directed by Sunhil Sippy, White Hill Studios, 2017.

Painter, Chad, and Patrick Ferrucci. "Gender Games: The Portrayal of Female Journalists in *House of Cards*." *Journalism Practice*, vol. 11, no. 4, Apr. 2017, pp. 493–508.

Poon, Angelia. "In Praise of Failed Men (and the Woman Writer): Gender Politics in the Singapore Novel." *Singapore Literature and Culture: Current Directions in Local and Global Contexts*, edited by Poon and Angus Whitehead, Routledge, 2017, pp. 217–36.

Ross, Karen, et al. "Women, Men, and News: It's Life, Jim, but Not As We Know It." *Journalism Studies*, vol. 19, no. 6, Apr. 2018, pp. 824–45.

Roth, Louise Marie. "Engendering Inequality: Processes of Sex-Segregation on Wall Street." *Sociological Forum*, vol. 19, no. 2, June 2004, pp. 203–28.

Scrolavezza, Paola. "Translating Family Violence in Contemporary Japanese Literature: Dynamics of (Cruel) Affectivity in *Zangyakuki* by Kirino Natsuo." *PAJLS*, no. 19, 2018, pp. 198–208.

Senz, Kristen. "Lack of Female Scientists Means Fewer Medical Treatments for Women." *Harvard Business School Working Knowledge*, 22 Feb. 2022, hbswk.hbs.edu/item/lack-of-female-scientists-means-fewer-medical-treatments-for-women.

The State of Women in Academic Medicine, 2018–2019: Exploring Pathways to Equity. Association of American Medical Colleges, 2019, store.aamc.org/downloadable/download/sample/sample_id/330/.

Steel, Gill. "Changing Women's and Men's Lives in Japan." Introduction. *Beyond the Gender Gap in Japan*, edited by Steel, U of Michigan P, 2019, pp. 1–21.

Tanaka, Yukiko, editor. *To Live and to Write: Selections by Japanese Women Writers, 1913–1938*. Seal Press, 1987.

Tham, Claire. "The Gunpowder Trail." *The Claire Tham Collection*, Marshall Cavendish, 2010, pp. 226–62.

———. *The Inlet*. Ethos Books, 2013.

"33% of Major Firms Listed in Japan Have No Female Executives." *Japan Times*, 5 Dec. 2021, www.japantimes.co.jp/news/2021/12/05/business/female-executives/.

Thornber, Karen Laura. "Comparison and Gender Injustice: Opportunities in Worlds of Pandemics." *Comparative Critical Studies*, vol. 20, nos. 2–3, 2023, pp. 201–21.

———. *Empire of Texts in Motion: Chinese, Korean, and Taiwanese Transculturations of Japanese Literature*. Harvard UP, 2009.

———. *Global Healing: Literature, Advocacy, Care*. Brill, 2020.

Tiyu huanghou. Directed by Yu Sun, Lianhua Film Production and Printing, 1934.

Tocco, Martha. "Made in Japan: Meiji Women's Education." Molony and Uno, pp. 39–60.

Trimble, Virginia, and David A. Weintraub, editors. *The Sky Is for Everyone: Women Astronomers in Their Own Words*. Princeton UP, 2022.

Turban, Stephen, et al. "Research: When Gender Diversity Makes Firms More Productive." *Harvard Business Review*, 11 Feb. 2019, hbr.org/2019/02/research-when-gender-diversity-makes-firms-more-productive.

"University of Tokyo to Double Number of Female Professors by Fiscal 2027." *Japan Times*, 26 Nov. 2022, www.japantimes.co.jp/news/2022/11/26/national/social-issues/tokyo-university-female-professors/.

Watanabe, Jun'ichi. *Beyond the Blossoming Fields*. Translated by Deborah Iwabuchi and Anna Isozaki, Alma Books, 2008.

———. *A Lost Paradise*. Translated by Julie Winters Carpenter, Kodansha USA, 2000.

Wilkinson, Tara. "Explaining Investment-Banking Gender Gap." *The Wall Street Journal*, 24 Sept. 2007, www.wsj.com/articles/SB119059299133436828.

"Women Overtake Men for First Time in Exam Pass Rate at Japan's Medical Schools." *Japan Times*, 16 Feb. 2022, www.japantimes.co.jp/news/2022/02/16/national/gender-balance-medical-exams/.

Yamaguchi, Kiyoko. "Going Back to Traditional Ethics? The Importance of Marriage for Female College Graduates in Japan from 1995 to 2010." *Gender and Family in East Asia*, edited by Siumi Maria Tam et al., Routledge, 2016, pp. 36–53.

Zhang, Letian. "An Institutional Approach to Gender Diversity and Firm Performance." *Organization Science*, vol. 31, no. 2, Mar. 2020, pp. 439–57.

Zimmer, Marc. *The State of Science: What the Future Holds and the Scientists Making It Happen*. Prometheus Books, 2020.

3. Humanizing Migrant Reproductive Workers

Claire Tham's "Gunpowder Trail," analyzed in the previous chapter, depicts Singapore as openly hostile to ambitious women who excel in male-dominated professions. Scorned by other women and abused by her male colleagues, Lina, Tham's protagonist, ultimately concludes that there is no place for her in the city-state. In contrast, for many far less privileged Asian women, Singapore and other wealthy Asian spaces are lands of relative opportunity, where at tremendous psychological and emotional cost they can earn enough to support their families.

Tens of millions of women have migrated within Asia since the late twentieth century. They have been driven by a dearth of economic opportunities as well as by gender injustices close to home, combined with increasing demands for reproductive labor in some of Asia's more prosperous cities and nations as more women there join the paid workforce.[1] Broadly understood, the term *reproductive labor* refers to a range of activities, both paid and unpaid, "conducted to achieve the reproduction of human beings intra- and inter-generationally" (Lan 1801).[2] Paid reproductive labor done by migrant women in Asia generally encompasses the frequently overlapping areas of care work and domestic work as well as entertainment jobs, including sex work.[3] Asia's recent mammoth reproductive labor migration has taken place internally, most notably in China, where a significant proportion of female rural-urban migrants—who number in the hundreds of millions—engage in paid reproductive labor (Michel and Peng 4).[4] Intra-Asian transnational reproductive labor migration has also occurred on a massive scale since the late twentieth century, from some of Asia's poorest to some of its wealthiest nations (Malhotra et al. 117).

Regardless of their educational qualifications or work experience at home, in most parts of the world, documented and especially undocumented individuals employed in lower-prestige positions are regularly subjected to any number of injustices and abuses, including low pay, contract or workplace violations, and little official oversight (Bada and Gleeson 33; Romero et al. 6, 13–19). At the same time, significant disparities generally exist between the experiences of male migrant workers and those of female migrant workers engaged in reproductive labor. These women tend to work out of the public eye and are isolated, even if regularly surveilled, in the homes of their employers. Their workplace, a single house or apartment, often is not considered a real job site, unlike the workplaces of migrant male workers. Furthermore, these women are regularly expected to invest emotionally in their work. And, as part of the global care chain, or at least the regional care chain, they often must leave the care of their own families to others while they care for wealthier families (Kittay; Ogawa, "Making" 134–36; Ueno, "Strategies" 239–40).[5] Sonya Michel and Ito Peng's observations concerning Asia hold true more broadly: "With migrant women from poorer regions and emerging economies now working in private households in wealthier cities and countries, we can see global and multiple forms of inequalities—gender, class, race, immigration status—playing out in the most intimate of spaces" (Introduction 4). These inequalities frequently lead to verbal, physical, and sexual abuse of domestic and care workers (Meyer et al.). Female migrant workers in the entertainment industry, which is even more exploitative, are at still greater risk.

The fiction spotlighted in chapter 2 features women struggling for equity in male-dominated professions in Japan, Pakistan, and Singapore. In contrast, this chapter focuses on narratives from Asia and its diasporas that humanize and draw attention to the importance of humanizing women engaged in much less visible yet even more arduous professions, namely reproductive labor that is poorly compensated and most frequently performed by women (Gallo and Scrinzi; see also Kofman and Raghuram 6–7). The chapter begins with an analysis of the short story "My Sister" (1995), by the Cambodian writer Mey Son Sotheary (Sotheary Meyson, 1977–), and the novel *Longevity Park* (*Tianhei de hen man*, 天黑的很慢, lit. *Getting Dark/Old Slowly*, 2018), by the Chinese writer Zhou Daxin (1952–). These two narratives feature educated rural-urban migrant women who, to support their families, perform different forms of reproductive labor—sex work, and eldercare and domestic work, respectively. Sotheary's and Zhou's writings highlight both the intrafamilial and broader social dynamics and especially injustices confronting young women who devote their lives to caring for others.

Internal rural-urban migration is a common phenomenon, particularly in developing nations (Qin and Liao 533). It is most striking in China, where since the early 1980s rural-urban migration has become "the largest single migration in human history" (Fu and Hao 1061). But even on smaller scales, internal rural-urban migration, including reproductive labor migration, has been significant in places as diverse as Japan and South Korea, two of Asia's wealthiest nations, and in Pakistan, Myanmar, and Cambodia, three of the poorest. As is true of most types of migrants, rural-urban migrants who engage in reproductive labor are frequently dehumanized, not only by employment policies and their employers but also by their home communities and even their families. Diverse Asian and Asian diaspora literatures decry such treatment, promoting dignity and agency and advocating justice for internal rural-urban migrant women engaged in reproductive labor, including entertainment as well as care and domestic work.

After an analysis of Sotheary's and Zhou's texts, this chapter turns attention to three short stories by and on Indonesian and Filipina women who serve as maids in Hong Kong and Singapore: "Susi" ("Potret Susi," lit. "Portrait of Susi," 2010), by the Indonesian writer and former domestic worker Ratna Khaerudina (Tri Ratnawati, 1982–), underscores the complicity of employment agencies and the Indonesian consulate in the exploitation of migrant domestic workers in Hong Kong. "My Employer" ("Awal Cerita yang Kusimpan," lit. "The Story I Kept," 2009), by the Indonesian writer and former domestic worker Ally Dalijo (Elly Trisnawati, 1979–), reveals the extreme desperation of these women. For its part, "Development" (2009), by the Singaporean American writer Wena Poon (1974–), implicates not only Hong Kong's and Singapore's biased government policies, and, in the case of Singapore, its cruel individual employers in the abuse of Filipina migrant domestic workers. This short story also exposes the Western media and both Western and local charities as responsible for secondary victimization, behaviors that intensify or take advantage of an individual's trauma. Together, the narratives discussed in this chapter humanize frequently dehumanized migrant women who engage in reproductive labor with little hope of justice.

Globally, there are between 50 and 67 million documented transnational migrant domestic workers, at least three-quarters of whom are female and nearly one-quarter of whom are from Southeast Asia (Van Bortel et al. 1–2). The past decade has witnessed a surge of female workers from less advantaged Asian nations, including Indonesia and the Philippines, moving to wealthier parts of the region, including Hong Kong and Singapore (Wang et al. 155).[6] As in much of the world, these women, many of whom engage in reproductive labor, are regularly subjected to abusive conditions. This includes the inability to change employers, long hours, low wages, mistreatment (including verbal and physical abuse), and nonrecognition of their work under local labor laws (Wang et al. 154, 156; Van Bortel et al. 1). Dramatically asymmetrical power relationships both in the Asian host nation and in the employer's household have created "openly exploitative relationships between employer and worker" that can result in horrific abuse and little recourse for employees (Kuo; Miquiabas; Yeoh et al., "Asian Women" 3; Yeoh et al., "Social Protection"). Unlike in the past, when domestic servants and their employers were often members of the same ethnic communities if not extended families, the transnational domestic workers employed by many middle- and upper-class Asians today are frequently perceived as "aliens" and "others," individuals who despite sometimes being nominally celebrated by their countries of birth are marginalized and subjugated in their workplaces and host nations (Yeoh et al., "Asian Women" 3).

Many domestic workers are passionate readers, and a number are also avid writers, penning diaries, notes, poems, and fiction for private consumption and participating in migrant worker poetry competitions and publishing their output (Suryomenggolo, "Significance" 204–06).[7] Recent edited collections of migrant writing, such as Karien van Ditzhuijzen's *Our Homes, Our Stories: Voices of Migrant Domestic Workers in Singapore* (2018), sponsored by the Humanitarian Organization for Migrant Economics (est. 2004), and Jafar Suryomenggolo's *At a Moment's Notice: Indonesian Maids Write on Their Lives Abroad* (2019), have provided an additional platform for Asia's migrant workers "to voice their concerns, their dreams and aspirations, so they become narrators of their own stories" (Kanwar 5) and to expose the abuses many experience.[8] For their part, narratives such as Poon's "Development" have additionally spotlighted the secondary victimization of Asian migrant domestic workers.

Humanizing Sex Workers: Mey Son Sotheary's "My Sister" (1995)

Conventional narratives, whether local or external, regularly dehumanize Cambodia's female sex workers, declaring them either "a ruined, destroyed and victimized woman . . . [or] a destroying body that threatens society" (Sandy 1–2).[9] Similarly, as Annuska Derks has observed, "[w]hile ideas about sex workers as immoral, loose women persist among many Cambodians, images of sex workers as slaves, commodities and viruses have come to dominate Western and NGO reporting on sex work" (89). The narrative structure and aesthetic strategies of Sotheary's "My Sister" counter such degrading discourse.[10] "My Sister" was published 45 years after Cambodia gained independence from France and in the early days of Cambodia's movements for the rights of sex workers, several years before the establishment of Cambodia's first sex worker organization. This group, the Association to Support Vulnerable Women, known also as the Cambodian Prostitute's Union (est. 1998), called public attention to the differences between voluntary and forced sex work and advocated for the occupational and human rights of sex workers (Sandy 12).

Sotheary's "My Sister" highlights the agency and resilience of Keo, a young woman from rural Prey Veng Province who attended college in Cambodia's capital, Phnom Penh. After her parents died, and unbeknownst to her siblings, she became a sex worker to finance their secondary and tertiary educations.[11] Keo's younger brother San, who had thought she worked at a foreign investment firm, is furious to discover the truth after several years, and he commands their younger sister Moum to "stop using [Keo's] indecent money" (Sotheary 49). When confronted, Keo is deeply ashamed, declares herself unworthy of being their sister, and disappears. Yet San is himself chastised by both Moum and their aunt and uncle, and he ultimately determines "to find Keo, to beg forgiveness for my cruelty" (52). "My Sister" not only draws attention to the limited employment possibilities for women in mid-1990s Cambodia, depicting sex work as the only viable option for women supporting family members. Incorporating complicated sibling relationships, Sotheary's story also reveals the devastating impacts of both family stigma and self-stigma and calls for destigmatizing both sex work and sex workers.

Notably, as its title suggests, "My Sister" is narrated neither by Keo nor in the third person but instead by San.[12] This aesthetic strategy means that readers learn far more about San than about Keo and that readers see and hear Keo and other members of their family only indirectly through San. At the same time, San, as the first-person narrator, provides an important window into the perspectives and experiences of a young man who, although recognizing his biases and privilege only belatedly and even then only partially, undergoes the type of transformation, however incomplete, that is so necessary on a broad scale.

San initially makes no secret about his disdain for sex workers. After spotting a group of "bargirls" while strolling with Moum in Phnom Penh one night, he agrees with Moum, and with many Cambodians, that these young women create "a bad impression, one that slowly destroys Cambodian values and traditions. . . . [T]hat kind of business is a big mistake for Cambodian girls. Even if they say it's for survival, that kind of work is still completely wrong" (Sotheary 47).[13] Instead, he thinks, "they could clean floors, or wash noodle dishes, or sell vegetables. They could survive that way too" (47). The following year, having just discovered how his sister Keo is earning a living, San asks a sex worker he meets at a bar why she is a prostitute, given that there are "so many decent jobs available" (50). Forcing a smile, the woman replies, "I'm not educated; I have no skills. What can I do? Even if I found another job, the most I could make is thirty or forty dollars a month" (50–51). When San declares this sufficient for a single person, she retorts, "Do you survive just for yourself and that's it? I have brothers and sisters, and they have to go to school. How can I pay for their education? You just want them to be illiterate and then get a job like me?" (51).

Rather than reflect on the woman's remarks, and her condemnation of his long-standing and somewhat contradictory assumptions that women have many opportunities and that they should be content just to "survive," a term repeated several times in just a few pages, San is "appalled at her demeanor," only to then feel "embarrassed" (Sotheary 51). Ultimately, it takes his aunt and uncle's unrelenting condemnation of San's own condemnation of Keo to convince San that he is in the wrong. Although at first protesting that Keo brings their family great shame and has ruined their reputation, San in the end relents: "Actually, my aunt is right. Whatever Keo did was for us. She didn't do anything wrong. I was the brute who dared to scold her" (52). And San vows to track down his older sister, "to let her know she's a great person regardless of that profession. She is still noble, I still respect her" (52).

San depicts himself as undergoing striking transformations: from appreciating Keo to being repulsed by her to admiring her courage and devotion to him and Moum. At the same time, even as San speaks of Keo as a "great person," as "noble," and as worthy of "respect," his modifiers "regardless" and "still" make clear his continued discomfort with his sister's work. San is silent on the disparities between his and Keo's experiences. After just a year studying in Phnom Penh, he lands a position as a radio broadcaster that provided sufficient income for him to help Keo with Moum's university fees (Sotheary 47). This is in sharp contrast with Keo, not to mention women without an education, whom "My Sister" depicts as being limited to sex work if they need to support anyone other than themselves and as determined that they create for their siblings a better life. Notable as well, and unremarked by San, is Keo's own capitulation, her self-contempt despite years of having made possible her siblings' educations, providing them with opportunities denied to her. Sotheary's short story reveals family stigma and self-stigma against sex work as just as powerful as external stigmas.

Sex work has a long history in Cambodia, as in most parts of the world. The economic and political opening up of the nation following the severe repression of the Khmer Rouge era (1975–79) and the suppressive People's Republic of Kampuchea (1979–89) led to a plethora of brothels, bars, and nightclubs in Phnom Penh and other major urban areas in the mid-1990s.[14] These establishments were staffed largely by rural-urban Cambodian migrants, and subsequent government crackdowns were unsuccessful although not without significant impact on the sex workers themselves (Derks 91, 115). The experiences of sex workers in Cambodia vary significantly based on family background, including ethnicity, and on the type of establishment for which they work, their employment contract, and many other factors. Yet overall, sex work generally is the most lucrative option for uneducated Cambodian women, even as they often do not reveal their profession to their families and friends (107, 174). Featuring a young rural woman who moves to the city to attend university and who becomes a sex worker to support her family, Sotheary's "My Sister" complicates typical understandings of rural-urban migration. This story reveals the importance of sex work to a broader range of women than is typically acknowledged. Keo appears infrequently and is given little voice in "My Sister," pointing to the continued silencing of sex workers. Yet by highlighting San's changing opinions—and, just as significantly, by depicting his aunt and uncle as defending Keo and chastising their nephew for attacking her (a recourse unavailable to many of the women described in chapter 6, which focuses on family violence)—this short story reveals the important roles families can play not only in perpetuating stigma but also in countering stigma and humanizing sex workers.[15]

Women in Cambodia have more options today than in the 1990s. Even so, the nation ranks 58th of 146 in economic participation and opportunity, having closed only 71% of its employment gender gap; 70% of women participate in the workforce, compared with 83% of men (*Global Gender Gap Report 2023* 17, 133). Women are particularly underrepresented in government and the judiciary, and they occupy just 31% of senior positions (*Women and Men* 53–61; *Global Gender Gap Report 2023* 133). Furthermore, working conditions and wages for many women remain dismal, including in the garment industry, by far the largest employer of Cambodian women, most of whom are internal migrants and more than two-thirds of whom are sexually harassed at work (*Women in Cambodia's Garment Industry*).[16] The deep albeit conditional regret San displays at the end of Sotheary's "My Sister" is unusual. Instead, the cruelty and injustices of reproductive labor practices frequently remain unacknowledged, including for care workers, for whom demand is steadily increasing amid aging populations, as exposed in Zhou's *Longevity Park*.

Humanizing Care Workers: Zhou Daxin's *Longevity Park* (2018)

Mainland China is aging at unprecedented speed and scale: whereas at the turn of the twenty-first century 10% of its population of 1.26 billion was over age 60, by 2007, 17.3% of its population of 1.35 billion had reached this milestone (Zhang et al. 2).[17] By 2050, more than one-quarter of China's anticipated population of 1.4 billion will be 65 or older, and 8% of the population will be over 80 (OECD 199). One of the many challenges facing aging, aged, and super-aged populations is meeting the long-term care needs of elderly individuals. A disproportionate number require assistance with the activities of daily living, even if they are not suffering from the debilitating conditions that tend to target the aged, such as Alzheimer's disease and other forms of dementia (Feng et al. 2767).[18]

Already more than half of China's aged population requires long-term care services (Zou et al. 389). As is true of most Asian societies, China has relied primarily on family—generally daughters and daughters-in-law—to provide the unpaid reproductive labor of eldercare. China's entrenched parent-centered caregiving tradition, rooted in concepts of filial piety, with some aspects now codified into law, calls for younger generations to fulfill the material and emotional needs of older generations (Chen 128–29; Nie 357). As is true in many societies, bedside nursing care generally is the responsibility of the family, even in hospitals (Hui et al. 1027). At the same time, socioeconomic changes are making it increasingly difficult for grown children to care for their aging parents and grandparents. These include extensive rural-urban migration, with hundreds of millions of Chinese having moved from China's impoverished countryside to its wealthier cities in recent decades. The so-called four-two-one problem, in large part a result of China's one-child policy (1980–2015), also means that one child is often responsible for caring for two parents and four grandparents, a phenomenon discussed further in chapter 4 (Feng et al. 2767).[19]

In the past, eldercare homes were reserved for those without family, work, or income, the "three-nos" (Hong 71). Although the number of such homes in China has increased dramatically in recent decades, demand far outpaces supply, with waiting lists into the thousands. This is the case even though placing a loved one in the care of strangers remains anathema to many Chinese. Those with financial resources who cannot themselves provide part-time, much less full-time care for elderly family members, whether because of the severity of their loved one's health conditions or their own health conditions, employment, or other commitments, generally hire nonfamily caregivers (Feng et al. 2768). Nearly all these individuals are underpaid female internal migrants from rural China, many of whom send home to the countryside a portion of their relatively meager wages, having left behind their own aging family members as well as their children.[20] As Liu Hong has argued, "At the intersection of the rural-urban divide and gendered segregation in the labor market, predominantly female care workers suffer a double inequity" (85).

Chinese literature has been hesitant to engage with the challenges of aging, both for the elderly and for caregivers, whether paid or unpaid. One prominent exception is Zhou's *Longevity Park*.[21] The novel is structured as a series of seven lectures given over the course of a week at Longevity Park (Wanshou Gongyuan) in Beijing. The first four lectures (Monday through Thursday) are given by various experts and are relatively short, focusing, respectively, on the mass-produced robot nurse Miss Weiwei and opportunities at the Biquan Nursing Home, the Lingqi Longevity Pill and the history of longevity in China, a virtual rejuvenation experience, and the future of humankind.[22] The lectures that take place on Friday through Sunday, which mark a sharp shift in content and narrative aesthetics and account for close to 90% of *Longevity Park*, are given by Zhong Xiaoyang, a young woman from rural Henan Province with a nursing degree from Nanyang Medical College. Xiaoyang is the paid caregiver, companion, and housekeeper of Xiao Chengshan (Uncle Xiao), a retired judge and academic lawyer in his seventies. In her monologue, Xiaoyang shares with the audience in Longevity Park how she had hoped to find a position in Beijing that would enable her both to pay for her boyfriend Lü Yiwei's education at Peking University and to support his parents and siblings as well as her own, echoing Keo's concerns in Sothcary's "My Sister." Yet competition for skilled positions was unexpectedly fierce, and she ultimately was hired by Uncle Xiao's daughter, Xinxin, to care for the family patriarch during the long hours Xinxin and her lawyer husband, Chang Sheng, were away at work.

On the one hand, as speaker and the most dominant voice in *Longevity Park*, Xiaoyang joins a growing number of Chinese female migrant care workers who are telling their own stories, countering their continued status as "politically voiceless, socially disadvantaged, and culturally invisible" (Xiao 47; see also Yu). For the past few decades, these women have participated in a range of literary initiatives, from writing contests to literature groups and online media platforms.[23] Sharing their experiences, including with gender injustice (not unlike Khaerudina's and Dalijo's narratives, discussed below), they have "restore[d] the value and dignity of labor and [built] meaningful affective ties with fellow laborers" (Xiao 51). They also have raised awareness "regarding labor rights and social justice," especially during the COVID-19 pandemic (53). On the other hand, although sizeable and steadfast, the audience at Xiaoyang's three lectures is "fellow carers for the elderly" (Zhou Daxin 41). It is also explicitly gendered: Xiaoyang thanks the "aunties, older sisters, and younger sisters" on Friday, Saturday, and Sunday evenings (41, 126, 223). In other words, while Xiaoyang's story likely resonates with and validates the experiences of her audience, forming important affective bonds, it does not reach a broader group, in sharp contrast with the opening four lectures of *Longevity Park*. Xiaoyang's story relies on the prominent male novelist Zhou Daxin for broader consumption, solidifying long-standing power structures.

Xiaoyang narrates her experiences chronologically and relatively directly, keeping the focus on herself and rarely addressing her audience in the park, except at the beginning and end of the three lectures. Her narrative strategy is to intersperse detailed descriptions of daily life as well as her thoughts and emotions with both dialogue and summaries of conversations. Life as a live-in caregiver, companion, and housekeeper is challenging at best. Initially, Uncle Xiao rejected Xiaoyang and questioned her basic nursing competence. He thwarted her at every turn, frequently refusing her care and companionship, despite her being responsible for him 24-7.[24] Xiaoyang likewise reveals that Uncle Xiao's girlfriends scorned her, one condescendingly instructing her how to disinfect the toilet. This disdain from privileged urbanites is not surprising given the low status of and deep stigmas attached to both migrants and care work in China's cities (Hong 74–76).

Xiaoyang shares how her responsibilities continued to mount, which meant that she was not able to travel home for the Lunar New Year, a holiday granted to nearly all rural-urban migrants in China, because Uncle

Xiao's daughter and her husband had moved to the United States and could not care for Uncle Xiao themselves. To be sure, unlike many rural-urban migrants, as Xiaoyang's responsibilities increased, so too did her salary. And Uncle Xiao's daughter, Xinxin, lavished money and presents on Xiaoyang. But Xiaoyang reveals that "I was very unhappy about the way she [Xinxin] was using money and gifts to buy off my opportunity to see my friends and family" (Zhou Daxin 173). And as Uncle Xiao's health deteriorated, physicians became more judgmental, interrogating Xiaoyang: "What kind of nurse are you? Haven't you been feeding him properly? . . . You've been very negligent! If anything like this happens again, we will have to call the police!" (182). Undeterred, Xiaoyang not only continued to care for Uncle Xiao but also took on the additional care burden of Xinxin when she returned from the United States, emaciated and suffering from severe depression, far worse even than that of Kim Jiyoung, discussed in chapter 1. Not long thereafter, Xinxin died by suicide, leaving Xiaoyang funds for funeral expenses and access to a bank account that would pay her salary for the next 20 years. But with these funds came a substantial burden: "As he [Uncle Xiao] got older, the demands on me as his carer would become greater, and I might well lose much of my freedom in the prime of my life. . . . I was just a random family carer that Older Sister had found. . . . [D]id that mean I had to put myself in lockdown for her?" (239).

Life as a female rural-urban migrant grew even more precarious when Xiaoyang became pregnant by her boyfriend, who cheated on her, abused her (as do the intimate partners discussed in chapter 7), and ultimately abandoned her. Xiaoyang recognized that "[n]o one was going to want to recruit me to work for them in my current state, and I had no choice but to view Uncle Xiao's apartment as my long-term place of residence" (Zhou Daxin 263–64). Moreover, she notes, "I had no mother to guide me [given the severe stigma in China of giving birth outside of marriage], and no girlfriends to share my experiences with" (266). Unlike Kim Jiyoung, Xiaoyang bounced back quickly from childbirth, but as is true of rural-urban migrants more generally, because of China's strict *hukou* (household registration) system, there were multiple barriers to registering her son's birth and applying for his residency permit, without which he would be greatly disadvantaged (e.g., he would not be able to attend school). Because she was a migrant worker, Xiaoyang could not register her son in Beijing, a task she describes figuratively as "more difficult than climbing up to heaven" (274). And Xiaoyang could not register her son in her home village because "the whole village would get to know that I had had a child outside marriage, and my parents would never be able to hold their heads up there again" (272). Uncle Xiao proposed that by marrying him and claiming that he was her son's father, Xiaoyang could register both herself and her son in Beijing, affording them a lifetime of advantages. As Uncle Xiao made clear, unlike Lina's boss in "Gunpowder Trail," discussed in chapter 2, he had no designs on her; he was just trying to help her and her son. In her final lecture at Longevity Park, Xiaoyang shares her experiences as Uncle Xiao's wife and then his ex-wife, particularly as his condition deteriorated. She relates how her devoted and repeated attempts to make his life more comfortable were invariably thwarted by his rapidly declining physical and mental health. *Longevity Park* ends as Xiaoyang recounts several desperate yet marginally successful attempts to alleviate Uncle Xiao's severe dementia and other impairments and as Xiaoyang's son wheels Uncle Xiao onto the lecture stage.[25]

Breaking numerous silences and foregrounding new voices, Zhou's novel provides a penetrating exposé of the realities of aging, especially in China, primarily from the perspective of a reproductive care worker. *Longevity Park* reveals not only many of the frequently suppressed details of the mental and physical changes that can take place as individuals advance in years but also the stigmas against aging, the aged, and care homes as well as the vulnerability of the elderly to fraudulent schemes. This supple narrative likewise addresses the inability of many families to care for their aging loved ones, whether because of their own family and employment commitments or because of their own health conditions, including mental illness. Just as significantly, *Longevity Park* exposes—through an eloquent first-person narrator in the throes of caregiving—some of the distinct challenges of being a rural reproductive care worker in urban China, including frequently low wages and mental, physical, and sexual harassment.

China's fourteenth five-year plan, approved by the National People's Congress in March 2021 and covering 2021–25, calls for China to promote the

> coordinated development of senior care and the elder care industry, improve the system of basic elder care services, vigorously develop inclusive elder care services, support families taking on the elder care function, and build an elder care system in which home-based, community-based, and institutional elder care are mutually coordinated and medical care is combined with health and wellness care. (*Outline* 117–18)

The plan also declares that China will "intensify the training of geriatric nursing talent . . . and better meet the needs of nursing services for the elderly with disabilities and dementia. . . . We will build a social environment of care, filial piety, and respect for the elderly and strengthen the protection of the rights and interests of elders" (118). *Longevity Park* reveals the urgency of these proposals. Just as important, Zhou's novel also draws needed attention to the rights and interests of the vulnerable rural-urban migrant women who serve as caregivers for the urban elderly. These women's reproductive labor offers significant relief to urban families even as the women's own families sometimes must go without care and as the women themselves suffer numerous injustices, articulated so clearly and directly by Xiaoyang. Yet while Xiaoyang remains in China, and Keo from Sotheary's story in Cambodia, many women, including the transnational migrant women in the writings analyzed in the following section, have no choice but to leave their nations of origin.

Humanizing Indonesian Migrant Domestic Workers: Ratna Khaerudina's "Susi" (2010) and Ally Dalijo's "My Employer" (2009)

Indonesian women—primarily from poorer rural areas—have been migrating abroad to serve as domestic workers since the late 1970s, nearly 30 years after Indonesia's independence from the Dutch. By the late 1990s they greatly outnumbered their male counterparts going to Singapore and Hong Kong as well as to Saudi Arabia and the United Arab Emirates (Hugo 58, 63; Silvey 89–94).[26] By the turn of the twenty-first century, in part a result of the 1997 Asian financial crisis, Indonesia had become one of the world's largest sources of migrant reproductive labor, and by the 2010s, more than half of both Hong Kong's and Singapore's foreign domestic workers, almost all of whom are women, were Indonesian citizens, the vast majority from Java (Hugo 68; Palmer 139, 142). Although the Indonesian government, as well as the governments of Hong Kong, Singapore, and other receiving nations, have all placed restrictions on who can migrate and on conditions for migrants, companies that recruit transnational migrant labor often falsify dates of birth to evade minimum age requirements and edit school records to circumvent minimum education requirements (Palmer 142–43). Once abroad, female Indonesian migrant workers, who make up 70% of officially documented migrant workers from Indonesia, are subjected to strict regulations and have limited protections

(Suryomenggolo, "Significance" 207, 209). Not only do middle- and upper-class Indonesians in Hong Kong and Singapore, including consular officials, distance themselves from Indonesian domestic workers. Even more significant, law enforcement in Hong Kong and Singapore regularly dismisses accusations of exploitation and abuse as "misunderstandings" (Palmer 145). Only occasionally do the international media report on cases of physical abuse of migrant domestic workers, even when this abuse is extreme, "serving to remind observers that Hong Kong and Singaporean residents do far too little to ensure foreign domestic workers' physical safety" (140). Despite the hardships experienced in their host countries, Indonesian women continue to migrate in large numbers for a range of reasons, including financial need, social constraints at home, and abusive family relationships (Suryomenggolo, "Significance" 208).[27] Already intolerable conditions were exacerbated during the height of the COVID-19 pandemic, when migrant Indonesian and Filipina domestic workers in Hong Kong were fired after becoming ill and were forced onto the streets (V. Wang), revealing that discrimination against foreigners in China is not unlike that against Chinese abroad.

The anthology *At a Moment's Notice* brings together a narratologically, aesthetically, and thematically diverse range of short stories by 23 Indonesian migrant domestic workers who have engaged in reproductive labor in Hong Kong, Malaysia, Singapore, and Taiwan (Suryomenggolo). As the editor and translator Jafar Suryomenggolo explains, these affective fictional narratives "explore the whole fabric of relationships within both sending and receiving societies, between the domestic worker and her fellow migrants, with her employer and her employer's family, with strangers she meets during her time abroad, and with her own children, parents and husband back in Indonesia" (Preface vii). Just as notable from a stylistic perspective, in these stories, as opposed to much writing on migrant women performing reproductive labor, including Poon's "Development," discussed later in this chapter, the women themselves are subjects, not objects (Suryomenggolo, "Significance" 207).[28] Particularly striking in *At a Moment's Notice* are Khaerudina's "Susi" and Dalijo's "My Employer," both of which use the short story form to highlight the extreme vulnerability and courage of migrant domestic workers and in particular their closely guarded feelings and emotions.[29]

Khaerudina draws on her experiences working in Hong Kong between 2003 and 2011 to expose in "Susi" the complicity of employers, employment agencies, and the Indonesian consulate in exploiting Indonesian migrant domestic workers in Hong Kong. Strikingly narrated in the third-person omniscient, and seemingly describing the events of a 24-hour period, "Susi" centers on the eponymous Susi, who works for a Hong Kong family with two children. The family, including the children, makes no secret of their disdain for their Indonesian maid, even greater than what Xiaoyang experiences in Zhou's *Longevity Park*. Khaerudina's story opens with Susi returning to her employer's apartment the evening of her weekly day off and being forced to work. When she questions this breach of contract, her employer paradoxically calls her "lazy" and without "initiative" (Khaerudina 33), threatens to fire her, and then does so. Susi is bereft, given that, as is true of most migrant reproductive workers, her parents and younger siblings at home in Indonesia depend on her earnings. Returning to the employment agency, she is encouraged to put the past behind her and work for a new family. Yet as Susi recognizes, employment agencies profit from terminations and replacements, so they have little incentive to resolve workplace conflicts. Speaking with other domestic workers at the agency, all of whom have had similar experiences; drawing attention to their dehumanization; and attempting to build solidarity, Susi asserts, "Sisters, they treat us like used goods" (35). This simile echoes her subsequent determination "to put an end to being treated like things rather than people" (36) and her protest to the Indonesian consulate that the agency is treating workers "like toys" (38).

Terrified for their own futures and knowing how much their families in Indonesia depend on their remittances, her fellow workers want nothing to do with her. And recognizing that Susi "was definitely not the usual type of domestic worker" who "would just do whatever the agent told them to do," the employment agency tosses her out (Khaerudina 37). Susi then calls the Indonesian consulate, only to have the consular officer on the other end of the line condescendingly dismiss her concerns, disparagingly remarking as he hangs up, "You should be grateful that you are working in Hong Kong. If you were in Indonesia, you would be working as a maid too. And your earnings would be lower. So why are you complaining? You should calm down" (38).

The short story form enables the narrator of "Susi" to provide a snapshot of life in Hong Kong that highlights both Susi's agency and the severe limitations she faces. Notably, unlike many third-person narrators—such as Watanabe Jun'ichi's in *Beyond the Blossoming Fields*, discussed in chapter 2, and Dạ Ngân's in *An Insignificant Family*, discussed in chapter 1—the narrator of "Susi" does not comment on the broader context in which the story is embedded. Rather, everything the reader learns about not only Susi but also female transnational migrant reproductive workers in

Hong Kong comes from transcriptions of Susi's conversations with her employer, the employment agency, and the Indonesian consulate and from translations of Susi's thoughts and feelings about her own situation and that of migrant domestic workers more broadly. At the same time, the omnipresence of the third-person narrator is a constant reminder of the constraints on Susi, encapsulated in the story's final image, after the Indonesian consulate dashes her confidence: "her hope melted instantly, like jelly in hot water" (Khaerudina 38).

Both Susi and Isa, the protagonist of the short story "My Employer," by the Indonesian writer and former migrant domestic worker Ally Dalijo,[30] are fired for daring to challenge a breach of contract. Yet the breach Isa experiences by her employers, Winnie (age 30, secretary at an insurance company) and Roby (age 32, recently unemployed) is far greater than what Susi encounters: Winnie and Roby replace housekeeping, of which there is very little to do in the couple's small apartment, with sexual assault. "My Employer" makes clear through the perspective of Isa just how desperate some migrant domestic workers are for work and how little agency they believe they have, the short story form bringing to the fore their anguish. At the same time, the choice of first-person narration points to Isa's strength, while her choice of imagery opens future possibilities.

Isa begins her story on a stormy night. She describes standing outside alone in a heavy rain, having been thrown out of Winnie and Roby's apartment, and thinking of heading to the agency that placed her with the couple. But unlike Susi, she does not know where the employment office is located "in this urban wilderness, this land of concrete" (Dalijo 75), a description of Hong Kong echoed elsewhere in the story. Alarmingly, and unlike Susi, particularly given what she soon reveals about her time with Winnie and Roby, Isa also blames herself: "I knew I had made mistakes. I wasn't an educated person. I felt that I couldn't blame her for hating me so much that she wanted to kick me out" (75). Isa then flashes back to her experiences with the couple and particularly to what happened when Winnie went to Japan on a business trip: Roby took her out to dinner, drugged her, and then raped her, a situation that echoes Itō Shiori's experiences in *Black Box*, discussed in chapter 5. Waking up naked in Roby's bed, Isa recounts, "I began sobbing when I realized what had happened to me. I wanted to attack and kick him but I had no energy at all. . . . My scream turned into a whispering moan. I surrendered, as I couldn't fight him, though my heart felt as though it had broken into pieces" (81).

When Isa shared with Winnie that she had been raped, Winnie surprised her by replying, "You know very well, Isa, that I can't perform my duties as a wife, even though I love him very much. That's why I took a maid. I want you to take over my duties. You're pretty enough" (Dalijo 81). Recognizing that Isa wanted no part of this scheme, Winnie fired her on the spot and sent her onto the street, informing her that she was welcome to return should she change her mind and that she would be paid five times her current salary for so doing (83). Outside in the pouring rain, Isa thinks of her four-year-old son, her disabled father, and her mother, who has an undiagnosed medical condition, all back in Indonesia: "The only reason I'd come to the land of concrete was to work hard, to help them" (83). Wet, shivering, and believing she has no choice, Isa returns to Roby and Winnie's apartment: "Let what must be come to pass. I give in" (83). The couple bathe Isa, then both join her in the bathtub, after which both "started hugging and kissing me" on their bed (84). In a plot twist, "My Employer" here implies that Winnie "can't perform [her] duties as a wife" not because she is too wrapped up in her career, as suggested earlier in the narrative, but instead because she is attracted to women, at least Isa, not men, at least not her husband, Roby.

"My Employer" ends as Isa describes her employers fondling her "like ants seeking honey on my body" (Dalijo 84). Not unlike the final lines of "Susi," where Khaerudina's character finds her hope dissolving, Isa's body, fresh from a hot bath, is violated. At the same time, Isa retains her voice and her humanity, while her employers are likened to insects. Furthermore, that Isa's employers are (still) "seeking" rather than (already) consuming suggests opportunities for resistance: ants are known to readily detect, flock to, and hungrily consume honey, and that Isa's employers-turned-insects are not (yet) consuming her leaves open the possibility, however remote, of escape.

Humanizing Filipina Migrant Domestic Workers: Wena Poon's "Development" (2009)

The Philippines are one of the world's largest sources of overseas labor. Since the 1970s, hundreds of thousands of individuals have left the archipelago annually for employment in more than 100 nations in other parts of Asia and around the globe, sending home remittances that play a significant role in the Philippine economy (Asis 22, 27).[31] While men from the Philippines occupy a range of mostly so-called unskilled occupations abroad, women from the Philippines, regardless of education, are most frequently hired as domestic helpers (23, 37). Women leave the Philippines not only because of economic precarity but also because of the gender inequalities and injustices they face in their communities, including intimate partner violence and the inability to divorce (Parreñas 31–40).[32] As Maria Allen Cellan, who worked in Singapore for four years, has candidly described, "It is very common to have partners who are drunkards, abusive, jobless, or irresponsible. Working abroad can help us getting back on our feet" (57). Over the decades, the Philippine government has established numerous protective mechanisms for its migrant workers abroad and their families at home. This has led international organizations to depict the Philippines as exemplary in "migration management" (Rodriquez). Yet the perception of paid reproductive work as "private and non-work" has left many female migrants exploited (Asis 30–34). And as Juliet Ugay, who served for a decade as a domestic worker in Singapore, has summarized, "The work is physically strenuous, and sometimes mentally exhausting. . . . Every single cent that we earn is the result of hard work, patience, sacrifice and sometimes suffering, all of that just to make sure that our families back home are taken care of" (51–52).

Poon's "Development" highlights the abuse and secondary victimization of Filipina domestic workers in Hong Kong and Singapore.[33] This short story incriminates not only Hong Kong's and Singapore's biased government policies and, in the case of Singapore, its brutal individual employers.[34] Unlike Khaerudina's "Susi" and Dalijo's "My Employer," Poon's "Development" also unrelentingly implicates the Western media, especially their persistent male gaze, and both Western and local charities and individuals who believe themselves charitable as responsible for secondary victimization, behaviors that intensify or take advantage of an individual's trauma.

Narrated in the third-person limited omniscient, "Development" stridently satirizes the attitudes, thoughts, and behaviors of MacGregor, a Scottish photojournalist dispatched by a California-based international women's charity first to Hong Kong, to provide photographs for its annual report on "domestic workers and labor problems around the world" (Poon 78), and then to Singapore, to photograph abused Filipina maids for a United Nations report (86). MacGregor embodies Western imperialism and colonialism as well as the dehumanization not only of those living within the "scenic poverty" (76) of rural Asia but also of women exploited within and outside Asia's wealthiest cities, including those engaged in reproductive labor. Just as important, although the third-person narrator focuses primarily on MacGregor, "Development" also draws attention to

Chinese charities in Hong Kong and Singapore as further enabling the secondary victimization of Filipina domestic workers in these cities. In so doing, Poon's short story spotlights not only how wealthy Westerners, on the one hand, and Hong Kong's and Singapore's official policies and individual employers, on the other, dehumanize Filipina domestic workers. Like "Susi," "Development" also reveals the dehumanization of women engaged in reproductive labor that is enabled and even inflicted by local intermediaries: MacGregor's Chinese guide in Hong Kong and the Chinese nun who provides him access to abused Filipina domestic workers in Singapore, respectively.

MacGregor passionately embraces "disappearing peoples" (Poon 77) anywhere there is "regress, not progress" (78) where he can run "towards the smoke and the bombs" (86) and then rapidly depart. Supporting him are his Oxford- and Cambridge-educated editors who lap up the "human drama" he sends them "from far corners of the world" (77). For this reason, he is less than enthusiastic when asked to go to Hong Kong, one of the "developed Asian nations" that are "slowly and thoughtlessly encasing themselves in concrete" (78), an image that echoes Isa's descriptions of the hardscape city in "My Employer." MacGregor's agent reassures him that he need only "capture the weekly outing of Filipina domestic workers" (79), something he can do on a single Sunday morning. Unlike the women he photographs, MacGregor fails to appreciate the contradiction between the California-based charity's needing material on "domestic workers and labor problems around the world" (78) and his photographing women on their weekly day off. To MacGregor, they are a mass of humanity rather than individuals with their own stories, a belief Poon's discourse accentuates. Looking out over Central (Hong Kong's core business district), MacGregor lets his gaze rest on Filipina women "gathered on the sidewalks, on the steps, in the plazas and on the overhead bridges, forming a noisy, uniform mass of black heads and brown humanity" (79). He experiences the soundscape as "a rat-a-tat-tat of rapid-fire Tagalog. . . . It sounded like a language of breathless excitement suspended on a single note" (79). Incredibly, although "he did not understand a word . . . he knew that among the voices there was no trace of anxiety" (80).[35] When MacGregor does speak with individual women, conversations facilitated by the many Filipina domestic workers who know English, it is from behind his camera lens, taking photographs his sole concern.

Enabling MacGregor in the secondary victimization of these reproductive laborers is his Hong Kong guide, Charles (Charlie) Tsang, a masculine-looking woman with "a butch haircut and a stiff voice" assigned to him by the California charity that commissioned his photographs (Poon 79). To be sure, Charlie rectifies many of MacGregor's misconceptions regarding the lives of Filipina domestic workers. What MacGregor presumes is a Filipino festival, thousands of maids congregating on their day off, Charlie clarifies is a routine weekly occurrence (80). What MacGregor finds incomprehensible—the maids gathering in Central, where the sun beats mercilessly and there is nowhere to sit—Charlie explains is their only option. And what MacGregor finds odd—the apparent dearth of "the *Chinese*" in Hong Kong—Charlie curtly justifies: "If these people [Filipina maids] were to go away tomorrow, our economy will collapse" (82). At the same time, Charlie leads MacGregor first to Central and then to Hong Kong Park, where she promises him "more girls" (82). Even more significant are her silences: Charlie generally confines herself to responding directly to MacGregor's questions, and after clarifying for a group of Filipina maids MacGregor's plans, she disappears from the narrative.

MacGregor's next assignment takes him to Singapore, where the Tan trial is underway. Mrs. Tan, who had served as a high school principal for three decades, was accused of physically abusing her grown son's Filipina maid. MacGregor's employer (the charity) has hired him to take photographs of "the girls for a U.N. report" (Poon 86). Even so, just as MacGregor arrives in Hong Kong, he enters Singapore "prepared to be bored" (87). He mistakenly believes Singapore is a place with "[t]oo little blood. . . . Too quiet. Too clean. . . . [Singapore] was a city of civil servants and coffee bars" (86–87). Much to his astonishment, MacGregor soon discovers something very different behind closed doors: scenes of exploitation, menace, and absolute horror (92–95), a place quite unlike the professional Singapore of Tham's "Gunpowder Trail," discussed in chapter 2.

There is no Charlie Tsang to greet MacGregor in Singapore, nor is there much to see on the streets and in the parks, since domestic workers in Singapore were not given a guaranteed weekly day off until 2013, several years after MacGregor's visit. Instead, MacGregor visits a house in a residential neighborhood. The door is answered by a Chinese nun, Sister Anne, who quickly becomes MacGregor's enabler. Sister Anne explains that the house is "a shelter for Filipina maids who have been abused by their employers" and who "have nowhere else to go. They come here while their case is being investigated" (Poon 88). One of these women is Recca (Rebecca), a maid in her 30s whom Mrs. Tan had "locked up for three days without food or water" (91) for burning a shirt she was ironing. Mrs. Tan had also physically abused Recca, the narrator graphically describing the horrific scars on Recca's back as the "clear imprints of six scorch marks, each the size of a paperback book. Red-brown against dull-brown skin, they formed a pattern like shadows of giant leaves. . . . She had lain on a bed, perhaps, naked, while this was done to her" (90–91). This depiction, even more extreme than the images in Khaerudina's and Dalijo's stories, echoes reports in the Singaporean press (Leow 205). After MacGregor has finished photographing Recca, Sister Anne provides him with "the other girls in the shelter . . . one by one" (93). As MacGregor later recalls in vivid detail, while developing the photographs in his friend's darkroom, providing a long list of body parts and weapons:

> The insides of elbows, wrists, ankles, the tender flesh of thighs, armpits, breasts, genitals—they had opened up to him, shown him. Razors, cigarettes, lit incense, kebab sticks, canes, needles, electric irons, kitchen utensils, sharpened pencils, letter openers, wooden clogs. When the horror of ordinary household items did not satisfy, there was recourse to the traditional blows of flesh upon flesh. (93)

Notably, even as MacGregor describes aspects of the violence that would not be immediately apparent from photographs alone, Sister Anne does not share with him, much less enable him, to listen to these women's stories, whether of their lives in the Philippines, their experiences in Singapore, or their hopes for the future. Instead, she facilitates the women's becoming mutilated bodies posed against a "very Third World" backdrop (89). Their voices, which MacGregor had heard earlier wafting in from the kitchen with the same "race-track commentary of Tagalog" (89) he had witnessed in Hong Kong, are now silenced. Even MacGregor—for whom horror has become routine and who thrives on "making even the most bruised face glamorous with a trick of the light" (91)—occasionally finds it "very odd that he was photographing a woman's most intimate details without any awareness of her history" (94).

After his trip to Singapore, MacGregor becomes "engrossed in the subject" (Poon 94) of Filipina maids. For two years, he photographs abused reproductive laborers and covers their trials and quests for justice. He is aware that these are "the pharmacists, the nurses, the secretaries, the farmers' wives, the polytechnic students who left in droves for the wealthier cities of Southeast Asia or the Middle East to clean house, push strollers, buy groceries for tiny households" (94). And he chastises his expatriate friends who have Filipina maids, reminding them that "[p]rostitutes have more freedom. . . . [Filipina maids] are practically under house arrest, and nobody checks on them. Nobody" (95). Yet his greatest concern is not the well-being of the maids. Instead it is the banality of evil, men and women "who drove their kids to school, bought groceries at the supermarket, and spent weekends playing golf" and yet "were capable of the casual infliction of pain on other human beings" (96). MacGregor likewise struggles to understand why the women continue to migrate, finally and dismissively asserting that it must be because they are Catholic and so "there's nothing to be done about it. You can't save them" (97).[36] Although he has expended significant effort observing and photographing Filipina migrant domestic workers, MacGregor has not spent much time speaking with them, much less listening to them. He sees them less as subjects with dignity than as objects for his camera. If he had spoken with the women as fellow human beings, he likely would have heard stories not only of economic exigencies but also of domestic violence. He also would have heard stories of great resilience and agency. Without question, as Joanne Leow writes, "[t]he story's ending depicts MacGregor's lack of understanding as a refusal to acknowledge his own complicity in the system" (207). Less recognized but equally important is that MacGregor's Chinese guides enable his secondary victimization of these women; Charlie and Sister Anne do little to humanize these women, and Sister Anne, however unwittingly, actively participates in denying justice to the Filipina migrant workers in her care. The story's focus on MacGregor and the narrator's frequent editorializing highlight Western complicity in the tragedies to which Asian female migrant reproductive workers are frequently subjected and underline their silencing by the very bodies purporting to bring them justice.

The Singaporean horror film *The Maid* (*Nüyong*, 女佣, 2005), on the experiences of Rosa, an 18-year-old Filipina domestic worker newly employed in Singapore, was an instant success at local box offices. For the director, Kelvin Tong, this film depicts "the plight of domestic workers" (Gomes 145). And as Catherine Gomes observes, Tong's use of the horror genre can be interpreted as "representing the 'horror' of alienation and unexpected dangers" experienced by foreign domestic workers (145). Yet local critical commentary on *The Maid* focused almost entirely on its place in Singapore's burgeoning film industry, remaining nearly silent regarding the film's social message (145–47).

Similar silences have long resonated globally, with internal and transnational migrant women engaged in reproductive labor in Asia and far beyond regularly exploited, abused, and dehumanized, their voices and stories ignored and suppressed and they and their families denied justice.

Creative narratives such as those discussed in this chapter amplify some of these stories from multiple perspectives, humanizing migrant reproductive workers while exposing disdainful attitudes, injurious behaviors, and horrific practices that are by no means limited to Asia. The varied literary aesthetics and narrative techniques of Sotheary's "My Sister," Zhou's *Longevity Park*, Khaerudina's "Susi," Dalijo's "My Employer," and Poon's "Development" resonate poignantly with dynamics generally underplayed if not unexamined outside literature, including both the plights and the dignity of diverse migrant reproductive workers throughout the region and, by inference, throughout the world. Also foregrounded in literature and other creative production from Asia and its diasporas is the undermining of reproductive autonomy and reproductive destinies, the focus of the following chapter.

NOTES

1. Unlike most scholarship on migration that focuses solely on economic motivators, Parrenas exposes gender, including gender-based violence, as "a constitutive element of the larger structural forces behind migration" (28). See also Xiao 51. Reproductive labor migration of women from Asia to other continents is also extensive.

2. This includes marriage migration, which together with paid domestic work are the two largest types of female migration in Asia (Cheng and Choo 655).

3. Scholars and activists have drawn attention to similarities between sex work and the types of work more frequently associated with reproductive labor. See, for instance, Cruz, who discusses migrant sex work as a form of "paid and unpaid sexually reproductive labour" (83), and Berg, who notes that "Marxist feminist theories of domestic (or reproductive) labor give us the tools to understand as work the historically un- and underpaid labor that maintains, or *re*produces, waged workers. Sex, paid or otherwise, is a fundamental piece of this maintenance" (697). See also Malhotra et al., who include sex work in their examination of late-twentieth-century gender and reproductive labor migration in Asia. Rodriquez makes a strong case for including service work as part of reproductive labor. Reproductive labor also can involve significant affective (i.e., emotional) labor. Unpaid reproductive work includes child-rearing, cooking, and housekeeping, work usually associated with women but also done by men, particularly in preindustrial societies (Uno 25–26, 30–34).

4. Internal rural-urban migration of female domestic workers occurred in many parts of Asia, including in Japan, from the late nineteenth century through the middle of the twentieth century, and maids are ubiquitous in modern Japanese literature (Nakamura 45).

5. The sociologist Arlie Hochschild identifies the "global care chain" as "a series of personal links between people [primarily women] across the globe based on the paid or unpaid work of caring" (250). Hochschild's work has been critiqued for its "presumed heteronormativity and essentialized notion of gender" (Nadasen 125).

6. Malhotra et al. chart women's migration flows within Asia between 1960 and 2000, while Wang et al. summarize Hong Kong's and Singapore's employment policies and working conditions for foreign domestic workers (157–61). For a detailed discussion of conditions in Hong Kong, see Wee and Sim; for conditions in Singapore, see Rahman et al. See also Palmer; Ueno, "Foreign Domestic Workers" and "Strategies." While one-third of Hong Kong households with children and one-eighth of Hong Kong households overall employ domestic helpers, 20% of Singaporean households employ foreign domestic workers (Leow 198).

7. Domestic workers are also artists in a range of media (Huang).

8. Paradoxically, given their sometimes graphic content, works of fiction have been considered "safer" than books on labor rights and have thus not been confiscated by employment agencies or employers (Suryomenggolo, "Significance" 209). Other, more popular fiction on migrant domestic workers includes the Singaporean novelist Balli Kaur Jaswal's murder mystery *Now You See Us* (2023), which depicts a range of working conditions and experiences for its three protagonists, Filipina domestic workers in Singapore.

9. These narratives were as prevalent in the 1990s as they are today. Sandy summarizes the changing relationships among feminisms and sex work (8–9). The term *sex work* emerged in the 1980s as an attempt to destigmatize and legitimize prostitution yet has come under fire in recent years for further harming the individuals involved. As Taina Bien-Aimé, of the Coalition against Trafficking in Women, argues, "Prostitution is neither sex nor work but a system based on gender-based violence and socioeconomic inequalities related to sex, gender, race, and poverty that preys on the most marginalized among us" (qtd. in Paul).

10. In addition to writing, Sotheary has worked as a television broadcaster in Phnom Penh. "My Sister" first appeared in Khmer in the newspaper *Rasmei Kampuchea*. I was unable to employ anyone to compare the source text and its English-language translation.

11. "My Sister" is one of many works of Southeast Asian literature that address the challenges facing rural-urban internal migrants (Yamada 45), although the family featured in this story is unusual in its access to higher education. Even today, only about 13% of women and men in Cambodia enroll in tertiary education (*Global Gender Gap Report 2023* 124). Phaenkār discusses rural-urban migration in Cambodia.

12. The Burgher Sri Lankan writer Jean Arasanayagam's English-language "Two Women and an Apple" is narrated by a sex worker who describes the immense challenges of providing for her unemployed husband and three

children. See also the Indian writer Mahasweta Devi's short story "Breast-Giver" ("Stanadāyinī," 1987), discussed in chapter 4. For its part, the Indo-Canadian writer Anosh Irani's novel *The Parcel* (2016) illuminates conditions for both sex workers and hijra in Mumbai. *Hijra* is a broad term that generally encompasses individuals who identify as transgender, intersex, or eunuchs; in much of South Asia these individuals are categorized as a third gender.

13. See Derks 12, 15; Ledgerwood 2. See also Anderson and Grace on the impact and continued significance of the Cambodian code of conduct for women, *Chbăb Srei*. See also Moore.

14. The Khmer Rouge (the Communist Party of Kampuchea) overthrew the Khmer Republic in 1975 and evacuated Phnom Penh and other major cities, displacing millions. One in five Cambodians died or were killed outright between 1975 and 1979 (Chandler vii; Sandy 42). Sex workers were regularly arrested and detained; many were beaten, raped, and even killed in detention (Sandy 45).

15. As Sandy emphasizes, it is crucial also to listen to the voices of sex workers themselves. See also Schuler. The Indonesian writer Eka Kurniawan's short story "My Lipstick Is Red, Darling" ("Gincu ini merah, sayang") reveals the devastating impact of social and spousal stigmas against sex work.

16. Nearly 20% of Cambodian women are employed in the garment industry (Jackson et al. 2).

17. China is the most dramatic example of broader global trends (OECD 250).

18. Other challenges facing aging populations involve labor supply, economic growth, family relationships, and ultimately restructuring social systems including eldercare, health care, housing, and the pension system (Yip). See also Wang and Mason. "Aging societies" are those in which more than 7% of the population is 65 or older, while "aged societies" and "super-aged societies" are those in which more than 14% and more than 21%, respectively, are 65 or older (Tahara 1102).

19. For a summary of internal migration in China, see "Migrant Workers"; Liang.

20. See Hong for more on rural-urban migration and eldercare in China. Zhang discusses women and internal migration more generally in China. See also Zhu and Xiao. For more on the role of foreign domestic workers in providing eldercare in other parts of Asia, see Wang et al.; Ogawa, "Making" and *Transnational Migration*. In South Korea, much eldercare is provided by Chinese Koreans (Bu [2 Jan. 2022]; Ogawa, "Making"). Also of note is the Korean director Park Chan Wook's film *Decision to Leave* (*Heŏjil kyŏlsim*, lit. *Resolution to Break Up*, 2022), on a Chinese Korean woman employed as an eldercare worker (Bu [7 Apr. 2023]). The Japanese film director Hayakawa Chie's dystopian *Plan 75* (2022), which depicts a Japan that offers Japanese citizens age 75 and over the option of euthanasia, features a Filipina caregiver; women from the Philippines have done care work in Japan since the 1980s (Ong and López 57).

21. Publishers initially were skeptical about this novel, given its topic (Jia). Zhou is the author of *After the Finale* (*Quzhong renzai*, 2015) and the semi-autobiographical *Fields of Joy* (*Anhun*, 2012), a conversation between a father and his deceased son. Other Chinese novels grappling with aging include Bei Cun's *The Baptizing River* (*Shixi de he*, 2005), Jiang Lin's *Being Mortal* (*Zuihao de gaobie*, lit. *The Best Farewell*, 2018), and Shi Tiesheng's *Ditan and I* (*Wo yu ditan*, 2005). (Thank you to Fangdai Chen for these references.) For different perspectives on the experiences of rural to urban female migrant workers, see Chinese science fiction such as Wanxiang Fengnian's *Through the Fog, a Distant Land Appears* (*Wuzhongxilai de yuanfang*, 2019).

22. Robots are increasingly used in eldercare and, given the gendered aspects of this work, are usually imagined as female. In Japan, the government promotes robots for economic, nationalistic, and xenophobic reasons; industry does so to save labor; and intellectuals believe them part of national identity (Frumer).

23. Xiao discusses these issues. The July 2021 issue of *Chinese Literature Today* contains a special section on Chinese women migrant workers' literature (47–127), guest-edited by Xiao and including Meng Yu's powerful "I Am Not Afraid of Being Infected," which focuses on abuses faced by migrant reproductive workers both in their own homes, perpetrated by husbands and other family members, and in the homes of their employers. See also X. Zhou.

24. Uncle Xiao's wrath is not confined to Xiaoyang; the retired judge is belligerent toward family and strangers alike. For background on nursing in China, see Hui et al.

25. Earlier in the novel, Xiaoyang thwarted Uncle Xiao's suicide attempt, claiming, "All we need now is time [for a cure]. . . . You have to keep on living" (Zhou Daxin 294). Xiaoyang was concerned with the impact Uncle Xiao's suicide would have on her career. For more on end-of-life decisions and care, see Thornber 386–584. Keimig discusses experiences of aging and caregiving from the perspectives of Chinese elders.

26. Between 1994 and 1999, male migrants numbered 22.9 and 1.7 per 100 female migrants to Singapore and Hong Kong, respectively (Hugo 58). Before the 1990s, most female migrant workers from Indonesia went to the Middle East (Suryomenggolo, "Significance" 204). For more on Indonesian domestic worker migration to and from Malaysia, see Killias.

27. Indonesia ranks 87th of 146 nations overall, having closed nearly 70% of its gender gap. Just 52.5% of women are in the workforce, in contrast with more than 80% of men (*Global Gender Gap Report 2023* 205).

28. Suryomenggolo likewise distinguishes this writing from more "mainstream literary production," addressing topics neglected by elite authors ("Significance" 208). See also the Singaporean playwright Haresh Sharma's *Model Citizens* (2010), on the relationship between a Singaporean family and an Indonesian maid (Leow 208–11).

29. Also notable is the section in *At a Moment's Notice* titled "Love and Sexualities" (87–137), which includes stories on "experiences of love and sex, and about perceptions of same-sex relations," common themes in post-1998 Indonesian literature by middle- and upper-class Indonesian female writers as well but in this anthology told through the workers' perspectives (Suryomenggolo, "Significance" 212). For more on canonical Indonesian literature, including post-1998 women's writing, see Allen; Arimbi; Budiman; and Smyth. Izharuddin explores gender and Islam in Indonesian cinema. See also Ahmed; Wadud. Despite significant searches, the Indonesian-language source texts for the translations in *At a Moment's Notice* were not found.

30. Dalijo worked in Hong Kong, Taiwan, Singapore, and Malaysia for more than a decade.

31. Overseas Filipino and Filipina workers today number more than 11 million, more than 10% of the population of the Philippines.

32. The Philippines ranks 16th of 146 nations in closing its gender gap, although only 44% of women participate in the labor force, compared with 69% of men (*Global Gender Gap Report 2023* 301).

33. Born in Singapore, Poon is a novelist, photographer, and lawyer. The author of sixteen books, many of which have been adapted for radio and the theater, she "reimagine[s] the Western canon from a global perspective . . . [and] challenge[s] contemporary notions of ethnicity, gender, and culture" ("About").

34. See also Crisanta Sampang's memoir *Maid in Singapore* (2005). Originally from the Philippines, Sampang worked as a maid in Singapore from 1984 to 1988. Anthony Chen's feature film *Ilo Ilo* (2013), which focuses on a Singaporean family and their recently hired Filipina domestic worker, insists "on the messy, embodied nature of domestic labor" (Leow 214).

35. See also Poon 89. Notable is Sampang's humanistic description of the voices of her compatriots on their day off: "The buses are abuzz with excited conversations in a variety of Filipino dialects, a sound so familiar to a Filipino's ear, that if one takes a moment to close her eyes, one almost feels she's back on the streets of downtown Manila" (73).

36. More than 80% of the Philippine population is Roman Catholic.

WORKS CITED

"About." *Wena Poon*, 2022, www.wenapoon.com/about.

Ahmed, Leila. *Women and Gender in Islam*. Yale UP, 1992.

Allen, Pamela, editor and translator. *Women's Voices: An Anthology of Short Stories by Indonesian Women Writers*. Longman, 1995.

Anderson, Emily, and Kelly Grace. "From Schoolgirls to 'Virtuous' Khmer Women: Interrogating *Chbab Srey* and Gender in Cambodian Education Policy." *Studies in Social Justice*, vol. 12, no. 2, Dec. 2018, pp. 215–34.

Arasanayagam, Jean. "Two Women and an Apple." *All Is Burning*, by Arasanayagam, Penguin Books, 1995, pp. 354–75.

Arimbi, Diah Ariani. "Indonesia Muslim Women Writers and Their Writings: Women, Islam, and Religious Identity." Michalik and Budianta, pp. 167–92.

Asis, Maruja. "Caring for the World: Filipino Domestic Workers Gone Global." Huang et al., pp. 21–53.

Bada, Xóchitl, and Shannon Gleeson. "A New Approach to Migrant Labor Rights Enforcement: The Crisis of Undocumented Worker Abuse and Mexican Consular Advocacy in the United States." *Labor Studies Journal*, vol. 40, no. 1, Mar. 2015, pp. 32–53.

Berg, Heather. "Working for Love, Loving for Work: Discourses of Labor in Feminist Sex-Work Activism." *Feminist Studies*, vol. 40, no. 3, 2014, pp. 693–721.

Bu, Chan Yong. Personal communication with the author. 2 Jan. 2022.

———. Personal communication with the author. 7 Apr. 2023.

Budiman, Manneke. "Emerging Women Writers in the *Reformasi* Period." Michalik and Budianta, pp. 143–66.

Cellan, Maria Allen. "Love, Lost and Found." Van Ditzhuijzen, pp. 57–59.

Chandler, David. *Voices from S-21: Terror and History in Pol Pot's Secret Prison*. U of California P, 1999.

Chen, Lin. "Deciding to Institutionalize: Caregiving Crisis, Intergenerational Communication, and Uncertainty Management for Elders and Their Children in Shanghai." *Journal of Gerontological Social Work*, vol. 58, no. 2, Feb. 2015, pp. 128–48.

Cheng, Catherine Man Chuen, and Hae Yeon Choo. "Women's Migration for Domestic Work and Cross-Border Marriage in East and Southeast Asia: Reproducing Domesticity, Contesting Citizenship." *Sociology Compass*, vol. 9, no. 8, Aug. 2015, pp. 654–67.

Cruz, Katie. "Beyond Liberalism: Marxist Feminism, Migrant Sex Work, and Labour Unfreedom." *Feminist Legal Studies*, vol. 26, no. 1, 2018, pp. 65–92.

Dalijo, Ally. "My Employer." Suryomenggolo, *At a Moment's Notice*, pp. 75–84.

Derks, Annuska. *Khmer Women on the Move: Exploring Work and Life in Urban Cambodia*. U of Hawai'i P, 2008.

Devi, Mahasweta. "Breast-Giver." *Breast Stories*, by Devi, translated by Gayatri Chakravorty Spivak, Seagull Books, 2010, pp. 38–133.

Feng, Zhanlian, et al. "China's Rapidly Aging Population Creates Policy Challenges in Shaping a Viable Long-Term Care System." *Health Affairs*, vol. 31, no. 12, Dec. 2012, pp. 2764–73.

Frumer, Yulia. "Agency and Ethics in Japanese Robotics Engineering." 4 Oct. 2022, Harvard University. Lecture.

Fu, Zhaohao, and Lingxin Hao. "Agent-Based Modeling of China's Rural-Urban Migration and Social Network Structure." *Physica A*, no. 490, Jan. 2018, pp. 1061–75.

Gallo, Ester, and Francesca Scrinzi. *Migration, Masculinities, and Reproductive Labour: Men of the Home*. Palgrave Macmillan, 2016.

Global Gender Gap Report 2023. World Economic Forum, 2023, www3.weforum.org/docs/WEF_GGGR_2023.pdf.

Gomes, Catherine. "Maid-in-Singapore: Representing and Consuming Foreign Domestic Workers in Singapore Cinema." *Asian Ethnicity*, vol. 12, no. 2, June 2011, pp. 141–54.

Hochschild, Arlie Russell. "Global Care Chains and Emotional Surplus Value." *Justice, Politics, and the Family*, edited by Daniel Engster and Tamara Metz, Taylor and Francis, 2014, pp. 249–61.

Hong, Liu. "Home Care for Elders in China's Rural-Urban Dualism: Care Workers' Fractured Experiences." Michel and Peng, *Gender*, pp. 67–89.

Huang, Junting. "Bordering Domesticity: Filipina Domestic Workers in Hong Kong's Contemporary Art." *Journal of Contemporary Chinese Art*, vol. 8, no. 1, 3 May 2021, pp. 33–48.

Huang, Shirlena, et al., editors. *Asian Women as Transnational Domestic Workers*. Marshall Cavendish, 2005.

Hugo, Graeme. "Indonesian International Domestic Workers: Contemporary Developments and Issues." Huang et al., pp. 54–91.

Hui, Jiang, et al. "Family-Paid Caregivers in Hospital Health Care in China." *Journal of Nursing Management*, vol. 21, no. 8, Nov. 2013, pp. 1026–33.

Irani, Anosh. *The Parcel*. Alfred A. Knopf Canada, 2016.

Izharuddin, Alicia. *Gender and Islam in Indonesian Cinema*. Palgrave Macmillan, 2017.

Jackson, James Lowell, et al. *The Supply Chain Ripple Effect: How COVID-19 Is Affecting Garment Workers and Factories in Asia and the Pacific*. International Labour Organization / Cornell University, Oct. 2020, www.ilo.org/wcmsp5/groups/public/---asia/---ro-bangkok/documents/briefingnote/wcms_758626.pdf.

Jaggar, Alison M., editor. *Gender and Global Justice*. Polity Press, 2014.

Jaswal, Balli Kaur. *Now You See Us*. William Morrow, 2023.

Jia, Mei. "New Focus on Old Age." *China Daily*, 23 Feb. 2018, www.chinadaily.com.cn/a/201802/23/WS5a8f681fa3106e7dcc13d80a.html.

Kanwar, Sheena. Foreword. Van Ditzhuijzen, pp. 5–6.

Keimig, Rose K. *Growing Old in a New China: Transitions in Elder Care*. Rutgers UP, 2021.

Khaerudina, Ratna. "Susi." Suryomenggolo, *At a Moment's Notice*, pp. 32–38.

Killias, Olivia. *Follow the Maid: Domestic Worker Migration in and from Indonesia*. NIAS Press, 2018.

Kittay, Eva Feder. "The Moral Harm of Migrant Carework: Realizing a Global Right to Care." Jaggar, pp. 62–84.

Kofman, Eleonore, and Parvati Raghuram. *Gendered Migrations and Global Social Reproduction*. Palgrave Macmillan, 2015.

Kuo, Lily. "How Hong Kong's 'Maid Trade' Is Making Life Worse for Domestic Workers throughout Asia." *Quartz*, 19 Feb. 2014, qz.com/176354/how-hong-kong-maid-trade-is-making-life-worse-for-domestic-workers-throughout-asia.

Kurniawan, Eka. "My Lipstick Is Red, Darling." Translated by Annie Tucker. *Kitchen Curse: Stories*, translated by Tucker et al., Verso, 2019, pp. 101–08.

Lan, Pei-Chia. "New Global Politics of Reproductive Labor: Gendered Labor and Marriage Migration." *Sociology Compass*, vol. 2, no. 6, Nov. 2008, pp. 1801–15.

Ledgerwood, Judy. *Changing Khmer Conceptions of Gender: Women, Stories, and the Social Order*. 1990. Cornell U, PhD dissertation.

Leow, Joanne. "Strangers, Surrogates, Lovers: Foreign Domestic Workers in Contemporary Singapore Texts." *Singapore Literature and Culture: Current Directions in Local and Global Contexts*, edited by Angelia Poon and Angus Whitehead, Routledge, 2017, pp. 198–216.

Liang, Zai. "Internal Migration: Policy Changes, Recent Trends, and New Challenges." Zhao and Guo, pp. 197–215.

Liu, Jieyu, et al., editors. *Routledge Handbook of East Asian Gender Studies*. Routledge, 2020.

Malhotra, Ragini Saira, et al. "Gender and Reproductive Labor Migration in Asia, 1960–2000." *International Journal of Sociology*, vol. 46, no. 2, Apr. 2016, pp. 114–40.

Meyer, Sarah R., et al. "Gender Differences in Violence and Other Human Rights Abuses among Migrant Workers on the Thailand-Myanmar Border." *Violence against Women*, vol. 25, no. 8, June 2019, pp. 945–67.

Michalik, Yvonne, and Melani Budianta, editors. *Indonesian Women Writers*. Regiospectra, 2015.

Michel, Sonya, and Ito Peng, editors. *Gender, Migration, and the Work of Care*. Palgrave Macmillan, 2017.

———. Introduction. Michel and Peng, *Gender*, pp. 3–22.

"Migrant Workers and China's Floating Population." *Facts and Details*, Oct. 2021, factsanddetails.com/china/cat11/sub72/item150.html.

Miquiabas, Bong. "After Another Nightmare Surfaces in Hong Kong's Domestic Worker Community, Will Anything Change?" *Forbes*, 31 Mar. 2015, www.forbes.com/sites/bongmiquiabas/2015/03/31/after-another-nightmare-surfaces-in-hong-kongs-domestic-worker-community-will-anything-change/.

Moore, Anne Elizabeth. *New Girl Law: Drafting a Future for Cambodia*. Microcosm Publishing, 2013.

Nadasen, Premilla. "Rethinking Care: Arlie Hochschild and the Global Care Chain." *Women's Studies Quarterly*, vol. 45, nos. 3–4, Dec. 2017, pp. 124–28.

Nakamura, Miri. "The Cult of Happiness: Maid, Housewife, and Affective Labor in Higuchi Ichiyō's 'Warekara.'" *Journal of Japanese Studies*, vol. 41, no. 1, Jan. 2015, pp. 45–78.

Nie, Jing-Bao. "Erosion of Eldercare in China: A Socio-ethical Inquiry in Aging, Elderly Suicide and the Government's Responsibilities in the Context of the One-Child Policy." *Ageing International*, vol. 41, no. 4, Nov. 2016, pp. 350–65.

OECD. *Health at a Glance 2021: OECD Indicators*. OECD Publishing, 2021.

Ogawa, Reiko. "Making Migrant Care Workers in East Asia." Liu et al., pp. 123–43.

———, editor. *Transnational Migration from Southeast Asia to East Asia and the Transformation of Reproductive Labor*. Kitakyushu Forum on Asian Women, 2010.

Ong, Michelle G., and Mario Ivan López. "Filipina Migrants and the Embodiment of Successful Aging in Japan: Individual Quests for Wealth, Health, and Meaningful Interdependence." *Southeast Asian Studies*, vol. 11, no. 1, Apr. 2022, pp. 49–77.

Outline of the People's Republic of China Fourteenth Five-Year Plan for National Economic and Social Development and Long-Range Objectives for 2035. Mar. 2021, cset.georgetown.edu/wp-content/uploads/t0284_14th_Five_Year_Plan_EN.pdf.

Palmer, Wayne. "Migration Systems and Identity: Javanese Domestic Workers in Hong Kong and Singapore." *Departing from Java: Javanese Labour, Migration, and Diaspora*, edited by Rosemarijn Hoefte and Peter Meel, NIAS Press, 2018, pp. 137–59.

Parreñas, Rhacel Salazar. *Servants of Globalization: Migration and Domestic Work*. Stanford UP, 2015.

Paul, Pamela. "What It Means to Call Prostitution 'Sex Work.'" *The New York Times*, 17 Aug. 2023, www.nytimes.com/2023/08/17/opinion/prostitution-sex-work.html.

Phaenkār, Krasuaṅ. *Migration in Cambodia: Report of the Cambodian Rural Urban Migration Project*. Ministry of Planning, 2012.

Plan 75. Directed by Hayakawa Chie, WOWOW / Dongyu Club / Loaded Films / Fusee / Urban Factory / Happinet Phantom Studios, 2022.

Poon, Wena. "Development." *The Proper Care of Foxes*, by Poon, Sutajio Uena, 2016, pp. 75–98.

Qin, Hua, and Tim F. Liao. "Labor Out-Migration and Agricultural Change in Rural China: A Systemic Review and Meta-Analysis." *Journal of Rural Studies*, vol. 47, 2016, pp. 533–41.

Rahman, Noor Abdul, et al. "'Dignity Overdue': Transnational Domestic Workers in Singapore." Huang et al., pp. 233–61.

Rodriquez, Robyn Magalit. "Service Workers or Servile Workers? Migrant Reproductive Labor and Contemporary Global Racial Capitalism." *LPE Project*, 12 Dec. 2019, lpeproject.org/blog/service-workers-or-servile-workers-migrant-reproductive-labor-and-contemporary-global-racial-capitalism/.

Romero, Mary, et al. "Care Work in a Globalizing World." *When Care Work Goes Global: Locating the Social Relations of Domestic Work*, edited by Romero et al., Ashgate, 2014, pp. 1–25.

Sampang, Crisanta. *Maid in Singapore*. Marshall Cavendish International, 2005.

Sandy, Larissa. *Women and Sex Work in Cambodia: Blood, Sweat, and Tears*. Routledge, 2014.

Schuler, Greta. "'At Your Own Risk': Narratives of Migrant Sex Workers in Johannesburg." *Urban Forum*, vol. 28, no. 1, Apr. 2016, pp. 27–42.

Silvey, Rachel. "Transnational Rights and Wrongs: Moral Geographies of Gender and Migration." Jaggar, pp. 85–99.

Smyth, David, editor. *The Canon in Southeast Asian Literatures*. Routledge, 2000.

Sotheary, Mey Son. "My Sister." *Virtual Lotus: Modern Fiction of Southeast Asia*, edited by Teri Shaffer Yamada, translated by Tomoko Okada et al., U of Michigan P, 2002, pp. 45–52.

Suryomenggolo, Jafar, editor and translator. *At a Moment's Notice: Indonesian Maids Write on Their Lives Abroad*. NIAS Press, 2019.

———. Preface and acknowledgments. Suryomenggolo, *At a Moment's Notice*, pp. vii–viii.

———. "The Significance of the Stories." Suryomenggolo, *At a Moment's Notice*, pp. 204–16.

Tahara, Yoshio. "Cardiopulmonary Resuscitation in a Super-Aging Society." *Circulation Journal*, vol. 80, no. 5, Apr. 2016, pp. 1102–03.

Thornber, Karen Laura. *Global Healing: Literature, Advocacy, Care*. Brill, 2020.

Ueno, Kayoko. "Foreign Domestic Workers in Singapore." *Asia's New Mothers: Crafting Gender Roles and Childcare Networks in East and Southeast Asian Societies*, edited by Emiko Ochiai and Barbara Molony, Global Oriental, 2008, pp. 140–56.

———. "Strategies of Resistance among Filipina and Indonesian Domestic Workers in Singapore." *Asian Women and Intimate Work*, edited by Ochiai Emiko and Aoyama Kaoru, Brill, 2014, pp. 239–61.

Ugay, Juliet. "Coming Home." Van Ditzhuijzen, pp. 48–53.

Uno, Kathleen S. "Women and Changes in the Household Division of Labor." *Recreating Japanese Women, 1600–1945*, edited by Gail Lee Bernstein, U of California P, 1991, pp. 17–41.

Van Bortel, Tine, et al. "Perceived Stressors and Coping Mechanisms of Female Migrant Domestic Workers in Singapore." *PLoS One*, vol. 14, no. 3, Mar. 2019, pp. 1–15.

Van Ditzhuijzen, Karien, editor. *Our Homes, Our Stories: Voices of Migrant Domestic Workers in Singapore*. Humanitarian Organization for Migrant Economics, 2018.

Wadud, Amina. *Qur'an and Woman: Rereading the Sacred Text from a Woman's Perspective*. Oxford UP, 1999.

Wang, Chieh-Hsuan, et al. "The Foreign Domestic Workers in Singapore, Hong Kong, and Taiwan." *The Chinese Economy*, vol. 51, no. 2, Mar. 2018, pp. 154–74.

Wang, Feng, and Andrew Mason. "Population Ageing: Challenges, Opportunities, and Institutions." Zhao and Guo, pp. 177–96.

Wang, Vivian. "Hong Kong, Buckling under Covid, Leaves Its Most Vulnerable in the Cold." *The New York Times*, 2 Mar. 2022, www.nytimes.com/2022/03/02/business/hong-kong-covid.html.

Wanxiang Fengnian. "Through the Fog, a Distant Land Appears." Translated by Nathan Faries. *Future: Science Fiction Digest*, no. 4, 16 Oct. 2019, future-sf.com/fiction/through-the-fog-a-distant-land-appears/.

Wee, Vivienne, and Amy Sim. "Hong Kong as a Destination for Migrant Domestic Workers." Huang et al., pp. 175–209.

Women and Men in Cambodia: Facts and Figures 2018. Ministry of Planning, National Institute of Statistics, 2018.

Women in Cambodia's Garment Industry: Their Work, Their Safety. CARE *Australia*, Mar. 2017, www.care.org.au/wp-content/uploads/2017/04/SHCS_Brief-Women-Cambodia-Garment-Industry-March-2017_CA.pdf.

Xiao, Hui Faye. "Caring for the Small: Gendered Resistance and Solidarity through Chinese Domestic Workers' Writings." *Chinese Literature Today*, vol. 10, no. 2, 2021, pp. 47–57.

Yamada, Teri Shaffer, editor. *Virtual Lotus: Modern Fiction of Southeast Asia*. U of Michigan P, 2002.

Yeoh, Brenda, et al. "Asian Women as Transnational Domestic Workers." Huang et al., pp. 1–17.

Yeoh, Brenda, et al. "Social Protection for Migrant Domestic Workers in Singapore: International Conventions, the Law, and Civil Society Action." *American Behavioral Scientist*, vol. 64, no. 6, May 2020, pp. 841–58.

Yip, Winnie. Personal communication with the author. 7 June 2021.

Yu, Meng. "I Am Not Afraid of Being Infected." *Chinese Literature Today*, vol. 10, no. 2, 2021, pp. 98–101.

Zhang, Nana. "Women and Migration in China." Liu et al., pp. 157–68.

Zhang, Xinjie, et al. "The Effect of the Universal Two-Child Policy on Medical Insurance Funds with a Rapidly Ageing Population." *BMC Public Health*, vol. 21, no. 1, July 2021, pp. 1–4.

Zhao, Zhongwei, and Fei Guo, editors. *Transition and Challenge: China's Population at the Beginning of the Twenty-First Century*. Oxford UP, 2007.

Zhou Daxin. *Longevity Park*. Translated by James Trapp, ACA Publishing, 2021.

Zhou, Xiaojing. *Migrant Ecologies: Zheng Xiaoqiong's Women Migrant Workers*. Lexington Books, 2021.

Zhu, Ping, and Hui Faye Xiao, editors. *Feminisms with Chinese Characteristics*. Syracuse UP, 2021.

Zou, Xiang, et al. "Gendered Caregiving and Structural Constraints: An Empirical Ethical Study." *Nursing Ethics*, vol. 28, no. 3, May 2021, pp. 387–401.

4. Capitulating to and Fighting against Reproductive Violence

As several of the narratives examined in the previous chapters illuminate, decisions about whether, how, and under what circumstances to have and raise children have never been entirely autonomous matters for people of any gender (Altunjan 98; Tone xv). Instead, in most parts of the world and for much of history, partner and familial expectations and demands, cultural norms, medical practices, technological innovations, court decisions, legislation, national mandates, and wartime aggression have variously interfered with if not violated reproductive autonomy (Tone xv).[1] What is now understood as reproductive coercion or reproductive violence—"behavior that undermines autonomous decision-making in areas of reproductive health" (Fay and Yee 518) and "acts which affect the victim's reproductive system, organs, process, or capacity to reproduce" (Altunjan 9)—has long been used to assert power and control over both individuals and collectivities, particularly women already vulnerable because of their race, ethnicity, class, age, ability, sexuality, and other factors. More specifically, for women, reproductive violence—a form of gender-based violence and gender injustice—can be understood as "the interwoven conditions of power, coercion, and bodily and mental harm that disrupt women's reproductive destinies at all stages of reproduction, including conception, gestation, birth, childrearing, and family making" (Hong 487).[2]

Reproductive violence takes many forms, including both forced and denied pregnancy, childbirth, or child-rearing either by preventing access to or by imposing fertility treatments, abortion, contraception, sterilization, adoption, childcare, and similar phenomena. Such violence also can occur on diverse scales: within an intimate relationship (e.g., sabotaging a partner's birth control, forcing a partner to continue or end a pregnancy), within a family (e.g., forcing a daughter-in-law to abort a female fetus, discussed in chapter 6; preventing a daughter from removing an intrauterine device; and, most commonly, representing childbirth and child-rearing as a necessary part of a daughter or daughter-in-law's future), nationally (e.g., in the United States, controlling Black women's reproduction from the time of slavery to the present and forcibly sterilizing members of marginalized communities; forced pregnancy and abortion in Cambodia and China, respectively), and internationally (e.g., Nazi eugenics and racial hygiene policies during World War II; forced abortions conducted in Asia on so-called comfort women, discussed in chapter 5; rape camps in the former Yugoslavia; Altunjan 79–84, 86; Griffin and Woods).[3] Reproductive violence regularly intersects with other forms of gender-based violence, including social violence (psychological, physical, and sexual violence perpetrated by individuals outside the family or intimate partner relationship), family violence, and intimate partner violence, the focus of chapters 5, 6, and 7, respectively.[4] Rates and intensity of reproductive violence vary greatly within and among communities and cultures, with few women immune and already marginalized women particularly affected.[5] As the organization Asian Communities for Reproductive Justice argues, "[T]he regulation of reproduction and exploitation of women's bodies and labor is both a tool and a result of systems of oppression based on race, class, gender, sexuality, ability, age and immigration status."

Writers from across Asia and its diasporas have grappled in their work with reproductive violence of myriad forms and dimensions, granting dignity to individuals and communities who have been systematically dehumanized. This chapter focuses on narratives that depict individuals both capitulating to and fighting against pervasive reproductive violence that is endorsed if not mandated by the government. *Breasts and Eggs* (*Natsu monogatari*, 夏物語, lit. *Natsu's Tale, Summer's Tale*, 2019), by the leading Japanese feminist writer Kawakami Mieko (1976–), exposes the personal toll of a system with significant barriers facing those who want children outside heteronormative relationships—paradoxical given Japan's grave concerns regarding its shrinking population. For their part, the documentary *One Child Nation* (2019), by the Chinese filmmakers Wang Nanfu (1985–) and Zhang Jialing, and the dystopian novel *The Dark Road* (*Yin zhi dao*, 陰之道, 2012), by the Chinese British writer Ma Jian (1953–), reveal even more drastic efforts to control women's reproduction, highlighting the horrors experienced by individuals ensnared in China's one-child policy (1979–2015). These included forced abortions, mandatory sterilizations (mostly of women), and birth control (primarily through intrauterine devices) as well as exorbitant fines for couples who had more than one child without authorization. The chapter ends with a discussion of the novel *Origins of Love* (2012), by the Indian writer Kishwar Desai (1956–), where paradoxically it is the relative absence of official policies regarding assisted reproduction that enables a thriving and exploitative commercial surrogacy industry that preys on socioeconomically disadvantaged women, several of whose stories of agency and resistance are brought to the fore.

Loretta Ross and Rickie Solinger identify storytelling as "an act of subversion and resistance" fundamental to reproductive justice, which encapsulates "1) the right *not* to have a child, 2) the right to *have* a child, and 3) the right to *parent* children in safe and healthy environments" (9, 59). The narratives discussed in this chapter are no exception, speaking to diverse aspects of struggles for reproductive justice in Asia and far beyond through a multiplicity of stories and storytellers.[6]

Restricting Reproduction: Kawakami Mieko's *Breasts and Eggs* (2019)

Having a child outside marriage, not to mention without a partner, is highly stigmatized in much of Asia (Saim et al. 466). In Vietnam, there is tremendous pressure on unmarried women who become pregnant either to terminate their pregnancy, resulting in one of the world's highest abortion rates, or to marry, leading to a booming fake-wedding industry where families go to considerable effort and expense to save face (Pike). In Malaysia, where pregnancy outside marriage is judged a "moral violation" and abortion is illegal except to protect a woman's physical or mental health, unmarried pregnant women have even fewer options: some turn to traditional and frequently dangerous methods of termination, while others are sent to special homes (Saim et al. 466). Stigmas against single mothers extend even to nations eager to reverse plummeting birth rates. In China, where the state is desperate to increase births after decades of the one-child policy, unmarried women are barred from freezing their eggs (Wang). Moreover, the Chinese government continues to promote heterosexual marriage as the only legitimate environment in which to birth and raise a child. As Xiaoyang describes in Zhou Daxin's *Longevity Park*, discussed in chapter 3, penalties levied against single mothers are severe: for instance, they are unable to register their children and are denied access to social welfare services and reproductive health resources (Zhao and Basnyat 1239–40).[7] Such policies reinforce China's "normative expectations of sexual conduct and motherhood" (1240).[8]

Having a child outside marriage, and especially without a partner, is also highly stigmatized and extremely rare in Japan. While an average of 41% of births across OECD (Organization for Economic Cooperation and Development) countries now take place outside marriage, a notable increase from 7% in 1970 and 24% in 1995, the rate in Japan remains unchanged, at 2–3% ("SF2.4").[9] The proportion of births by single women who choose to become pregnant outside a committed relationship is smaller still. Japan likewise has the lowest rate of single-parent households among OECD nations, at just 2.63% (2.36% single-mother and 0.27% single-father households; "SF1.1"). The Japanese government does not impose on single mothers the types of penalties found in China. But conventional gender norms surrounding marriage, childbirth, child-rearing, and employment mean that single mothers suffer from much higher poverty rates than the overall population, the highest rates in the OECD (Nonoyama-Tarumi 916).[10] To be sure, single mothers have a significantly higher work participation rate than their married counterparts. Yet in a society where women's incomes are generally much lower than men's, full-time positions often do not provide Japan's single mothers financial stability, regardless of education (Ezawa xvii, 63–64).

Japanese women who are single and who require medical intervention to become pregnant encounter even greater obstacles. Take, for instance, Natsuko, the first-person narrator of Kawakami Mieko's best-selling *Breasts and Eggs*. Natsuko, a writer in her 30s, poignantly describes the process of having a child on her own (the novel concludes with the birth of her daughter) after great struggle with social expectations and Japan's fertility industry, considerable research, and much soul-searching.[11] Her aesthetically imaginative narrative style intersperses her singular story with numerous flashbacks to her impoverished and abusive childhood, entries from her adolescent niece Midoriko's journal, long transcriptions of conversations with her sister Makiko, and considerable and sometimes biased (e.g., transphobic) commentary and questioning regarding day-to-day events (part 1 [Kawakami, *Breasts* 9–147], which takes place in summer 2008). The narrative also incorporates extensive dialogues with diverse interlocutors as well as summaries of numerous external sources (part 2 [149–430], which takes place between 2016 and 2019). In these ways, the narrative places Natsuko's own adversities in the larger context of socioeconomic inequality and rigid understandings of gender, sexuality, reproduction, and motherhood.

In part 1 of *Breasts and Eggs*, Natsuko describes Makiko and 12-year-old Midoriko's visit to her apartment in Tokyo; desperate for breast implants, the Osaka-based and beauty-obsessed Makiko has come to Tokyo to consult with surgeons, while Midoriko is horrified both with her mother and with her own rapidly changing body.[12] Part 1 personalizes the challenges of single mothers in Japan, and Natsuko draws parallels between her sister and their mother: "[Makiko] still works at a bar five nights a week, living pretty much the same life as our mom. Another single mother, working herself to death" (Kawakami, *Breasts* 20).[13] Early on, Natsuko also reveals intolerance toward gender nonconforming individuals, in a lengthy discussion of the thoughts, questions, and elaborate scenarios that race through her mind after a "pair of women" enter the bathhouse, one of whom "had to be a man" (59), her empathy extending only so far. Although told primarily from Natsuko's perspective, part 1 also includes several of Midoriko's journal entries, in which Midoriko not only disparages gender disparities and declares herself childfree (meaning she has no desire to have children) but also reveals body dysmorphia—horror with her rapidly changing body—that suggests possible gender dysphoria. Interestingly, Natsuko does not comment on her niece's writings, as she does on many other matters, sometimes quite extensively, pointing to her own discomfort, again despite her own departure from social norms and her own sexual identity, revealed early in part 2.

Part 1 of *Breasts and Eggs* ends somewhat precipitately, with Natsuko gazing at her naked body in the mirror, and part 2 begins just as abruptly, eight years later, with Natsuko transcribing a disheartening conversation with some of her former colleagues, all of whom, she quickly notes, are married and most of whom have children. Having successfully launched her career as a writer; thinking about Midoriko, who is now seemingly more at peace with her body, in college, and planning to move in with her boyfriend; and reflecting on her time with her ex-boyfriend Naruse, who has just had a child with his wife, Natsuko ponders her future. She reveals that she had wanted to build a life with Naruse but that she is asexual: "the sex was never enjoyable or comforting or fulfilling. . . . I lacked the [sexual] appetite [my friends] took for granted. . . . Passion and sex were incompatible for me. They didn't connect" (Kawakami, *Breasts* 174–75). And she wonders:

> Would I ever have a child? If so, when? I didn't have a partner, and I wasn't looking for one. Could I really have a baby if I couldn't handle sex? What was I supposed to do? Visit a sperm bank? . . . Married couples could only register if they met certain criteria, but there was

no room for unmarried women. It might be different in a freer country, but I couldn't speak a word of English. (179)[14]

Tirelessly piling questions one atop another, something she does frequently, Natsuko draws attention not just to her dearth of English, the lack of infertility treatment for Japanese speakers abroad, and her logistical plight in a society that places clear limits on who is deemed worthy of having children. She also highlights her tangled thoughts and emotions, in sharp contrast with Keiko in Murata Sayaka's *Convenience Store Woman*, who, as discussed in chapter 1, is unwavering in her determination to remain unpartnered and childfree.

In part 2 of *Breasts and Eggs*, Natsuko superimposes various individual stories. In addition to sharing her own emotions and experiences, she adroitly includes transcripts and summaries of recent conversations with strangers, colleagues, friends, and family as well as quotations and précis from the media and other sources. She thereby creates an even more polyvocal narrative than in part 1, yet one that is less temporally encompassing.[15] This aesthetic strategy effectively foregrounds many of the conflicting emotions and active legal, political, and social debates surrounding motherhood in contemporary Japan and reveals their deeply personal impact. Shortly after sharing a conversation she had with her married friends, most of whom have children, Natsuko recaps a television program that reports infertility treatment as having existed in Japan for over six decades and having yielded more than 10,000 live births. Until recently this option had been available only to "married couples who had undergone conventional infertility procedures and discovered that the husband was sterile. Unmarried women who wanted kids were not allowed access to treatment, and same-sex couples were obviously out of luck" (Kawakami, *Breasts* 184).[16] And Natsuko shares her doubts: "At this stage of the game, I need to plan ahead, for myself and for my family [my sister and niece]. Why add a child to the picture? The idea was absurd, no matter how you slice it. More than impossible" (187). At the same time, Natsuko resents the lack of choice, again piling question atop question: "What if you were alone? . . . What about the rest of us, who were alone and planned to stay that way? Who has the right to have a child? Does not having a partner or not wanting to have sex nullify that right?" (275–76).

Significantly, Natsuko consults with and cites at length a range of people, including her editor, Sengawa Ryōko; her sister Makiko; and an activist for Children of Donors, Zen Yuriko, who are opposed to her having a child. Yuriko, reflecting on her own experience, is most adamant: "You force this other being into the world, this other being that never asked to be born. . . . [Parents are] only thinking about themselves. They never think about the poor kid being born. No one gives a damn how that child is going to feel" (Kawakami, *Breasts* 349–51).[17] Yet Yusa Rika, a writer Natsuko meets through her editor, suggests that given the dearth of writing in Japan on unconventional paths to motherhood, were she to have a child, Natsuko could offer tremendous hope to other women, particularly the minority who are financially stable: "You could give women something real. Real hope. Precedent. Empowerment" (321).[18]

Ultimately, Natsuko decides to have a child, using donor sperm from her friend Aizawa Jun, a physician and staunch advocate for individuals such as himself who were born from donor sperm; the two deceive a fertility doctor by claiming to be in a relationship. But because it includes so many different voices and opinions, and because it shares such a panoply of experiences, emotions, and inner conflicts so openly, *Breasts and Eggs* is by no means a pronatalist appeal—a call made by so many in the Japanese government and media—for Japanese women writ large to have (more) children. Instead, Kawakami's novel, which humanizes individuals who resist social norms and which integrates discourse on the relationship between pregnancy and publishing, highlights the necessity of reproductive choice and, ultimately, justice.

Kawakami's Akutagawa Prize–winning novella *Breasts and Eggs* (*Chichi to ran*, 乳と卵, 2008), precursor to the 2019 novel, "detonated like a bomb" (McNeill) in the male-dominated Japanese literary establishment because of its explicit discussion of breasts, menstruation, reproduction, beauty practices, and mothering. Tokyo's then governor Ishihara Shintarō, himself a former Akutagawa Prize recipient, proclaimed, "The egocentric, self-absorbed rambling of the work is unpleasant and intolerable" (Hernon). Not one to be silenced, Kawakami asserted, "I don't care if people criticize my work, especially if they have no interest in the subject matter. . . . What I do have a problem with is the patriarchal system in this country and the religious-like pressure that people are put under to conform here" (qtd. in Hernon). Natsuko enjoys sufficient privilege to undermine this system and seek justice, yet her future is uncertain, given Tokyo's high cost of living and the unpredictability of her income, not to mention the severe stigmas she will face as a single mother in Japan, all of which she herself highlights throughout *Breasts and Eggs*.

Banning Reproduction: Wang Nanfu and Zhang Jialing's *One Child Nation* (2019) and Ma Jian's *The Dark Road* (2012)

When compared with the reproductive violence experienced by Kawakami's Natsuko, significantly greater reproductive violence is enacted on individuals subjected to forced contraception, abortion, or sterilization. Banning reproduction can take place within individual relationships, as in the well-publicized cases of the American singers Britney Spears (forced under the terms of her guardianship to use an IUD to prevent pregnancy) and R. Kelly (who compelled a woman with whom he had had an abusive relationship to have an abortion). Asian and Asian diaspora writers describe analogous dynamics: for example, in the Indian writer Kishwar Desai's *Witness the Night* (2010), discussed in chapter 6, the protagonist's sister-in-law escapes from India back to the United Kingdom in order to avoid a family-mandated sex-selective abortion; in the Vietnamese American writer Quan Barry's *She Weeps Each Time You're Born* (2014), a Vietnamese grandmother unilaterally aborts her granddaughter's fetus; and in the Vietnamese writer Dạ Ngân's *An Insignificant Family*, discussed in chapter 1, the Vietnamese protagonist's lover compels her to have an abortion.[19]

Banning reproduction also can be a matter of national policy. Beginning in the early twentieth century, preventing individuals from having children was often done in the name of eugenics, the "science of improving the human race by better breeding" (Otsubo 225) and a form of "instrumental and selective procreation" (Robertson 191) intended to reduce the number of individuals seen as "unfit" (196) and undesirable. The United States has a long history of forcibly sterilizing individuals from marginalized populations, especially impoverished, mentally ill, and incarcerated Black, Latinx, Native American, and Puerto Rican individuals.[20] In 1907 the United States passed the world's first eugenics sterilization law—the Indiana Eugenics Law—authorizing the involuntary sterilization of "confirmed criminals, idiots, imbeciles and rapists" (Lombardo 98; see also Cohen; Manian; Manjeshwar; Torpy). As part of broader "racial hygiene" and extermination campaigns, in early-twentieth-century Europe, the Nazis systematically sterilized hundreds of thousands of Jewish and Eastern European men and women in addition to those deemed "hereditarily diseased" and otherwise likely to have "inferior" offspring (Altunjan 80–82). In wartime Japan, individuals with intellectual or physical disabilities, mental illnesses, or diseases such as leprosy and alcoholism, as well as members of other stigmatized groups, were targeted by Japan's National Eugenics Law (Kokumin Yūseihō, 1940–48).[21] For its part, Japan's postwar Eugenic Protection Law (Yūsei Hogohō, 1948–96) allowed for forcibly sterilizing and inducing abortions in people with certain hereditary diseases as well as mental illnesses and intellectual disabilities in order to prevent "the birth of eugenically inferior offspring" (Hovhannisyan 386; Robertson 194).

Forced sterilization and abortion have also been used as a form of state population control, in India from the 1970s to the 2010s and most aggressively and sweepingly in China under the one-child policy (1979–2015).[22] To be sure, the particulars of the Chinese mandate changed over time, and in practice it was a strictly one-child policy for only about a third of couples, with exceptions for second and occasionally third children for the majority of families (Greenhalgh, "Controlling" 7; Gu et al.). Yet for 35 years, the Chinese state engaged in forced contraception, sterilization, and abortion (including late-term) on a massive scale, a practice that affected all genders, particularly women. Initially, some Chinese population scientists raised concerns about class bias (i.e., that China's one-child policy had a greater impact on peasants than on urbanites, the wealthiest of whom could pay the exorbitant fines for policy violations). At the same time, nothing was said regarding "the real-world impact of a one-child policy on rural women and girls" (Greenhalgh, *Just* 264). As Susan Greenhalgh continues, "It was peasant women's bodies [80% of Chinese women in 1980 were peasants] that would be defined as overly reproductive and thus requiring abortions and sterilizations" (266). Indeed, not only are three of the "four operations" (*sizhong shoushu*) on which population control depended—IUD insertion, tubectomy (tubal ligation), induced abortion, and vasectomy—performed on women. Strong resistance from men regarding vasectomies meant that most sterilizations were conducted on women, despite vasectomies being a lower-risk procedure than tubectomies and abortions (Greenhalgh, "Controlling" 8).[23] Moreover, the traditional preference for sons meant that infant girls were disproportionately aborted or abandoned at birth, leading to distorted sex ratios, child trafficking, and illegal adoptions.

Neither the award-winning documentary film *One Child Nation* nor the dystopian novel *Dark Road* comprehensively depicts life under China's one-child policy. Scholars such as Greenhalgh have rightly exposed the film's many lacunae, its distortions (including overgeneralizations), and its failure to address the one-child policy from a broader perspective, especially the policy's substantial benefits to significant numbers of women

(Li et al.). These perspectives are also elided in *Dark Road*, which, as Julia Lovell explains, "rarely makes use of the stylistic flourishes that the freedom of the novel permits" and "radiates a misanthropy towards China that is terrifying in its absoluteness." *One Child Nation* and *Dark Road*, both of which are banned in China, ultimately tell pointed stories not of the "nation" in its entirety but instead of particular individuals, families, and communities in China whose experiences were widespread.

One Child Nation highlights some of the pervasive propaganda for the one-child policy—posters, songs, operas, theatrical performances, films, and relentless mass media campaigns—and eloquently probes how destructive this policy was and continues to be for countless individuals, families, and communities (Li et al.).[24] Although, as Jie Li and colleagues have noted, the film's "domineering voiceover and melodramatic score" tend to obscure and discredit witnesses' lived experiences, Wang's interviews with a range of individuals take deft advantage of the cinematic form in order to compellingly reveal the traumas and emotions that millions experienced and continue to endure. Victims, enablers, and enforcers alike, separately and together in small groups, boldly express anger, guilt, despair, helplessness, resignation, and justification. Common refrains are that there was "no way out" (*mei banfa*; 没办法) and that individual sacrifice was necessary to ensure the future of China. The film powerfully reveals the horrors of forced abortion (often late-term) and sterilization, infant abandonment and infanticide (mostly of infant girls, as happens in other overwhelmingly patriarchal societies including India, discussed in chapter 6), and the abduction and trafficking of children. It also spotlights families who were heavily fined, whose homes were demolished, or who were evicted from their villages for having more than one child as well as families searching decades later for children stolen from them and adopted by Western families who had believed they were orphans or that they had been abandoned.

One Child Nation resonates with other recent cultural productions that expose the terrors of the past and the painful legacies experienced in the present because of China's one-child policy. Particularly notable is Ma's *Dark Road*, which, unlike *One Child Nation*, takes place during the time the one-child policy was still in effect.[25] Narrated in the third-person omniscient, with its protagonists an impoverished rural couple—Meili and Kongzi (Eng. Confucius)—this striking novel interweaves exceptionally graphic discourse on many of the abuses fundamental to China's one-child policy with countless references to other injustices on the Chinese mainland, including sexual violence by family, acquaintances, partners, and strangers alike, discussed in the following chapters, as well as extreme environmental degradation.[26]

Meili and Kongzi have a daughter, Nannan, but Kongzi, as the seventy-sixth generation male descendent of Confucius, believes it his Confucian duty to produce a male heir. So, when Meili becomes pregnant with their second child without government authorization, the family flees their village, becoming internal migrants whose working and living conditions are even more perilous than those of the internal migrants discussed in chapter 3. The Chinese state is brutal: family-planning officers discover Meili and Kongzi, and they strangle the couple's second child at birth after unsuccessfully attempting to abort him at eight months. Kongzi, too, is vicious. Among many other abuses, he sells off their third child, a baby girl who needs a brain operation and likely a lifetime of care the couple cannot afford, and he has no interest in Meili beyond her ability to bear sons (Ma, *Dark Road* 314).

In her youth, Meili had believed that just as the government protects and cares for its people, husbands protect and care for their wives. But ultimately, she "discovered that women don't own their bodies: their wombs and genitals are battle zones over which their husband and the state fight for control—territories their husbands invade for sexual gratification and to produce male heirs, and which the state probes, monitors, guards and scrapes so as to assert its power and spread fear" (Ma, *Dark Road* 187). Meili faces innumerable barriers and unspeakable violence as she traverses a China overrun with corruption and scarred by ecological catastrophe, described in meticulous detail. From the opening pages, the narrator of *Dark Road* fills the novel with vivid imagery and explicit depictions of death and destruction of all kinds. To be sure, near the end of *Dark Road*, Meili is compared to "the heroine of a Victorian novel, rebelling against oppressive convention in the pursuit of happiness" and is described as having an "air of stubborn defiance" (352).[27] But Ma's narrative ends with Nannan's disappearance and possible abduction and with Meili drowning after giving birth to a green stillborn infant that she carried for six years, the narrative's one "leap into fantasy" (Lovell). Kongzi, for his part, ignores Meili, extracts himself and the stillborn infant from the river, and makes his way across a vast landscape of electronic waste, not unlike that featured in Wang Jiuliang's ecodocumentary *Beijing Besieged by Waste* (*Laji weigong*, 垃圾圍城, 2011). As Howard Choy argues, through depicting China's landscapes as severely degraded, "Ma's literary imagination effectively probes into the question of whether the baby has the right to be or not to be born" (280) and, by extension, whether couples have the right to continue to have children. Kawakami's *Breasts and Eggs* and Wang and Zhang's *One Child Nation* each make a strong case for enabling everyone to have (more) children, regardless of identity, marital status, or current family size. In contrast, *Dark Road* at once condemns forcibly preventing pregnancy and implicitly challenges initiatives to increase or even sustain birth rates given global environmental precarity.

Moreover, whereas Kawakami's narrative concludes with Natsuko contentedly clutching her healthy, screaming newborn to her chest, and Ma's novel with Kongzi stretching his stillborn infant up to the dawn while his wife is drowning, *One Child Nation* explicitly addresses transnational futures of reproductive freedom. In its final minutes, the film speaks explicitly of similarities between China and the United States. Wang comments, "I'm struck by the irony that I left a country where the government forced women to abort, and I moved to another country [the United States] where governments restrict abortions. On the surface, they seem like opposites. But both are about taking away women's control of their own bodies" (*One Child Nation* 1:23:18–1:23:38).[28] She then observes that after 35 years of the one-child policy, "there aren't enough young people in China to work and care for the elderly. So, China is introducing a new family-planning policy" (1:23:55–1:24:06). *One Child Nation* concludes with examples of the propaganda for this new two-child policy, which in 2021 became a three-child policy.[29] Birth rates have continued to decline despite these measures, and some fear that in the future the Chinese government will actively compel women to have children, particularly educated urban women who already have been targeted through aggressive media campaigns (Fincher 174–75). Both *Dark Road* and *One Child Nation*, by personalizing the immediate and longer-term effects of the one-child policy, respectively, encourage readers and viewers to think more deeply about the policies of their own governments and the impact of those policies on individuals. Other nations might not be as extreme as China under the one-child policy, but in much of the world, and possibly in the coming years in China as well, these policies interfere deeply and dangerously with personal reproductive freedoms and justice, including in the arena of surrogacy, discussed in the following section.

Reconceiving Surrogacy: Kishwar Desai's *Origins of Love* (2012)

Surrogacy—understood broadly as a woman carrying and delivering a child for an individual or couple who will become the child's parent or parents after birth—has been part of human societies for thousands of years and has frequently taken advantage of social and economic disparities (Fixmer-Oraiz 129–30; Klock and Lindheim 889). This dynamic comes to light in the Old Testament stories of Sarah's handmaiden Hagar bearing a child for Sarah and Abraham close to four millennia ago and of Rachel's maid Bilhah—featured in an epigraph of Margaret Atwood's *The Handmaid's Tale* (1985)—and Leah's maid Zilpah being forced to bear children with Rachel's husband, Jacob. The rapid development of assisted reproductive technology and in vitro fertilization in the late twentieth century made possible gestational surrogacy, wherein the surrogate carries the fertilized egg of another woman. In gestational surrogacy, unlike in earlier forms of surrogacy, the surrogate is not genetically related to the child they are carrying (Fixmer-Oraiz 130; Klock and Lindheim 890). With demand far exceeding supply, and regulations and cost across and even within nations ever-changing and enormously uneven, transnational gestational surrogacy soon became a booming business, and economically disadvantaged women around the world, including women in Asia, were targeted as surrogate mothers (Whittaker 3–4).

India legalized commercial surrogacy in 2002, and by 2012 surrogacy there was a 2-billion-dollar industry, with more than 25,000 children born annually, at least half for overseas couples (Desai, "India's Surrogate Mothers"). Before India banned international commercial surrogacy in 2015, overseas individuals were attracted by the nation's combination of qualified physicians and reliable medical facilities, on the one hand, and, on the other, the fact that surrogacy in India involved far fewer regulations, much lower costs, and a much greater certainty of outcome than at home (Srivastava 144).[30] For instance, legal, cultural, and financial factors make Indian surrogate mothers less likely than their counterparts elsewhere to claim the baby as their own (Shetty 1633; Srivastava 144). To be sure, surrogacy provided many Indian women with the opportunity to earn in a year what ordinarily would have taken two decades (Shetty 1634).[31] But it also led to significant exploitation and disregard for the surrogate's health—to implanting a dangerous number of embryos; to completely controlling surrogates during pregnancy, including regulating what they ate and drank, how much they exercised, and how often they saw their families; to performing an unnecessarily high rate of cesarean sections to accommodate the schedules of physicians and intended parents; and even sacrificing the surrogate's life for that of the fetus (Desai, "India's Surrogate Mothers"; Shetty). As Desai describes in the article "India's Surrogate Mothers Are Risking Their Lives," "In many cases the surrogate's life is secondary. . . .

[Surrogates] usually agree to assume all medical, financial, and psychological risks. . . . Medical practitioners involved in [surrogacy] are rarely troubled about the fate of the women [surrogates]."

Desai elaborates on these and similar forms of reproductive violence in *Origins of Love*.[32] This muckraking novel—which, as with *Breasts and Eggs*, *One Child Nation*, and *Dark Road*, incorporates multiple storytellers—exposes a highly profitable system of reproductive and fertility tourism that brutally exploits young, vulnerable, and impoverished Indian women, whom the novel brings to the fore. Reproductive and fertility tourism also takes advantage of non-Indian couples desperate to become parents, particularly same-sex couples. The catalyst of *Origins of Love* is the suspicious deaths of Mike and Susan Oldham, the intended British parents of newborn Amelia. Despite extensive testing of both her intended and surrogate parents, Amelia is HIV-positive. Moreover, her surrogate Indian mother, Preeti, has disappeared from the Madonna and Child Clinic on the outskirts of Delhi. The clinic directors, Doctors Subhash and Anita Pandey, call on Simran Singh, Anita's cousin and their unofficial adviser, to find a member of Amelia's family to adopt her. In the opening pages of *Origins of Love*, Simran explicitly distinguishes herself from women across India, declaring, "These millions of women have no choice [but to become pregnant]. Luckily, I do" (Desai, *Origins* 3). Unlike Kawakami's Natsuko, whose mother is deceased and whose sister begs her not to procreate, Simran's mother wants nothing more than for her daughter to have a biological child, but like Natsuko, Simran ultimately controls her own reproduction.

Origins of Love not only moves back and forth in time, and from India to the United Kingdom and back again, but also alternates between Simran's first-person narration and an omniscient third-person narrator. This aesthetic strategy further separates Simran from the surrogates: she tells her own story, while theirs are told by others, even as their struggles and inner lives are highlighted. Between its narrators, *Origins of Love* introduces a colorful palette of characters and subplots. These include physicians and entrepreneurs seeking to push the boundaries of medicine. One of the subplots of *Origins of Love* involves Freedom Hospital in Mumbai. There, illegal medical experiments and medical miracles are performed using embryonic stem cells. Some of these are from local embryos, and some are taken from embryos sent by couples in the United Kingdom to the Madonna and Child Clinic that instead are confiscated at customs in Mumbai by Nazir Ali, who "had been conducting a private jihad against surrogacy ever since his sister had been lured away" to serve as surrogate "to a rich childless sheikh from Saudi Arabia"

(Desai, *Origins* 99, 254). Another important subplot involves the extreme difficulties faced by queer couples attempting surrogacy; there are multiple references throughout *Origins of Love* to the blatant homophobia of everyone from religious and political leaders both within and outside India to Subhash and Ashok Ganguly, the managers of the clinic.

Yet the primary focus of the novel is the personal impact of the surrogacy industry's neocolonial exploitation of impoverished Indian women who have few options to support themselves and their families. The surrogate mothers introduced in the pages of *Origins of Love* include 16-year-old Radhika, whom Ganguly "groomed" for surrogacy (77). Ganguly told the intended parents of the baby Radhika carried that she was "a 22-year-old mother who needed the money to buy a flat" (77). In truth, Ganguly had found Radhika by the side of a road, distraught over her husband's head injury. He had reassured her that he could care for her husband and that she could pay for his treatment by becoming a surrogate, only to take full advantage of her. As the third-person narrator describes, "Like a bonded slave, she was trapped by Sharma into (what he hoped was) an endless cycle of surrogacy. Now passed over to Ganguly, she became an ideal candidate for his experiments" (78). The narrator's clarification that Sharma "hoped" Radhika would be permanently ensnared, and that she is an ideal "candidate" rather than an ideal subject, tempers somewhat his likening her to a "bonded slave," but opportunities for escape are few.

Sonia is another surrogate whose story is told in *Origins of Love*. A Dalit, a member of India's lowest social class, whose husband deserted her and left her penniless, Sonia attempts to "earn enough money to get her children back" (Desai, *Origins* 26). Sharma, the supplier for the Madonna and Child Clinic, claims that Sonia is "totally free" (26). But she is in fact controlled by Sharma's acquaintance Rohit, a "monster" of a man who abuses her financially, mentally, physically, and sexually and turns her into a "hunted animal" (141, 145), the narrative embracing figurative language here and elsewhere to elaborate on the injustices inflicted on surrogates. Sonia becomes even further ensnared after Rohit arranges for her to bear the child of Renu Mishra (the Delhi health minister and Rohit's employer) and Renu's mentor, Vineet Bhai, both Brahmins (members of India's highest caste) and eager for a political heir. Vineet, who took a vow of abstinence decades ago, declares himself "the savior of the poor and the defenseless, and especially of the minorities and the Dalits" (292). In truth, he abuses Sonia, and after he forcibly ejaculates into her mouth, "[Sonia] felt like an animal with no feelings. . . . More and more the realization was dawning on her that they were all using her. The hospital doctors, Renu

Madam, Vineet Bhai and Rohit. Everyone was getting something out of it, but her. . . . And watching what had happened with Reena, she realized that she couldn't even run away" (294).[33]

As traumatic as surrogacy is for the women at the Madonna and Child Clinic, conditions are even worse elsewhere. In one popular clinic, Subhash is shocked to find surrogates "kept on rope *charpoys* in an open ward. They had no privacy" (Desai, *Origins* 68). At Delhi's NewLife Fertility Clinic, Kate, a British woman considering surrogacy, is reminded of "chickens in a coop" when she sees "a tiny, cramped room where about seven women in different stages of pregnancy were sitting or lying down" (372). Simran believes surrogacy, "this cheap rent-a-womb . . . [is] a sort of slave trade" that "completely and thoughtlessly exploited" vulnerable young women (110–11).[34] To be sure, in addition to likening surrogacy to forms of slavery, *Origins of Love* repeatedly links international commercial surrogacy with European colonialism.[35] For Kate's husband, Ben, whose British grandfather had worked for the colonial government in India and taken advantage of Indian women, to use a "poor, illiterate woman" as a surrogate would be to continue the family's imperial "exploitation" (369). As Ali exclaims, "*Our* women do the work, and *their* population goes up. Don't you see it's a plot? A new way to colonize us" (40).

At the same time, Ali is just as furious with the rising demand from "West Asia [and] the Arab countries" for Muslim Indian surrogates that he believes will lead Indian wives to refuse to have children with their husbands so they can serve as wombs for wealthy sheikhs (Desai, *Origins* 410). Even more important, in *Origins of Love*, the young Indian women serving as surrogates are most directly abused, both illegally and legally, by fellow Indians, everyone from partners and family members to neighbors, physicians, politicians, and strangers. Just as Ma's *Dark Road* is a scathing indictment of China's present and recent past, Desai's novel includes numerous denunciations from a range of characters of other tremendous injustices women and children face across India, including high maternal mortality rates (285, 399), high infant mortality rates (94), deaths of baby girls being "a routine occurrence" (283), the proliferation of child trafficking (320, 420), the colorist preference for light-skinned and "fairer babies" (250), and the rejection of children with special needs or HIV (194, 464). *Origins of Love* condemns the exploitation inherent in much international commercial surrogacy, exploitation that led India to ban this type of surrogacy in 2015, three years after the novel's publication. At the same time, Desai's narrative highlights the significant responsibility of local actors in dehumanizing economically disadvantaged Indian women and in denying them justice by treating them as nothing more than, in Simran's words, "a vagina or womb" (110), much as surrogates are depicted in cultural productions that comment on China's one-child policy.[36]

Kawakami's *Breasts and Eggs*, Wang and Zhang's *One Child Nation*, Ma's *Dark Road*, Desai's *Origins of Love*, and countless other narratives from Asia, its diasporas, and beyond highlight the pervasiveness and severity of reproductive violence against women that is sanctioned if not mandated by the government as well as the short- and long-term effects of such violence on individual and collective health and well-being. The narrative strategies and aesthetic choices of the above works also offer unparalleled access to these women's interior lives and restore to them humanity and dignity that regularly are stripped away. As in Kawakami's and Desai's novels, some cultural products that highlight reproductive violence depict heterosexual cisgender women of some means, those less vulnerable to structural violence, as attaining some measure of gender justice. But most narratives emphasize how few women can escape unscathed. Although men are not at all immune, and gay and transgender men are particularly vulnerable, women in these narratives generally have far fewer options than men of similar gender and sexual identities and socioeconomic status do and virtually no choice but ultimately to capitulate to power no matter how much they might try to resist. Moreover, as the narratives analyzed in this chapter make clear, reproductive violence that is mandated or sanctioned by the state does not exist in a vacuum. This violence also regularly accompanies other forms of aggression, including widespread ecological destruction, as well as social, family, and intimate partner violence, endemic throughout the world—the focus of the following three chapters.[37]

NOTES

1. Tone's insights into conditions in the United States hold true for much of the world.

2. Hong's observations concerning cisgender women are also true for transgender women and transgender men, who generally face even greater injustices.

3. For additional examples of reproductive violence globally, see Altunjan 78–92. For examples in intimate partner relationships, see Grace and Anderson 374.

4. Hong distinguishes reproductive violence from sexual violence, arguing that the former "encompasses many different violations of women's autonomy and health relating to their reproductive and family lives" (487).

5. Even the most socioeconomically and culturally privileged women can experience reproductive coercion, including the Harvard- and Oxford-educated former diplomat Empress Masako of Japan, who for many years was under extreme pressure to have a son in order to continue the direct imperial line. Attitudes toward female imperial succession are slowly changing in Japan.

6. On reproductive justice in literature and culture, see Capo and Lazzari, "Reproductive Justice." Also noteworthy are narratives on women forced to have as many children as possible, including the Pakistani writer Bina Shah's dystopian *Before She Sleeps* (2018), often likened to Margaret Atwood's *The Handmaid's Tale* (1985) and notably lacking LGBTQIA+ individuals. See Thornber, "Comparison." Also significant are writings on *kogoroshi* (killing or abandoning to die a child of any age) in the context of Japanese repatriation after World War II (Xie 262).

7. As of March 2023, the one exception is Sichuan Province, which in February 2023 lifted limits both on the number of children a person can have and on marital status.

8. See also the Chinese American writer Vanessa Hua's *A River of Stars* (2022), where a character who became pregnant by her married boss in China lives in a secret maternity home in Los Angeles.

9. This OECD data is from 2018.

10. Single fathers generally fare better financially, but their children face similar educational disadvantages (Nonoyama-Tarumi).

11. Raised by a working-class single mother, Kawakami has been celebrated both in Japan and abroad while also being harshly criticized for her activism. Published 45 years ago, the Japanese writer Tsushima Yūko's novel *Territory of Light* (*Hikari no ryōbun*, 1979) reveals that very little has changed across the decades.

12. See also the Korean American writer Frances Cha's *If I Had Your Face* (2020), a gripping exposé of Korea's thriving cosmetic surgery industry.

13. The sisters were raised for six years by their impoverished single mother after their abusive father abandoned the family. After their mother died of breast cancer, they lived with their grandmother, who died from lung cancer when Natsuko was fifteen, leaving the sisters alone.

14. Translated more literally, "If so, when?" would read "Is it ever going to happen?" (そんなときがくるのだろうか; Kawakami, *Natsu monogatari* 214).

15. Alzate and Yoshio discuss the polyvocality of Kawakami's narrative (468–69, 473–75), while Alzate examines the place of menstruation, beauty ideals, and mothering in *Breasts and Eggs*.

16. Same-sex couples have each other, as Natsuko also observes, but their options in Japan are as limited as those of single women ("To"). Additionally, married women who pursue assisted reproductive technology face legal barriers that men do not (King). Fassbender analyzes discourses surrounding reproduction in contemporary Japan, while Terazawa provides historical perspectives.

17. Translated more literally, the final sentence would read, "In this world, there isn't a single parent who conceives a child for the child's sake" (子どものことを考えて、子どもを生んだ親なんて、この世界にひとりもいないんだよ; Kawakami, *Natsu monogatari* 435).

18. Natsuko describes having "more of a [financial] cushion than I knew what to do with," more than many parents in their thirties, thanks to her frugality (Kawakami 236). As Ezawa notes, women who do not interrupt their employment "in line with the expected life course of a woman of their generation" fare much better as single mothers (113).

19. The protagonist of Dạ Ngân's novel had two additional voluntary abortions some years earlier and remembers the lack of empathy with which she was confronted, the "repeated reminders from the [hospital] staff that 'you made your bed, now you can lie in it'" (76).

20. See, for instance, Quiara Alegría Hudes's *My Broken Language: A Memoir* (2021).

21. As the South Korean writer Kim Soom (Kim Sum) graphically describes in the novel *One Left* (*Han myŏng*, 2016), discussed in chapter 5, during World War II, those serving as "comfort women" for Japanese troops were also subjected to brutal forced abortions that included tearing out their uteruses, rendering them permanently unable to give birth.

22. Although significantly smaller in scale and of much shorter duration, the Peruvian president Alberto Fujimori's National Population Program (Programa Nacional de Poblacíon, 1995–2000) facilitated the coerced, forced, and clandestine sterilization of thousands of marginalized and primarily Indigenous Peruvians (Altunjan 85–86; Boesten 6, 14).

23. Additionally, women were subjected to repeated pelvic exams, and their menstrual cycles were tracked.

24. Wang is also known for the documentaries *Hooligan Sparrow* (2016), which exposes child rape, and *In the Same Breath* (2021), on the COVID-19 pandemic.

25. Ma's work, beginning with his first short story collection, published in 1987, has long been banned in China. Ma relocated to Hong Kong in the mid-1980s and to the United Kingdom in 1997. Also noteworthy is the Nobel Prize–winning Chinese writer Mo Yan's novel *Frog* (*Wa*, 2009), which reveals the traumas not only of women subjected to mandatory abortions and forcibly and often unknowingly sterilized or inserted with an IUD but also of the individuals compelled to enforce the one-child policy (Thornber, "Abusive Medicine"). Very few works of Chinese fiction grapple with the one-child policy (thank you to Coco Ruan for this insight).

26. Lovell lists the "tragedies and injustices from China's present and recent past" that are exposed in *Dark Road*. See also Thornber, *Ecoambiguity*.

27. In the Chinese source, Meili is likened explicitly to Jane Eyre, Charlotte Brontë's nineteenth-century heroine (Ma, *Yin zhi dao* 315).

28. On 24 June 2022, the United States Supreme Court overturned *Roe v. Wade* (1973), enabling individual states to ban abortion.

29. Unlike their majority Han counterparts, Uyghur women in Xinjiang are being pressured to reduce birth rates if not forced to use IUDs or be sterilized (Fincher 180–81; Qin). Stevenson summarizes Chinese leader Xi Jinping's pronatalist rhetoric.

30. After India outlawed international commercial surrogacy, the industry moved to Thailand, Nepal, and Cambodia and then to Laos, after being banned in the former nations (Whittaker 170). In Cambodia, dozens of surrogates and intended parents have been accused of trafficking and imprisoned unless the surrogates raise the children themselves, despite their own very limited resources (Beech). India's Surrogacy (Regulation) Bill, which was introduced in 2019, endeavors to prohibit commercial surrogacy altogether in India but permits altruistic surrogacy (Srivastava 146).

31. India ranks 142nd of 146 nations in women's health and survival and has one of the largest gender disparities in economic participation and opportunity, ranked 142nd, with a mere 36.7% of the gap filled. Only 28.26% of women in India are part of the paid workforce, a gap with men of just under 50% (*Global Gender Gap Report 2023* 17, 18, 203).

32. Born and raised in northern India, Desai, whose work has been widely translated, is best known for the Simran Singh series: the award-winning *Witness the Night* (2010), on infanticide and sex-selective abortions, discussed in chapter 6; *Origins of Love* (2012); and *Sea of Innocence* (2014), on gang rape, discussed in chapter 5. Desai is also a professional journalist and has written several works of nonfiction. For very different perspectives on surrogacy, see the Japanese science fiction writers Kakiya Miu's *Dairibo, hajimemashita* (*Hey There, Surrogate Mother*, 2021) and Tanaka Chōko's *Chōsansei* (*Birth Service*, 2018). Ruan analyzes both novels (121–30).

33. Reena had a difficult pregnancy and after giving birth to a healthy baby boy became so attached that she attempted to flee with him. Although sympathetic, Preeti, who was also abused by her physician at the clinic, Dr. Ashok, had no choice but to snitch on Reena, knowing that Preeti's family's financial future depended on her salary as a surrogate (Desai, *Origins* 287–89). Yet Preeti never made it home; after giving birth to Amelia and becoming gravely injured trying to escape Ganguly, she ended up in Freedom Hospital, where she was given an experimental embryonic stem cell treatment (434–35, 446).

34. Surrogacy also allows for the creation of "designer babies" and the inscription of racial and caste-based preferences (Karmaker and Parui 330).

35. See the special issue on slavery in early modern Asia in the *Harvard Journal of Asiatic Studies* (Howell).

36. The prominent and prolific Bengali writer and social and tribal activist Mahasweta Devi's short story "Breast-Giver" ("Stanadāyinī," 1987) adds breasts to vaginas and wombs. As Gayatri Spivak, Devi's English-language translator, has commented, this story "builds itself on the cruel ironies of caste, class, patriarchy" (viii). "Breast-Giver" centers on Jashoda, a woman whose name recalls that of the mother of Krishna, a major Hindu deity (thank you to Aniket De for this observation). Jashoda becomes a wet nurse for 50 members of the wealthy Halder family after her husband, Kangali, is no longer able to work. To keep her milk flowing, she also becomes a "professional mother," giving birth to 20 children in 30 years, from the 1950s to the 1980s (Devi 53). Jashoda is tossed aside after her fertility wanes and her milk dries up, and she dies a horrific death of breast cancer. For historical context on "Breast-Giver," see Banerjee.

37. As noted above, many of these writings also expose LGBTQIA+ individuals as particularly vulnerable to reproductive and other forms of violence.

WORKS CITED

Altunjan, Tanja. *Reproductive Violence and International Criminal Law*. Springer, 2021.

Alzate, Juliana Buriticá. "Embodiment and Its Violence in Kawakami Mieko's *Chichi to ran*: Menstruation, Beauty Ideals, and Mothering." *Japanese Language and Literature*, vol. 54, no. 2, Oct. 2020, pp. 515–49.

Alzate, Juliana Buriticá, and Hitomi Yoshio. "Reimagining the Past, Present, and the Future of Reproductive Bodies in Contemporary Japanese Women's Fiction." Capo and Lazzari, *Palgrave Handbook*, pp. 465–86.

Asian Communities for Reproductive Justice. *A New Vision for Advancing Our Movement for Reproductive Health, Reproductive Rights, and Reproductive Justice*. 2017. *Forward Together*, forwardtogether.org/wp-content/uploads/2017/12/ACRJ-A-New-Vision.pdf.

Banerjee, Swapna. "Blurring Boundaries, Distant Companions: Non-kin Female Caregivers for Children in Colonial India." *Paedagogica Historica*, vol. 46, no. 6, 2010, pp. 775–88.

Beech, Hannah. "They Were Surrogates. Now They Must Raise the Children." *The New York Times*, 26 Nov. 2022, www.nytimes.com/2022/11/26/world/asia/surrogacy-cambodia.html.

Boesten, Jelke. "Free Choice or Poverty Alleviation? Population Politics in Peru under Alberto Fujimori." *European Review of Latin American and Caribbean Studies*, no. 82, Apr. 2007, pp. 3–20.

Capo, Beth Widmaier, and Laura Lazzari, editors. *The Palgrave Handbook of Reproductive Justice and Literature*. Palgrave Macmillan, 2022.

———. "Reproductive Justice in Literature and Culture." Capo and Lazzari, *Palgrave Handbook*, pp. 1–20.

Cha, Frances. *If I Had Your Face*. Ballantine Books, 2020.

Choy, Howard Y. F. "On the One-Child Policy of China: Reading Ma Jian's Novel *The Dark Road*." Capo and Lazzari, *Palgrave Handbook*, pp. 269–85.

Cohen, Adam. *Imbeciles: The Supreme Court, American Eugenics, and the Sterilization of Carrie Buck*. Penguin Books, 2016.

Dạ Ngân. *An Insignificant Family*. Translated by Rosemary Nguyen, Curbstone Press, 2009.

Desai, Kishwar. "India's Surrogate Mothers Are Risking Their Lives." *The Guardian*, 5 June 2012, www.theguardian.com/commentisfree/2012/jun/05/india-surrogates-impoverished-die.

———. *Origins of Love*. Simon and Schuster, 2012.

Devi, Mahasweta. "Breast-Giver." Devi, *Breast Stories*, pp. 38–133.

———. *Breast Stories*. Translated by Gayatri Chakravorty Spivak, Seagull Books, 2010.

Ezawa, Aya. *Single Mothers in Contemporary Japan: Motherhood, Class, and Reproductive Practice*. Lexington Books, 2016.

Fassbender, Isabel. *Active Pursuit of Pregnancy: Neoliberalism, Postfeminism and the Politics of Reproduction in Contemporary Japan*. Brill, 2022.

Fay, Kathryn, and Lynn Yee. "Reproductive Coercion and Women's Health." *Journal of Midwifery and Women's Health*, vol. 63, no. 5, Sept. 2018, pp. 518–25.

Fincher, Leta Hong. *Betraying Big Brother: The Feminist Awakening in China*. Verso, 2018.

Fixmer-Oraiz, Natalie. "Speaking of Solidarity: Transnational Gestational Surrogacy and the Rhetorics of Reproductive (In)Justice." *Frontiers*, vol. 34, no. 3, Jan. 2013, pp. 126–257.

Global Gender Gap Report 2023. World Economic Forum, 2023, www3.weforum.org/docs/WEF_GGGR_2023.pdf.

Grace, Karen Trister, and Jocelyn C. Anderson. "Reproductive Coercion: A Systematic Review." *Trauma, Violence, and Abuse*, vol. 19, no. 4, 2018, pp. 371–90.

Greenhalgh, Susan. "Controlling Births and Bodies in Village China." *American Ethnologist*, vol. 21, no. 1, Feb. 1994, pp. 3–20.

———. *Just One Child: Science and Policy in Deng's China*. U of California P, 2008.

Griffin, Shana, and Clyde Woods. "The Politics of Reproductive Violence." *American Quarterly*, vol. 61, no. 3, Sept. 2009, pp. 583–91.

Gu, Baochang, et al. "China's Local and National Fertility Policies at the End of the Twentieth Century." *Population and Development Review*, vol. 33, no. 1, Mar. 2007, pp. 129–47.

Hernon, Matthew. "Award-Winning Japanese Author Mieko Kawakami: 'I Have a Problem with the Patriarchal System in This Country.'" *Tokyo Weekender*, 6 Aug. 2020, www.tokyoweekender.com/art_and_culture/award-winning-author-breast-and-eggs-mieko-kawakami/.

Hong, Mai-Linh K. "'The Deep Root Snapped': Reproductive Violence and Family Un/Making in Quan Barry's *She Weeps Each Time You're Born*." *The Palgrave Handbook of Magical Realism in the Twenty-First Century*, edited by R. Perez and V. A. Chevalier, Palgrave Macmillan, 2020, pp. 483–501.

Hooligan Sparrow. Directed by Nanfu Wang, Little Horse Crossing the River, 2016.

Hovhannisyan, Astghik. "Preventing the Birth of 'Inferior Offspring': Eugenic Sterilizations in Postwar Japan." *Japan Forum*, vol. 33, no. 3, 2021, pp. 383–401.

Howell, David, editor. *Slavery in Early Modern East, Inner, and Southeast Asia*. Special issue of *Harvard Journal of Asiatic Studies*. Vol. 81, nos. 1–2, 2021.

Hua, Vanessa. *A River of Stars*. Ballantine Books, 2022.

Hudes, Quiara Alegría. *My Broken Language: A Memoir*. OneWorld, 2021.

In the Same Breath. Directed by Nanfu Wang, HBO Documentary Films, 2021.

Kakiya Miu. *Dairibo, hajimemashita*. Chūō kōronsha, 2021.

Karmaker, Manali, and Avishek Parui. "'These Were Made-to-Order Babies': Reterritorialised Kinship, Neoliberal Eugenics, and Artificial Reproductive Technology in Kishwar Desai's *Origins of Love*." *British Medical Journal*, vol. 46, no. 3, 2020, pp. 323–32.

Kawakami, Mieko. *Breasts and Eggs*. Translated by Sam Bett and David Boyd, Europa Editions, 2020.

———. *Natsu monogatari*. Bungei Shunjū, 2019.

King, Rachel. "Comment: Redefining Motherhood: Discrimination in Legal Parenthood in Japan." *Pacific Rim Law and Policy Journal*, vol. 18, no. 1, Jan. 2009, pp. 189–216.

Klock, Susan C., and Steven R. Lindheim. "Gestational Surrogacy: Medical, Psychosocial, and Legal Considerations." *Fertility and Sterility*, vol. 113, no. 5, May 2020, pp. 889–91.

Li, Jie, et al. "What a Picture of China's One-Child Policy Leaves Out." *China File*, 6 Feb. 2020, www.chinafile.com/reporting-opinion/culture/what-picture-of-chinas-one-child-policy-leaves-out.

Lombardo, Paul A. *A Century of Eugenics in America: From the Indiana Experiment to the Human Genome*. Indiana UP, 2011.

Lovell, Julia. "A Dystopian Vision of China." *The Lancet*, no. 382, 13 July 2013, p. 117.

Ma Jian. *The Dark Road*. Translated by Flora Drew, Penguin Books, 2013.

———. *Yin zhi dao*. Yunchen wenhua shiye gufen youxian gongsi, 2012.

Manian, Maya. "Immigration Detention and Coerced Sterilization: History Tragically Repeats Itself." *ACLU*, 29 Sept. 2020, www.aclu.org/news/immigrants-rights/immigration-detention-and-coerced-sterilization-history-tragically-repeats-itself.

Manjeshwar, Sanjana. "America's Forgotten History of Forced Sterilization." *Berkeley Political Review*, 4 Nov. 2020, bpr.berkeley.edu/2020/11/04/americas-forgotten-history-of-forced-sterilization/.

McNeill, David. "Mind the Gender Gap: Kawakami Mieko, Murata Sayaka, Feminism and Literature in Japan." *The Asia-Pacific Journal: Japan Focus*, vol. 18, no. 21, Nov. 2020, apjjf.org/2020/21/McNeill.html.

Mo Yan. *Frog*. Translated by Howard Goldblatt, Viking, 2014.

Nonoyama-Tarumi, Yuko. "Educational Achievement of Children from Single-Mother and Single-Father Families: The Case of Japan." *Journal of Marriage and Family*, vol. 79, no. 4, Aug. 2017, pp. 915–31.

One Child Nation. Directed by Nanfu Wang and Jialing Zhang, Chicken and Egg Pictures, 2019.

Otsubo, Sumiko. "Engendering Eugenics: Feminists and Marriage Restriction Legislation in the 1920s." *Gendering Modern Japanese History*, edited by Barbara Molony and Kathleen Uno, Harvard UP, 2005, pp. 225–56.

Pike, Matthew. "Why Vietnam's Single Mothers Are Staging Fake Weddings." *Culture Trip*, 16 Mar. 2018, theculturetrip.com/asia/ridge/articles/why-vietnams-single-mothers-are-staging-fake-weddings.

Qin, Amy. "China Targets Muslim Women in Push to Suppress Births in Xinjiang." *The New York Times*, 10 May 2021, www.nytimes.com/2021/05/10/world/asia/china-xinjiang-women-births.html.

Robertson, Jennifer. "Blood Talks: Eugenic Modernity and the Creation of New Japanese." *History and Anthropology*, vol. 13, no. 3, Jan. 2002, pp. 191–216.

Ross, Loretta, and Rickie Solinger. *Reproductive Justice: An Introduction*. U of California P, 2017.

Ruan, Coco. *Illusion of Babies, Babies of Illusion: Writing Pregnancy in Low Fertility East Asia*. 2023. Harvard U, MA thesis.

Saim, Nor Jana, et al. "Teenagers' Experiences of Pregnancy and the Parents' and Partners' Reactions: A Malaysian Perspective." *Journal of Family Violence*, vol. 29, no. 4, Apr. 2014, pp. 465–72.

"SF1.1: Family Size and Household Composition." *OECD*, 2015, www.oecd.org/els/family/SF_1_1_Family_size_and_composition.pdf.

"SF2.4: Share of Births Outside of Marriage." *OECD*, 2018, www.oecd.org/els/family/SF_2_4_Share_births_outside_marriage.pdf.

Shah, Bina. *Before She Sleeps*. Delphinium Books, 2018.

Shetty, Priya. "India's Unregulated Surrogacy Industry." *The Lancet*, no. 380, 10 Nov. 2012, pp. 1633–34, https://doi.org/10.1016/S0140-6736(12)61933-3.

Spivak, Gayatri Chakravorty. Introduction. Devi, *Breast Stories*, pp. vii–xvi.

Srivastava, Astha. "The Surrogacy Regulation (2019) Bill of India: A Critique." *Journal of International Women's Studies*, vol. 22, no. 1, Jan. 2021, pp. 140–51, vc.bridgew.edu/jiws/vol22/iss1/8.

Stevenson, Alexandra. "China's Male Leaders Signal to Women That Their Place Is in the Home." *The New York Times*, 2 Nov. 2023, www.nytimes.com/2023/11/02/world/asia/china-communist-party-xi-women.html.

Tanaka Chōko. *Chōsansei*. Shichōsha, 2018.

Terazawa, Yuki. *Knowledge, Power, and Women's Reproductive Health in Japan, 1690–1945*. Palgrave Macmillan, 2018.

Thornber, Karen Laura. "Abusive Medicine: Constructing the Japanese Empire and Its Aftermaths in East Asian Literatures." *The Routledge Handbook of Modern Japanese Literature*, edited by Rachel Hutchinson and Leith Morton, Routledge, 2016, pp. 213–26.

———. "Comparison and Gender Injustice: Opportunities in Worlds of Pandemics." *Comparative Critical Studies*, vol. 20, nos. 2–3, 2023, pp. 201–21.

———. *Ecoambiguity: Environmental Crises and East Asian Literatures*. U of Michigan P, 2012.

"To Get Pregnant." *Japan Healthcare Info*, 2011–19, japanhealthinfo.com/pregnancy-and-childbirth/to-get-pregnant.

Tone, Andrea. Introduction. *Controlling Reproduction: An American History*, edited by Tone, SR Books, 1997, pp. xiii–xxii.

Torpy, Sally J. "Native American Women and Coerced Sterilization: On the Trail of Tears in the 1970s." *American Indian Culture and Research Journal*, vol. 24, no. 2, Jan. 2000, pp. 1–22.

Tsushima Yūko. *Territory of Light*. Translated by Geraldine Harcourt, Farrar, Straus and Giroux, 2019.

Wang, Vivian. "For China's Single Mothers, a Road to Recognition Paved with False Starts." *The New York Times*, 31 May 2021, www.nytimes.com/2021/05/31/world/asia/china-mothers-children-birth.html.

Whittaker, Andrea. *International Surrogacy as Disruptive Industry in Southeast Asia*. Rutgers UP, 2018.

Xie, Miya. *The Literary Territorialization of Manchuria: Rethinking National and Transnational Literature in East Asia from the Frontier*. 2017. Harvard U, PhD dissertation.

Zhao, Xiaoman, and Iccha Basnyat. "Gendered Social Practices in Reproductive Health: A Qualitative Study Exploring Lived Experiences of Unwed Single Mothers in China." *Sociology of Health and Illness*, vol. 43, no. 5, June 2021, pp. 1237–53.

5. Prosecuting Cultures of Shame, Silence, Rape, and Murder

Given its brutality and frequently lifelong consequences, rape (nonconsensual sex) by a non-partner is criminalized in most of the world, including across Asia. Yet the traumas of those who have been raped—overwhelmingly women and children, particularly from marginalized populations, including gender and sexual minorities—are frequently minimized if not dismissed entirely. Victims and survivors are regularly dehumanized, blamed for the rape, and even blame themselves.[1] Furthermore, perpetrators are only very rarely investigated, prosecuted, and punished for their crimes (Bowdler 4, 164). Similarly, even though taking the life of another is generally outlawed, some illegal homicides (i.e., murders) are treated far more seriously than others, with murders of marginalized individuals disproportionately tolerated. Although works of literature have often supported dominant legal, political, and social discourses, much creative writing counters such narratives, providing far more complete and nuanced accounts of rape, murder, and their aftermaths (Sehgal 64). By honoring the subjectivity and complex stories of victims and survivors, memoirs, short stories, novels, and other genres have highlighted their voices, humanity, and dignity amid broader cultures that condone and even encourage these heinous crimes.[2]

This chapter spotlights four such narratives: the memoir *Black Box* (*Burakku bokkusu*, ブラックボックス, 2017), by the Japanese journalist, documentary filmmaker, and feminist activist Itō Shiori (1989–), in which Itō contextualizes her 2015 rape by an esteemed journalist and her tenacious pursuit of justice within Japan's broader rape culture; the short story "The Mayor of the Roses" (1999), by the Filipina American writer Marianne Villanueva (1958–), narrated in the first person by a Filipina American woman reflecting on the 1995 trial of Antonio Sanchez, who was convicted and imprisoned for gang-raping and murdering Mary Eileen Sarmenta and for murdering Sarmenta's boyfriend, Allan Gomez; the novel *One Left* (*Han myŏng*, 한명, lit. *One Person*, 2016), by the South Korean writer Kim Soom (Kim Sum, 1974–), whose third-person narrator, while focusing on one traumatized elderly survivor, gives voice to myriad victims and survivors of Japan's wartime comfort women system, in which more than 200,000 women and girls throughout Asia were compelled into sexual service; and the memoir *Shamed* (2013), by the British Indian police community support officer Sarbjit Kaur Athwal, in which Athwal describes her childhood as part of the Punjabi diaspora in London, her married life, and her pursuit of justice in the aftermath of the honor killing in India of her British Indian sister-in-law Surjit Athwal. These narratives engage with the pursuit of justice for cisgender straight women from a range of class, educational, ethnic, religious, and national backgrounds who have been raped by acquaintances or strangers, murdered, or both. Narratives on violence committed by family members other than intimate partners are the focus of chapter 6, and violence committed by intimate partners the topic of chapter 7.

The World Health Organization estimates that as of 2018, 6% of women globally aged 15–49 years had been subjected at least once to non-partner sexual violence (*Violence* 85). Non-partner sexual violence is understood as "a woman's self-reported experience of one or more acts of sexual violence by someone other than a current or former husband or male intimate partner [e.g., by other family members, friends, acquaintances, or strangers] since the age of 15," with sexual violence understood as "being forced, coerced or threatened to perform any unwanted sexual act; this could include rape, attempted rape, unwanted sexual touching or non-contact forms of sexual violence" (5, 7). According to World Health Organization data, Oceania and the Americas have the highest estimated prevalence of lifetime non-partner sexual violence (16% and 13%, respectively), with the lowest prevalence estimates in East Asia (7%), Southeast Asia (4%), and South Asia (2%; 31–32).[3] These percentages are significantly smaller than the prevalence estimates of intimate partner violence, discussed in chapter 7. Yet the numbers are large, involving at the very least nearly 200 million women. Furthermore, the World Health Organization strongly cautions that data on non-partner sexual violence is quite limited, and the prevalence of non-partner sexual violence, as with intimate partner violence, is likely "much higher than the reported or estimated rates of this form of violence in low- and middle-income countries" (xv). Prevalence of non-partner sexual violence in high-income nations is also likely to be notably greater than currently reported or estimated. As Itō argues in *Black Box*, statistical disparities across cultures result less from differences in prevalence than from the number of female law enforcement officers, understandings of what constitutes rape, and treatment of rape survivors, among other factors (139–44).

The near certainty in patriarchal families, communities, and societies that victims of sexual violence are blamed, shamed, isolated, and ostracized has prevented most survivors from coming forward and most perpetrators from being convicted and brought to justice (*Violence* xv). Until recently, most legal systems essentially disregarded rape, especially rape committed by an individual with a professional or personal relationship with the victim (e.g., acquaintance, date, and spousal rape), and some legal systems even justified if not encouraged rape (Brownmiller, *Against*; Garland and Bennett 10–12). Rape cultures—sites with "casual, pervasive commodification of women's bodies and relentless normalizing of a masculinity steeped in conquest and control"—remain ubiquitous (Nicholls 67). And myths surrounding rape remain pervasive in many parts of the world and impose even greater burdens for individuals who are already disadvantaged in their particular societies (Begum and Barn; Crenshaw; Garland and Bennett 14–18).[4] Common myths surrounding rape assert that most rape claims are false; women are to blame for rape since only "bad" or "badly behaving" women are raped (e.g., women are "asking for" rape by wearing "provocative" clothing, drinking excessively, walking alone at night, or otherwise transgressing gender norms and engaging in precipitant behavior); "real" rapes are those committed by strangers; women secretly want to be raped; and "no" means "yes." Such myths "teach women to blame themselves for their own victimization" (Hanser 42). And they carry over into criminal justice systems, with "police, prosecutors, and jurors often treat[ing] the victims as criminals [and] leading them to conclude that there is no basis to their claims" (Garland and Bennett 13). Severe stigmas against individuals who are raped also greatly impede healing; the physical and psychological impacts of sexual violence and responses to this violence are often quite serious and can be lifelong.

Rape Culture, Silence, and Me Too on Trial: Itō Shiori's *Black Box* (2017)

Following the March 1997 murder of Watanabe Yasuko, a 39-year-old Tokyo Electric Power Company female executive who also engaged in sex work, "I am Tōden OL" became a mantra in Japan, "allegedly uttered by women empathizing with her as a feminine subject of distress, rage, and acting out" (Yoda 196).[5] Resonating with "I am Tōden OL," the phrase "me too" was coined by the American civil rights activist Tarana Burke in 2006 as "a strategy to communicate with sexual abuse, assault, exploitation, and harassment survivors" (Gieseler 2). The phrase went viral a decade later, with the American actress Alyssa Milano's tweet on 15 October 2017: "If you've been sexually harassed or assaulted write 'me too' as a reply to this tweet. Me Too." Within 10 days, 1.7 million tweets had poured in from 85 countries; *Facebook* reported 12 million Me Too posts in less than 24 hours (Gieseler 2). The resulting Me Too movements, their offshoots and adaptations, the other forms of feminist digital activism (many of which date back years if not decades, and some of which have even lengthier genealogies), and the frequently severe backlashes against those who share their stories have taken diverse trajectories in different parts of the world, as noted in chapter 1.[6]

On 29 May 2017, five months before Milano's tweet, Itō went public about her April 2015 "quasi-rape" by the prominent Japanese journalist Yamaguchi Noriyuki. The Japanese penal code defines "quasi-rape" (*junkyōseiseikōtōzai*) as the rape of an individual who has lost consciousness or is otherwise unable to resist, regardless of whether the rapist causes this loss or inability (Itō, *Black Box* 148). As Itō trenchantly explains, like hers, many cases of "quasi-rape" involve alcohol, date rape drugs, or both (148). On 29 May 2017 Itō also shared her appeal to the Committee for the Inquest of the Prosecution to reopen the investigation into her rape. Four months later, on 22 September 2017, the committee claimed that "because the assault occurred behind closed doors, the incident was a 'black box'" and therefore was "nonprosecutable" (2). Four weeks later, on 20 October 2017, and just five days after Milano's tweet, Itō published *Black Box*.[7]

Itō adroitly uses the genre of memoir to both personalize and contextualize her rape, its immediate aftermath, and her lengthy pursuit of justice. *Black Box* is mostly chronological, with several prominent flashbacks, and it artistically weaves together multiple narratives. These include graphic first-person descriptions of mental and physical violence perpetrated by Yamaguchi (both during and well after the rape) and secondarily by law enforcement (including compelling Itō to tell her story multiple times, asking her repeatedly whether she had been a virgin before the sexual encounter with Yamaguchi, and requiring her, surrounded by male officers, to reenact her assault with a life-size dummy). Itō reveals profound lapses in Japan's legal, justice, and medical systems; the local media (which, unlike the international media, refused to pick up her story); the broader public; and other constituencies.[8] Itō also includes numerous transcripts of her post-rape email exchanges with Yamaguchi, set off in italics in the English translation, which expose readers even more directly than in cited dialogue to Yamaguchi's demeaning discourse, deception, and despicability. Itō likewise depicts childhood encounters with sexual harassment, echoing the experiences of Kim Jiyoung, the protagonist of Cho Namjoo's *Kim Jiyoung, Born 1982*, discussed in chapter 1. And she speaks extensively on sexual assault policies in Japan, at times citing relevant materials and contextualizing them nationally and globally. Throughout, Itō talks openly about the impact of this violence on her thoughts, feelings, and overall well-being, and she speaks transparently about her mental health struggles: she suffered from post-traumatic stress disorder and contemplated suicide, feeling as though "everything inside me had been obliterated. . . . [A]ll that was left was an empty husk of my former self" (172).[9] Yet, inspired by a photograph of Carri Leigh Goodwin, a member of the United States Marine Corps who was sexually assaulted by another service member, bullied for reporting the rape, and ultimately took her own life, Itō resolved that "[m]y job was to bear witness. To remain silent would condone the crime that had been committed" (172).

And bear witness she does. Itō shares in *Black Box* her acute exacerbation at the highly irregular decision of the Tokyo Metropolitan Police not to execute the June 2015 arrest warrant the prosecutor had issued against Yamaguchi—in retrospect no surprise given Yamaguchi's ties to the then prime minister Abé Shinzō. Together, these factors led to the July 2016 dismissal of her case: "What confounded me was seeing the various doors of the investigative authorities, followed by those of the press, close one after another before my eyes." The dismissal of the case "was a gagging attempt to silence me" (Itō, *Black Box* 168). As Itō likewise discusses, the 2017 amendment to Japan's 1907 penal code regarding sexual offenses—the first modification of this part of the penal code in 110 years—expanded definitions of rape, acknowledged that men also are victimized, and no longer required victims to file a complaint for a case to be prosecuted, among other modifications.[10] Yet as Itō perceptively determines, "If we are to change the status quo . . . it will require significantly more reform to the justice system" (159).[11]

Reflecting on the past few years in the epilogue to the 2021 English translation of *Black Box*, Itō reaffirms her absolute commitment to truth and comments more broadly on gender justice in Japan. She attributes Japan's relatively muted Me Too movement to "a lack of understanding about sexual violence and sexual harassment, as well as deeply rooted prejudices and biases against victims" (220), among other factors. She laments both the significant barriers to joining Me Too in Japan and the lack of support for those who speak out, many of whom, herself included, are viciously attacked for so doing. Itō explains that many Japanese prefer We Too (support for the victims) over Me Too, "in an effort to overcome that anxiety and to demonstrate that, as members of society, these problems concern all of us. This is based on the attitude that we cannot be passive bystanders, that we cannot tolerate any harassment or sexual violence" (220–21).

Harassment and sexual violence are part of most Japanese women's lives from childhood. In one particularly powerful flashback, Itō shares that her first experience of *chikan* (public groping) occurred in second grade, when a man looked up her skirt at the library (204). Itō also reveals how readily girls are blamed for the violence enacted against them, describing how when at age 11 a male stranger grabbed her in the pool, her friend's mother declared, "It's because you're wearing such a cute bikini" (207).[12] While Itō remembers being confused, tremendously afraid, and repulsed by being assaulted, she was "shattered" (207) by the response of her friend's mother. Advocating for all victims of sexual assault and incorporating multiple narratives and perspectives, *Black Box* creatively illuminates the many ways individuals and broader systems alike deny justice by reinforcing cultures of rape, shame, and silence.[13] At the same time, Itō's narrative strategies and aesthetic choices, especially her candid sharing of her vulnerability and her determination to speak her truth, enable her engaging memoir to assert the humanity, dignity, and agency of victims and survivors alike, across cultures and identities. This is especially vital given that, as Itō pronounces, "an unfathomable number of people around the world" who have been subjected to similar and even greater violence and suffering have even less recourse (218).[14]

Multiple-Perpetrator Rape on Trial: Marianne Villanueva's "The Mayor of the Roses" (1999)

Among the individuals to whom Itō is referring are those who have been subjected to multiple-perpetrator rape, also referred to as gang rape, group rape, and streamlining, in addition to other terms. Defined as "any sexual assault involving two or more perpetrators" (Horvath and Kelly 94), multiple-perpetrator rape occurs globally, making up an estimated 2% to 50% of rapes (83). In general, multiple-perpetrator rape tends to involve more severe sexual abuse and greater physical violence than single-perpetrator rape (Ullman 202). Some cases receive considerable local, national, and international attention and are quickly prosecuted. One striking example from India is the assault of 23-year-old Jyoti Singh Pandey, a medical student who died two weeks after six men raped and tortured her on a private bus in South Delhi the evening of 16 December 2012. Pandey's rapists objected to her being out at night with a male friend and resolved to "teach her a lesson" (*India's Daughter* 00:20:54).[15] As the Indian writer Kishwar Desai's novel *The Sea of Innocence* (2013) unsparingly describes, "All her reproductive organs had been ruptured and her intestines pulled out by one of the rapists with his bare hands, after he had inserted an iron rod inside her. In the multiple surgeries that followed only five per cent of her intestines were retained" (102).[16] Demands for justice and reform were almost immediate, with large demonstrations erupting across India and other parts of the world protesting "the increasing incidence of sexual violence against women and the almost institutionalized indifference to the suffering of victims" (Desai 95).[17] In response, Indian officials established five fast-track courts to handle cases of sexual violence against women and brought Pandey's case to trial in February 2013. One defendant died in jail in March 2013, the one juvenile defendant was sentenced to three years in a reform facility (the maximum for his age), and in September 2013, the four remaining defendants were found guilty and sentenced to death. Their multiple appeals were unsuccessful, and they were executed in March 2020 (Shandilya 467–68).

Pandey's case was an anomaly, both in terms of the attention it received and with respect to the prosecution of the perpetrators.[18] To be sure, as with South Korea's 2016 Gangnam Station incident, discussed in chapter 1, the image of Pandey as everywoman brought together disparate activist organizations and Indians from all backgrounds to fight against the status quo. Their voices drowned out the extreme and frequently repeated patriarchal assertions resonating through media. For instance, the documentary film *India's Daughter* (2015) exposes the claim of one of Pandey's rapists that "a decent girl won't roam around at 9 o'clock at night. A girl is far more responsible for rape than a boy" (00:05:42–00:05:50). It also cites one of the defense attorney's proclamations that, "[i]f my daughter or sister engaged in pre-marital activities and disgraced herself and allowed herself to lose face and character by doing such things, I would most certainly take this sort of sister or daughter to my farmhouse and in front of my entire family, I would put petrol on her and set her alight" (00:53:40–00:53:58).[19] At the same time, as Krupa Shandilya rightly observes, "the category [of everywoman] was co-opted to mean a Hindu, upper-caste, middle-class woman" (468).[20] Notably, in the years following Pandey's assault and murder, rape cases involving rural, lower-caste, non-Hindu, and poor women—whether single- or multiple-perpetrator—have been met with continued silence and apathy (Shandilya 478–79).[21] Indeed, women of all backgrounds are still raped with alarming frequency in India, as in much of the world.

Even as conventional attitudes justifying horrific forms of sexual violence against "misbehaving" women remain prevalent, denials of this violence are common, not only by the accused, including in the Pandey case, but also by the broader public, who can find it difficult to believe that such heinous acts are perpetrated. This dynamic comes to the fore in Villanueva's powerful and personal short story "The Mayor of the Roses," which focuses on the aftermath of the 1993 rape and murder of Mary Eileen Sarmenta and murder of Sarmenta's boyfriend, Allan Gomez, both students at the University of the Philippines, Los Baños.[22] Sarmenta and Gomez had been selected by Antonio Sanchez's nephew (their classmate) as a "gift" to Sanchez (Maguddayao), who had served as mayor of Calauan, Laguna Province, the Philippines. The couple were abducted from campus by Calauan police and taken to Sanchez, who after repeatedly raping Sarmenta, handed her over to his men, six of whom also raped her. Ultimately, both students were killed in what Judge Harriet O. Demetriou described as a "plot seemingly hatched in hell" (qtd. in Maguddayao). Although Sanchez was convicted in 1995 and sentenced to 280 years for his crimes, he enjoyed many luxuries while in prison and was approved for early release in 2019. Public outrage was so extreme that the authorities called off his release, and Sanchez died in prison in March 2021 (Maguddayao).

The first-person Filipina American narrator of Villanueva's "The Mayor of the Roses" graphically describes Sanchez's trial, parts of which she attended while visiting family in the Philippines. At the beginning of the narrative, she asserts that "[t]he other story, the one I am about to tell you now, is true. I know it really happened" (Villanueva 255). The narrator is certain these events "really happened" not solely because of the stories her family tells her—fragments of which are interspersed throughout "The Mayor of the Roses"—but also because of what she witnesses in the courtroom. She admits, "I myself didn't know why I wanted to listen to those things. The number of times the girl was raped. The way they tied her down. The shot in the face, at close range" (256). But as gruesome as the evidence is, the narrator understands, "I had no choice. I had to see it played out: the mayor, his bodyguards (beefy and mean-looking, just as in my dreams), his wife, the girl's mother. I had to see them all, arrayed in the courtroom, figures obscured by smoke and dim light. I had to see them, to convince myself this was real, it had really happened. It wasn't a nightmare" (259). The stories circulating through her community compel the narrator to attend Sanchez's trial, but it takes witnessing the trial, where Sarmenta's mother sits silently and stoically day after day, to convince the narrator that the stories of violence are all too real.

The stories others tell about Sarmenta, including those voiced at the trial, enable the narrator herself to construct another story about Sarmenta on the night she was raped and killed. The narrator's story not only elaborates on the violence committed against Sarmenta but also foregrounds her humanity by integrating chronological span and psychological depth. Immediately after citing the prosecutor's question to the former mayor about Sarmenta's screams, the narrator shifts focus and begins describing the attack from Sarmenta's perspective: "They were holding her arms so tight, so tight. She couldn't breathe. . . . They were laughing and calling her names now. Cunt. Bitch" (Villanueva 260). The narrator pivots again, flashing back to the following scene: "Today was her mother's birthday. In the morning, before leaving for school, she had handed her mother a *gumamemela* flower from the garden" (260). And then she flashes back further, to Sarmenta's childhood, before rapidly moving forward in time to the attack: "She [Mary] was suddenly helpless and small. She was the little girl hiding behind the *santan* flowers. She was the little girl hiding in the closet. . . . She had been naughty; she shouldn't have worn shorts that day. She could feel fingers at the edges of her shorts" (260). The narrator imagines what Sarmenta must have thought and felt and what she did not know and did not feel: "When they took her to that house, she recognized it. That was the terrible thing. . . . After he was through, she relaxed a little. She thought now he will let me go. I've survived. But she didn't realize he would hand her over to the others. . . . She didn't feel the gun blast that spattered her brains over the floor of the jeep" (260–61). The narrator's discursive choices repeatedly highlight how, unlike Itō, who survives to tell her own story, Sarmenta depends on multiple storytellers.

Even when perpetrators are convicted, punishments vary widely. "The Mayor of the Roses" ends with the narrator opening a newspaper some years after the trial to find a picture of Sanchez luxuriating in a bathtub. The accompanying article reports that "the Mayor's bathwater was sprinkled with rose petals provided by his loving wife, Bai, the new Mayor of Calauan" (Villanueva 262). Even while further publicizing a horrific case of multiple-perpetrator violence that rather unusually resulted in some justice for its victims, Villanueva's short story draws attention both to the near impossibility of truly punishing perpetrators who are socially privileged and to the significant barriers to believing that something so horrific could be so real.[23] Through its aesthetics and narrative strategies, "The Mayor of the Roses" also highlights how the stories of others can at once debase and humanize those no longer able to speak for themselves.

Wartime Sexual Violence and Shame on Trial: Kim Soom's *One Left* (2016)

Although the broader context of sexual violence against women is evoked in both Itō's memoir *Black Box* and Villanueva's short story "The Mayor of the Roses," it is even more central in Kim's *One Left*. So, too, are the lifelong ramifications for those who survive, including the decades-long struggle for dignity.

Mass rape and other forms of sexual violence—including sexual mutilation and sexual humiliation as well as forced prostitution and forced pregnancy—have been part of armed conflict since ancient times (*Sexual Violence* 3). Yet all too often, reports of sexual violence in conflict zones are downplayed if not ignored, denied, or dismissed as rhetoric or propaganda, and the survivor of wartime rape becomes a "symbol of her nation's defeat. A pariah. Damaged property. A pawn in the subtle wars of international propaganda" (Brownmiller, "Making"). Sexual violence primarily against women is regularly used in conflict zones as an instrument of genocide and a strategy of ethnic cleansing, including during the Bosnian War (1992–95), where as many as 50,000 primarily Muslim women were systematically raped by ethnically Serbian soldiers; the Bangladesh Liberation War (1971), where between 200,000 and 400,000 women and girls from East Pakistan (now Bangladesh) were raped by troops from West Pakistan (now Pakistan), the sexually violent genocidal seeds of which were sown during the partition of British India into India and Pakistan (1947); and the Rwandan genocide (1994), where between 250,000 and 500,000 Tutsi women were raped, many by HIV-positive Hutu men (Heineman 5; Jones 218–19; Peletz 77–81; Sharlach 94–98).[24] As Lisa Sharlach has noted, a "striking similarity" among these three examples is the "preexisting stigma against raped women in the ethnic group targeted for genocide" (101).

Although distinct from the sexual violence in the above examples, the atrocities to which the Japanese military subjected its so-called comfort women (*ianfu*) during the Pacific War (1937–45) have also been described as "genocidal" (Yang 63).[25] Comfort women, estimated to number in the hundreds of thousands, were primarily Korean and Chinese but also, among other Asian and European nationalities, Japanese, Taiwanese, Indonesian, Filipina, and Dutch girls and young women who suffered extreme sexual violence and abuse. Many were raped by Japanese soldiers dozens of times daily and physically tortured for resisting authority. The majority of Japan's comfort women came from societies where female chastity was highly valued (Coomaraswamy; Oh, "Japanese Imperial System"; Qiu 5; Soh xii, 5, 151; Yang 65–66).[26] Even so, comfort women were forcibly recruited not only by the Japanese military but also by local "entrepreneurs" (Soh 22); some were sold to the Japanese by their fathers and husbands (Yang 65).[27] C. Sarah Soh's insights concerning Korean comfort women apply more broadly to comfort women in other parts of the Japanese empire: "The abuse and maltreatment of daughters and wives in the patriarchal system, with its long-standing masculinist sexual culture, contributed as much as did the colonial political economy to the ready commodification of these women's sexual labor. . . . Korean comfort women [were not] victims *solely* of the Japanese military and colonialism" (xvi). In other words, both Japanese colonial and wartime policies and patriarchal systems in the comfort women's homelands were often responsible.

Most comfort women were unable to return to their families or even their homelands. If not killed during the war or by retreating Japanese troops, they were "simply abandoned to their fate" (Coomaraswamy). The fewer than 10% who did manage to find their way back to their countries of birth most frequently led impoverished, precarious, and "hidden lives" (Oh, Foreword xi), their voices silenced for nearly half a century in part because their societies deemed survivors of rape "impure" and a "disgrace" to their families, if not, particularly given the nationality of their rapist, "as having served the nation's enemy" (Qiu 5).

Indeed, although much was written in Japan between the late 1940s and the end of the Shōwa period (1989) on the comfort stations, publications on comfort women were not readily available in Korea until the mid-1960s (Soh 145–73). In the early 1970s, Korean women's groups staged protests against Japanese sex tourism to Korea. They were joined by Japanese feminists, who articulated the connections between the Japanese military "comfort system" and contemporary Japanese sex tourism (Kang 26). The late 1970s and 1980s saw continued inter-Asian feminist coordination against sexual exploitation (30). But it was not until the 1990s that the wartime experiences and continued suffering of comfort women received broad international attention and their rape moved away from the "shame of the victim" and closer to the "crime of the perpetrator" (Ueno 71).[28] This change resulted in part from the success of the international women's movement in declaring rape an issue not of honor but instead of gendered sexual violence (Yamamoto xix–xx).

Also contributing to this paradigm shift was the 1990 founding of the Korean Council for the Women Drafted for Military Sexual Slavery (Hanguk Chŏngsindae Munje Taech'aek Hyŏbuihoe), which was enabled by and enjoyed alliances with feminists and feminist groups across East and Southeast Asia (Yang 54). Equally important were the testimonies of individual former comfort women, beginning with Kim Haksun. Propelled by the Korean women's movement, in 1991 Kim became the first former Korean comfort woman to speak publicly regarding her wartime experiences and in so doing "opened the floodgates, sending a tidal wave across the globe" (Oh, Foreword xii).[29] Especially powerful was the 1996 *Report on the Mission to the Democratic People's Republic of Korea, the Republic of Korea and Japan on the Issue of Military Sexual Slavery in Wartime*, by Radhika Coomaraswamy, the UN special rapporteur on violence against women, which declared the comfort women system a form of sexual slavery, a conclusion unanimously accepted by the UN's Commission on Human Rights (Ueno 87).[30] The growth of Asian American studies in North America was also significant (Kang 43; Thoma). The decades since have witnessed continued attention to and controversies regarding the comfort women system and its aftermath, within and far outside East Asia and across the globe. These include the international outcry following the Harvard professor J. Mark Ramseyer's unsubstantiated assertions in January 2021 that the "Japanese army did not . . . use Korean women as sex slaves" and that instead, the comfort station system relied on voluntary contracts between women and brothel owners.[31]

Often suppressed in the perpetual comfort women debates have been the voices and subjectivities of individual women, who after being silenced for 50 years have for the past three decades been caught in "conflicting national agendas" (Choi 397). Kim's *One Left* is one of a growing body of creative works that counter this tendency.[32] Narrated in the third person, and documented even more extensively than Cho's *Kim Jiyoung*, discussed in chapter 1, this nonfiction novel is grounded in the testimonies of dozens of comfort women, to which readers are guided by more than 300 endnotes.

The protagonist of *One Left* is a 93-year-old Korean woman named P'unggil, who is haunted by horrific memories of the brutality to which she and other girls and young women were subjected at a Japanese comfort station in Manchuria (northeastern China). Through its many vivid and extensive flashbacks, the novel speaks explicitly of the horrific abuses to which P'unggil was subjected while being held captive for seven years (from the age of 13 to 21), including being raped by an estimated 30,000 Japanese soldiers. The 93-year-old P'unggil is also haunted by memories of the treacherous five-year journey back to her native village in Korea after Japan's surrender and of the difficult and isolated 65 years she has endured since her return. One night, P'unggil learns on the evening news that Yun Kŭmshil, the last known Korean comfort woman, is near death. Although P'unggil has remained silent about her traumas for nearly seven decades, she determines to visit this woman and let her know that even after she (Yun) passes, there still will be "one left."

Part of Kim's motivation for writing *One Left* in 2016 was knowing that "there soon will be a day when only one [former comfort woman] is left. And that there will be one day when not one survivor is around, when that last one passes away" ("Author Talks" 00:10:20–00:10:42). Kim has spoken of believing that "my writing is bringing back the memories they tried to erase, those they had erased" (00:12:00–00:12:13). Moreover, Kim feared that with survivors dying, "the true details and extent of their horrific experiences would be lost" and that "the comfort women's *real, excruciatingly painful* experiences might be forgotten unless depicted in a personal narrative" (Oh, Foreword ix). Without question, the narrator of *One Left* depicts in extreme detail "the gut-wrenching suffering of the victims" (x). From the very beginning, the novel speaks candidly of P'unggil and other impoverished and illiterate young women as kidnapped and transported to distant military comfort stations where they were treated like livestock. Through P'unggil, the narrator describes how the women were leashed if they tried to escape or otherwise did not obey, beaten and even shot for refusing a soldier's demands, and subjected to regular injections of an arsenic compound that left many sterile as well as to forced abortions, hysterectomies, and countless other atrocities. The narrator repeatedly refers to the comfort station as a "living hell," one where in addition to being raped dozens of times daily, often by men who refused to wear "mandatory" condoms, "the girls were flogged with *soekkudae*, whips with metal handles; beaten with red-hot fire pokers or with metal bars; hit with the flat of a sword; or kicked indiscriminately. *And they stuck red-hot metal rods into the girls' vaginas*" (Kim 42).

Just as penetrating as the novel's descriptions of Japanese brutality is its heart-wrenching evocation of the continued suffering of the comfort women in the decades following Japan's surrender. In the opening chapter of *One Left*, the narrator notes that "for seventy years now there hasn't been a single night that [P'unggil] slept soundly" (Kim 14), making immediately clear her enduring and relentless trauma. In chapter 2, the narrator observes that P'unggil has never gone public "out of shame [and] embarrassment" (19). She has not shared her experiences with her natal family, much less gotten married. Even when at the comfort station, she knew she could never tell her family: "considering what she'd done in the comfort station, she'd be better off dead" (65). In 1991 she watched Kim Haksun and others go public and thought, "'Me too, I'm a victim.' 'Me too, a victim.' 'Yes, me too, a victim.' 'Me too, I'm a victim'" (105), one of many precursors to the Me Too movement. But P'unggil also witnessed those who registered with the Korean government as former comfort women (largely to receive much-needed government assistance) being abandoned by their families and friends. The stigma against rape and the belief that comfort women had betrayed their families and their nation remained as powerful as ever even decades after Japan's defeat. The narrator describes P'unggil as having stayed silent; living a lonely, precarious life; teaching herself how to read; surviving as a maid for 35 years; and for the past three decades taking on odd jobs before finally having no choice but to live off her savings. P'unggil is terrified that her nephew will confine her to a facility, whereas she wants nothing more than a quiet death at home.

One Left concludes with P'unggil going to the university hospital where Yun Kŭmshil lies dying and realizing anew "[t]hat she [P'unggil] still lives in fear. And she's still at the comfort station in Manchuria, a 13-year-old girl" (Kim 187). The narrator does not specify whether P'unggil reaches Yun in time, whether the "last one" ever learns there is (at least) one more. Instead, *One Left* concludes with P'unggil still submerged in painful memories of the past and facing an uncertain future, the narrative from beginning to end collapsing together traumatic pasts, presents, and futures. Without question, as Kim has declared, "[a]s young girls [the comfort women] faced unimaginable suffering, and they continued to live with distortion and untreated traumas for the rest of their lives. Nevertheless, they lived, they survived from day to day. They are still living. The novel contains their own inner resilience, their ability to heal" ("Author Talks" 00:18:06–00:18:53). At the same time, *One Left* also highlights the tremendous barriers to healing. These include social structures and patriarchal demands that make it nearly impossible for women subjected to rape, not to mention repeated rape under wartime colonialism, ever to be reintegrated into their families and communities, much less find justice.[33] Kim's narrative strategies and aesthetic choices highlight shared culpability and enduring trauma on a broad scale. They also foreground P'unggil's humanity, depicting her as a dignified girl and woman with a powerful story and mission yet with a voice that remains silenced, entirely dependent on Kim's translation.

Prosecuting Honor-Based Violence: Sarbjit Kaur Athwal's *Shamed* (2013)

As exposed in Kim's *One Left*, former comfort women were shunned and otherwise abused throughout their lifetimes in part because of their perceived assaults on family and national honor. Even more extreme is honor-based violence, a form of gender-based violence perpetrated in the name of maintaining or restoring the reputation and honor of a family or community. Honor-based violence can involve forced marriage; verbal, financial, psychological, and physical abuse; and, in extreme cases, murder. Victims of honor-based violence are usually women and girls believed to have "defied the accepted social norms by behaving improperly or violating sexual boundaries" and in so doing to have significantly shamed their families or communities (Gregory et al. 365; see also Sedem and Ferrer-Wreder). Today, in families and communities globally—and particularly in South Asia, the Middle East, Turkey, the Mediterranean, and Latin America as well as in diasporic communities from these sites in Europe and North America—hundreds of thousands of women and girls are subjected annually to honor-based violence.[34] These individuals are harshly punished for being too westernized or independent (e.g., interacting with men outside their families, wearing makeup, cutting their hair, or attending college or university); refusing an arranged marriage, asking for a divorce, or having a relationship outside their religion or caste; disobeying their husband or father; being raped or sexually assaulted; having sex or becoming pregnant outside marriage; being lesbian, bisexual, or transgender; or having a mental or physical illness (Begum and Natarajan 376; Gregory et al. 366; Lowe et al. 284). Although many perpetrators are male, women also support and actively participate in honor-based crimes, particularly mothers and mothers-in-law concerned with the impact a shamed and unpunished woman will have on other members of the family (Chesler, "When"; Julios 44–45; Kirti et al. 345–46).

Death by honor killing is frequently preceded by torture (e.g., the woman or girl is raped or gang-raped and then attacked with acid, strangled, bludgeoned, stabbed, stoned, or burned to death). Honor killings are also generally perpetrated by multiple members of the woman's or girl's family of origin and occasionally by her in-laws or other members of the community (Chesler, "Worldwide Trends" 4). Estimates of numbers of women killed in the name of honor vary widely. Most frequently cited is the 2000 United Nations Population Fund claim that every year 5,000 women and girls are killed for honor-related reasons. This statistic likely represents just the tip of the iceberg (Chesler, "Worldwide Trends" 3; Gregory et al. 367).

Honor-based violence shares much in common and frequently coexists with family violence, the focus of chapter 6, and intimate partner violence, the focus of chapter 7. At the same time, honor-based violence is generally distinguished from family violence and intimate partner violence in several important respects. These include the extensive participation of both the extended family and the cultural or religious community—that is, both acquaintances and strangers—in arbitrating honor and shame, deciding punishment, and perpetrating and concealing violence (Idriss 4). Moreover, far from being condemned, the perpetrator is frequently accepted, even praised, by the family and community for "redeeming" or "cleansing" the family's honor (Cooney 9).[35]

Athwal's *Shamed* highlights the significant role played by the community in both perpetrating and concealing honor-based violence, including murder. Just as Itō's *Black Box* is one of a growing corpus of personal narratives on rape, Athwal's *Shamed* is one of an expanding list of memoirs on honor-based violence. At the same time, *Shamed* is far more Athwal's story than it is the story of the family's primary victim of honor-based violence, Athwal's sister-in-law Surjit, whose murder was arranged by their mother-in-law. As with Kim's and Villanueva's narratives, the primary victim or victims are no longer alive to seek justice.

Athwal describes, largely chronologically and straightforwardly, her sheltered and highly gendered upbringing in an extremely insulated Punjabi Sikh community in Hounslow, West London; her forced marriage as a teenager; her discovery of her in-laws' complicity in the honor killing of her sister-in-law Surjit; and the long struggle to bring her in-laws to justice, including the author's own difficult transformation from silent and obedient daughter-in-law to advocate for Surjit.[36] Providing a detailed account of her childhood and young adulthood enables Athwal to contextualize her sister-in-law's murder within broader structures of gender injustice. From the beginning of her memoir, Athwal underscores her isolation from greater Hounslow, not to mention London, and the all-encompassing control her diasporic Punjabi Sikh family and their community exert over the lives of their members.[37] She details how her family's sole objective was for her to learn the "Indian way" and become a good Indian daughter, wife, and mother (36). She was forbidden from speaking English and wearing Western attire at home; prohibited from talking with her male classmates inside and outside school and even her female classmates outside school; sent to India at age 10 to live with her extended family for two years, where she was both taught to "be a woman" (i.e., to look after a family, run a house, clean, and cook "the Indian way," a continuation of everything she was doing at home in the United Kingdom [28]) and physically and verbally abused "just because I was a young woman" (48); and compelled on her return to the United Kingdom to care for her siblings and extended family at the expense of her education.

Moreover, Athwal describes how, after she scraped through high school, her parents forced her to marry a man she did not know, even though—having been groped by men in India—she had no desire to get married. As she perceptively summarizes in *Shamed*, in one of several passages connecting her experiences with the insular norms of her tight-knit Sikh community:

> Everything a Sikh does is governed by one simple question. . . . Will I bring honour or shame on my family? And where our faith is concerned, a family isn't just two or three other people. . . .
>
> There are only around 400,000 Sikhs living in the UK—but sometimes it can feel that they all have a say in your life! My parents not only had their close family to please, but also distant aunts and uncles, all their neighbours plus every member of their local temple got a say as well. The worst thing a Sikh could do, it seemed to me growing up, was lose the respect of the community. . . . For Sikhs, the community is something to be ignored at your peril. (21–22)

In *Shamed*, Athwal comments repeatedly on her learned submissiveness, first to her natal family and then to her in-laws, fealty drilled into her since earliest childhood. Her in-laws are openly abusive, and her mother-in-law, Bachan Kaur Athwal, the family's domineering matriarch, works her daughters-in-law—both of whom are also employed outside the home—as though they were "slaves" (197, 241). Yet as Athwal declares, "I knew the ways of the community. I knew how quickly judgements were passed. I was an Athwal now. I needed to be loyal to them. To us. To our family name" (103).

Athwal was very different from her sister-in-law Surjit, a customs and excise officer at Heathrow Airport and the wife of Athwal's husband Hardave's older brother Sukhdave Singh Athwal. Athwal depicts Surjit as having little concern for family honor and regularly rebelling against her in-laws: she describes her sister-in-law as openly complaining about her subservient role in the family, frequently fighting with her husband, spending time with her friends, shopping for Western clothing, cutting her hair without her husband's permission, leaving the family home, having an affair, becoming pregnant with her lover, and preparing to divorce her husband. This was all too much for Sukhdave, and particularly for Athwal's mother-in-law, Bachan Kaur. As Athwal describes, at a family gathering in late November 1998, Bachan Kaur announced that she had "spoken to a contact in India" and that everything was "going to be taken care of" (147). Bachan Kaur then claims, "It's her own fault. She's out of control" (148). Her mother-in-law likewise accuses Surjit of "bringing shame on the family" and making them "the laughing-stock of the community" (148). Not leaving space for anyone else to speak, she concludes, "We have to get rid of her" (148). Although Sarbjit's husband, Hardave, challenged his mother, Bachan Kaur remained adamant: "It's decided. . . . I won't have her shaming our family. . . . We have discussed it. . . . The decision is made" (149).

Athwal shares her discomfort with this startling turn of events and admits her lack of courage and justification for her silence: "I knew I had to do something but I didn't know what. . . . However despicably I thought they were behaving, I wasn't to meddle in family business. I had to protect the family's honour" (154). Moreover, having been raised to believe "everything could be sorted out within the family," she could not fathom going to the local police (155). She did, however, call an anonymous helpline a few hours before her sister-in-law and mother-in-law were scheduled to depart London for India, Surjit having been lured by promises of a coveted shopping spree abroad. The following week, with Surjit and Bachan Kaur in India, and frightened that were she to go to the local police station a fellow Sikh would alert her mother-in-law, Athwal wrote a "long, detailed [anonymous] letter imploring [the police] to act" (163).

But the British authorities ignored these warnings. And Athwal poignantly describes how in January 1999, her mother-in-law informed her that her sister-in-law had been killed in India for "bringing too much shame on the family" (180). Athwal's in-laws demanded her silence, her husband threatening, "You also know the same thing will happen to you if you dare breathe a word of this to anyone" (184). Unable to keep completely silent, Athwal told her sister Inder. As she discovered only years later, Inder in turn went to the authorities, who interviewed her several times but ultimately did "nothing about it. It was the third time they'd been told, and third time they'd failed to respond. Why? Did they think it was just a family matter? Or maybe the disappearance of one more Sikh girl wasn't enough to trouble them?" (187).

Historically, many who participate in honor-based violence, including individuals who kill in the name of honor, have not been held fully accountable. In fact, for millennia, laws around the world have condoned and, in many cases, continue to condone honor-based violence (e.g., through reduced or minimal sentences for harming an individual, usually a woman, in the name of "honor"). Laws have also explicitly called for violence against women who have had premarital sex or committed adultery (Goldstein 29).[38] Even women and girls subjected to honor-based violence who live in nations where this violence is not condoned have long struggled for justice. Every year in the United Kingdom, for instance, tens of thousands of women are subjected to honor-based violence perpetrated not only by first-generation immigrants but also by individuals whose families migrated to the United Kingdom several generations ago (Julios 5, 45–46).[39] Although the numbers continue to increase, few perpetrators are brought to justice (7).

The case of Surjit Athwal is particularly striking, both in that her husband and mother-in-law were convicted by a jury and sentenced to prison and in that they were the first individuals in UK legal history to be held accountable for an honor killing planned in the United Kingdom but implemented abroad (Julios 50).[40] Notably, however, delays in prosecuting this case, which did not go to trial until 2007, highlight the role of family and community in at once promoting and obstructing justice. To be sure, in part 2 of *Shamed*, Athwal describes the determination of Surjit's natal family and especially her brother Jagdeesh Singh Dhillon to hold both the Athwal family and British authorities accountable. The Dhillons left no stone unturned, even after the police dismissed the case in 2000 for lack of evidence. As Athwal notes, Jagdeesh appeared "on numerous radio shows throughout the early 2000s and in many more local and national newspapers" (234), worked with BBC's *Newsnight*, and contributed to a documentary that "told her [Surjit's] whole tragic story" (234–35). Jagdeesh contrasted the United Kingdom's initial apathy toward the disappearance of Surjit with its urgent response in July 2000 to the disappearance of Lucie Blackman in Tokyo, "as if Surjit was less British than Lucie," who was a blue-eyed blond (234).[41]

Without question, the British police could have taken Surjit's case more seriously from the beginning (Julios 49–50), and had she been white they likely would have. At the same time, they did more than did the police in India, who believed "[t]his is family business. It [has] nothing to do with the police" (Athwal 299). The police in India wondered why their counterparts in London were "wasting" so many of their resources looking for Surjit (299). Because Surjit's body was never found, the case against Sukhdave and Bachan Kaur was circumstantial and almost certain to fail without a member of the Athwal family coming forward. Athwal describes in *Shamed* how for years she was too terrified to do so, echoing P'unggil's fear in *One Left*. It was only in October 2005, encouraged by her father, who was becoming increasingly appalled with how she was being treated by her in-laws, that she met with Detective Chief Inspector Clive Driscoll and made an official statement. She knew that testifying would "put me up against murderers. Murderers who knew where I lived and had a key to my house. My children kept coming to my mind and holding me back. . . . [But] I knew I had to do this. I had to do it for Surjit. I had to get justice for Surjit. I had to get justice for her family, her brother—and her precious children" (248). Later, Athwal explains, "The reason I'd kept silent about Surjit for so long was because I had been worried about my own safety. That fear, however, was nothing to the dread I had now that my children—and my community—would never forgive me" (293). This is precisely what happens, Athwal noting that even years after the trial, "[w]hen I do go [to the local temple], it is rare that I am not accosted by someone who accuses me of bringing shame on my family by having my mother- and brother-in-law arrested" (308).

In the final paragraphs of *Shamed*, Athwal declares Driscoll to be the "one hero in this terrible story" (313). Not only had he built a successful case, he had also believed in her, rescued her and her children "from a life of terror . . . won justice for Surjit Athwal . . . [and] shown the whole world that murders in the name of so-called 'honour' and 'shame' would not go undetected. Not in England. Not any more. Not on DCI Driscoll's watch" (314). Athwal's confidence is somewhat misplaced, given that honor-based violence continues unabated in the United Kingdom, as in many parts of the world. More important, Athwal underplays her own vital contribution in bringing her in-laws to justice, an exceptionally difficult yet invaluable role that comes to the fore in *Shamed* and is recognized by both Driscoll and the presiding judges (Julios 48). Even as family (her in-laws) and community took everything from Surjit, family (Surjit's parents and brother, sister-in-law's father, and particularly sister-in-law) risked everything to make certain that those who plotted her murder would be held accountable.

As with Mary in Villanueva's story "The Mayor of the Roses," Surjit is silenced forever. To be sure, *Shamed* depicts transformation as possible under even the direst circumstances. This memoir highlights the singularity both of those subjected to honor-based violence and of those who seek justice for victims of such violence despite tremendous personal risk. At the same time, as emphasized in Itō's, Villanueva's, Kim's, and Athwal's narratives as well as countless others, society's tolerance and even encouragement of violence against women (Bowdler 264), coupled with the inability of most people to break from family, community, religious, and social norms to prevent further violence, let alone save a life, expose just how much more needs to be done in societies around the world to dismantle cultures of shame, silence, rape, and murder in order to attain justice. This is particularly true given the prevalence of family and intimate partner violence, the topics of the following two chapters, respectively.

NOTES

1. Sexual and gender minorities experience rape at disproportionately higher rates than straight cisgender individuals (Bowdler 1).

2. Sehgal's observations about partition fiction are true more broadly.

3. Abrahams et al. provide additional statistics.

4. Chapter 10 of the Indian writer Anita Nair's novel *Ladies Coupé* (222–82) is especially revealing in this regard.

5. "OL" stands for "Office Lady," female office workers who do clerical tasks. "Tōden" refers to Tokyo Electric Power Company, also known as TEPCO.

6. Loney-Howes et al. examine the global digital footprints of Me Too, while Ghadery describes Me Too and the movements emanating from it as "a transnational feminist consciousness-raising endeavour" (254). Fincher discusses the Chinese government's "sweeping crackdown" against feminist activists, including those involved in Me Too (4–5). Hasunuma and Shin contrast South Korea's vocal Me Too movement with Japan's more muted response, even though many in both South Korea and Japan believe that women should "endure harassment rather than upset group dynamics" (107). In April 2020, the mayor of Busan resigned in response to outcries over his sexual assault of an employee, while in July 2021 the mayor of Seoul, long a proponent of gender equity, died by suicide after a subordinate accused him of sexual harassment. Itō herself collaborates with counterparts in Asia, in Africa, and around the world (Itō, #MeToo Movement). The novel

The Disaster Tourist (*Pam ŭi yŏhaengjadŭl*, 2013), by the contemporary South Korean writer Yun Ko-Eun (Yun Koŭn), reveals some of the barriers facing South Korean women who have been sexually assaulted. See Holland and Hewett for a broad discussion of Me Too and literature.

7. Although the criminal case against Yamaguchi was dropped, in December 2019 Itō won the civil trial against him, the court determining that she had not given consent; the courts also dismissed Yamaguchi's countersuit. Itō has twice been awarded damages for defamatory tweets.

8. Matsushita outlines the differences between Japanese and international journalistic portrayals of Itō.

9. See also the Taiwanese writer Lin Yi-Han, who died by suicide shortly after publishing the autofictional *Fang Si-Qi's First Love Paradise* (*Fang Si-Qi de chu lian leyuan*, 2018). After her death, Lin's parents took to social media, not only revealing the book—about a teacher in his 50s who rapes his teenage students—as "a truthful record and reflection of the pain and depression our daughter experienced after she was seduced by a famous cram school teacher" but also declaring that Lin wrote *Fang Si-Qi* "in the hopes that the world's parents, boys, girls, and men will protect the Fang Si-chis of this world" (qtd. in Cho).

10. The amendments were adopted by Japan's National Diet (parliament) on 16 June 2017 and enacted on 13 July 2017.

11. Doing so will require fundamental changes both to Japan's civil society (O'Dwyer) and in attitudes toward sexual assault.

12. Unlike Itō's mother, parents often blame their daughters, themselves, or both. Both phenomena are addressed in the Lao American writer Phet Mahathongdy's short story "Mother Love" (2009), narrated in the first person by a young woman who grew up "in traditional Lao culture in America," where "sex was something we never discussed. . . . To recognize that I was a woman with a body that could be desired or violated by men was taboo" (53–54). During her brutal rape her sophomore year in college, she "stared up into the black sky and thought how awful it would be for my mother were I to die in such a way. Beaten, raped, and killed. What would she do? She would be so brokenhearted. She would blame herself because she had let me go" (54). The first-person narrator does not tell her mother about her rape because "I was frightened she would blame me like the police had. I didn't want her to be mad at me. After all, it was I who had chosen to go out in a pretty dress. And it was I who chose to walk home alone. And it was I who wanted to attend a college so far away from home" (54).

13. Doing so more subtly are short stories such as "Trisanku" (1988), by the Indian writer Ambai (C. S. Lakshmi), in which a young woman is abused first by her father's boss and then by one of her professors, experiences that traumatize her for years. Even though she eventually overcomes her paralyzing timidity, in the final lines of the story she recognizes that "it was impossible to reveal anything freely, without fear or shame" (179). "Trisanku" alludes to but does not explicitly address broader cultures of rape, shame, and silence. See also the

Indonesian writer Intan Paramaditha's "Vampire" ("Vampir," 2005), which describes the experiences of a "highly trained professional" (100) whose boss ultimately invites himself into her home. This short story ends ambiguously; the narrative not only implies that the boss rapes his secretary but also leaves space for her to fight back. In contrast, the Vietnamese writer Di Li's "The Well" ("Giếng," 2009) features a "prosperous businessman and eligible bachelor with hundreds of women trailing after him" who is acquitted of rape charges. The court cannot believe he would attack an "ordinary girl with nothing special about her, well below his position." Instead, the judge becomes frustrated with his accuser, a "brazenly slanderous girl" (52).

14. Isa, in Ally Dalijo's "My Employer," discussed in chapter 3, is an example. One of many cases from China, where Me Too has been severely suppressed, is Zhou Xiaoxuan, a prominent activist who in August 2022 lost her appeal against the television anchor Zhu Jun, whom she accused of sexually assaulting her in 2018 (Stevenson and Wang). See also Suzuki's analysis of the Japanese writer Tamura Toshiko's short story "Temptation of the Wolfberries" ("Kuko no mi no yūwaku," 1914), where an adolescent girl who has been raped "remains trapped in a society that normalizes rape while punishing and silencing the victim" (Suzuki 100).

15. Pandey's male friend Awindra Pratap Pandey (no relation) was brutally beaten in the Delhi attack as he attempted to save Pandey.

16. Desai's novel, which centers on the first-person narrator Simran Singh's search for the truth behind the multiple-perpetrator rape and murder of the British tourist Liza Kay in Goa, is dedicated to Pandey; to Scarlett Keeling, a 15-year-old British tourist who was raped and murdered in Goa in 2008; and to "the thousands of women who have been raped and murdered in India—in the hope that one day they will get justice." *The Sea of Innocence* repeatedly references both the Pandey case and the Keeling case. Other novels by Desai are discussed in chapters 4 and 7.

17. Phillips et al. examine media responses to the Delhi case.

18. See also the 2019 case of a young veterinarian in Hyderabad who was gang-raped and killed by four men. Those men were then killed in a police shootout that many believe a "straight-up case of extrajudicial killing" (Gettleman).

19. Similarly, in the short story "Spirit on the Wind" ("Param ŭi nŏk," 1986), the South Korean writer Oh Jung-hee (O Chŏnghŭi) describes a gang rape where one of the men assaulting Ŭnsu blames her for the attack: "Pathetic, stupid broad! Unless you're fixing to die, you don't wander around a place like this [the mountains, where Ŭnsu had gone to rest]." After the men finally leave, Ŭnsu wonders, "Was a thirty-four-year-old woman supposed to cry if she was stripped naked in broad daylight and gang-raped?" She quickly determines, "No, the right to cry after being raped was reserved for girls who didn't know any better" (67).

20. Pandey's father is, in fact, a laborer, and her family is working-class. They had invested their life's savings in their daughter's education.

21. Wilkerson links the caste systems of India, the United States, and Nazi Germany.

22. Villanueva was born and raised in the Philippines, attended Stanford University for graduate school, and has lived in the United States for many years. She has published several short story collections, including *Ginseng and Other Tales from Manila* (1991), *Mayor of the Roses* (2005), and *The Lost Language* (2016), in addition to the novella *Jenalyn* (2014) and other narratives. The version of "Mayor of the Roses" cited in this chapter is from the anthology *Virtual Lotus: Modern Fiction of Southeast Asia*. A slightly different version opens *Mayor of the Roses*, an anthology that speaks to Filipino American immigrant experiences.

23. This is in part because of the increased blame placed on victims of multiple-perpetrator rape (Adolfsson). In other cases, blame is placed on the family of the victim, as in the Vietnamese writer Đỗ Tiến Thụy's "Wounds of the City" ("Vết thương thành thị," 2009). This short story is narrated in the first person by the husband of a young woman who is gang-raped on her commute home. The crowd that gathers around his blood-soaked wife demands of him, "What kind of husband lets his wife go home alone in the dark through such a neighborhood? Such a husband should be thrown to the dogs!" ("Wounds" 112). The Vietnamese source does not include the phrase "through such a neighborhood." Instead, the crowd is outraged that the husband lets his wife walk home alone in the dark ("Vết thương" 180). Although his wife declares that she has been defiled and has "nothing left to give you" ("Thế là em chẳng còn gì cho anh"; "Vết thương" 183), translated as "nothing for you to know" ("Wounds" 112), the narrator stands by her side and encourages her to seek justice. She refuses, fearing the publicity. This short story also decries the abuse of Vietnamese laborers by their Korean manager.

24. The partition led to one of the largest mass migrations in history (10–15 million people), the deaths of an estimated million people, and violence against tens of thousands of women and girls (Chua et al. 221). Chua et al., Daiya, Dey, Misri, Sehgal, and Stokes are among the many scholars who discuss literature that engages with gendered violence during partition and in its aftermath, including Sahuna Singh Baldwin's *What the Body Remembers* (2015), Amit Majmudar's *Partitions* (2011), Krishna Sobti's *To Hell with You Mitro* (*Mitro Marjani*, 1969), and Bapsi Sidhwa's *Ice-Candy-Man* (1988), also known as *Cracking India* (1991). As Daiya argues, "[T]his archive of migration . . . represents a hidden or subaltern history of women's experiences that often have no other official archive" (50). See also the roundtable "The Dawn of Freedom, the Pain of Partition" at the February 2017 Karachi Literature Festival, where partition is configured as an ongoing process ("KLF-2017"). Chowdhury "turns a feminist critical eye to contemporary, woman-centered Muktijuddho films coming out of Bangladesh" (17). This book examines "how these cultural texts imagine, disrupt, and reinscribe a gendered nationalist landscape of trauma, freedom, and justice" (17–18).

25. See also Soh 131; Ueno 75. Ueno writes of the sexual violence to which Japanese soldiers subjected non-Japanese women during World War II, including in the Nanking Massacre of 1937 and at the comfort stations, as manifesting "the patriarchal logic that women are the 'spoils of war'" (75).

26. Soh discusses the political connotations and sociolinguistic denotations of official and popular terms for the wartime comfort women (69–76). See also Kang 46–49. The Japanese established military comfort stations (brothels) everywhere from Sakhalin and Hokkaido in the North to Indonesia in the South, and from Burma in the West to Micronesia in the East (Coomaraswamy). Estimates vary as to the total number of comfort women; recent research suggests approximately 400,000 women, at least half of whom were Chinese, were forced to serve as comfort women (Qiu 6).

27. As of 2012, an estimated 4.5 million individuals worldwide were being sexually exploited (i.e., trafficked; Urban and Dioguardi 62). Asian narratives on child trafficking include Nair's *Chain of Custody* (2016) and the Cambodian activist Somaly Mam's *The Road of Lost Innocence* (*Silence de l'innocence*, lit. *Silence of Innocence*, 2005); Mam was later accused of fabricating her own story and those of others. The Afghan American writer Khaled Hosseini's *The Kite Runner* (2003) speaks of the Afghan and Pakistani practice of *bacha bazi* (lit. "boy play"), where boys are kidnapped or sold by their families to become the sexual slaves of powerful men. See also the journalist Najibullah Quraishi's documentary film *The Dancing Boys of Afghanistan* (2010).

28. Kang discusses the silence of US-anglophone feminist discourse regarding comfort women in the 1970s and 1980s (32–35).

29. Leading Japanese feminists assisted their Korean counterparts; the connections between Matsui Yayori and Yun Chong-ok, for instance, are well known (Kimura 156). Kimura addresses the range of activists (feminists, journalists, lawyers, scholars) involved in discussions of the comfort women and the hesitancy of many feminists to support the comfort women.

30. For additional examples, see Kang 41–43; Oh, "Japanese Imperial System" 15–20; Soh 43–46.

31. For rebuttals against Ramseyer, see "Letter"; Stanley et al. Curtis discusses the vicious attacks on scholars who have challenged Ramseyer. Memorials to the comfort women in the United States, Korea, and other parts of the world have also been sites of protest and debate. See, for instance, the Japanese American Miki Dezaki's documentary film *Shusenjo: The Main Battleground of the Comfort Woman Issue* (2018). Muta attributes the contemporary controversy regarding comfort women to Japan's "long history of systemic and deeply embedded bifurcation of women . . . into 'good' and 'bad'" (621). Alekseyeva's graphic essay places Dezaki's film within a broader context that includes Tiffany Hsiung's film *The Apology* (2016). Choe describes the "comfort stations" for American-led United Nations troops during the Korean War, which also exploited Korean women ("Brutal Sex Trade").

32. Kim has won multiple major Korean literary awards for her six short story collections and more than a dozen novels on a range of topics, including, as in her novella *Divorce* (*Ihon*, 2017), family violence and intimate partner violence. For more on creative production on comfort women, see Choi; Lee; Qiu; Soh 51–56, 145–73. See also the Indonesian writer Eka Kurniawan's *Beauty Is a Wound* (*Cantik ita Luka*, 2002), which contains graphic scenes of Japanese troops raping Indonesian women, including the protagonist Dewi Ayu (87–92). The Korean American poet Emily Jungmin Yoon draws on a range of testimonies by Korean comfort women in "The Testimonies," a series of seven poems in *A Cruelty Special to Our Species* (2018), where former Korean comfort women share their experiences (viii, 13–27). Only a few dozen former comfort women are still living. See Y. Yoon for Okinawan writing on Korean comfort women.

33. This is of course also true for women who are raped by their colleagues, including women in the Korean military (Choe, "'Only Exit'"). See also the Indian Malaysian writer K. S. (Subramaniam Krishnan) Maniam's short story "The Kling-Kling Woman" (1997), which describes the rape of a female laborer, on the double subalternity of these women in colonial Malaysia (Pillai 152). In contrast, the Hindi-language Indian Dalit writer Mohan Das Namishray's short story "Our Village" ("Apna Gaon," 1998) depicts an impoverished Dalit woman who is paraded through the streets naked because her husband is unable to pay his debts. Shamed that they "stood there watching while our daughter-in-law was stripped naked," the villagers decide to leave en masse and create a new community, where one of their first priorities is building a school, "a place where our children can study and become something." In this new place "their strength redoubled, returned, and doubled" (Namishray). See also Yasir, which describes the case of a 16-year-old girl who after being raped was publicly shamed; she was tied to the rape suspect and paraded through fields and markets.

34. Precise numbers are almost impossible to determine (Julios 5–6). Gay and bisexual men as well as those with physical or mental disabilities are likewise subjected to honor-based violence, as are transgender men and women. Honor-based violence also occurs in other parts of the world. For instance, the Chinese American writer Ha Jin's short story "Man to Be" (1997) describes a brutal case in China: angry at his wife for cheating on him, a husband has five of his friends gang-rape her, to "teach her a good lesson" (26). The story focuses on Nan, one of the men who participate in the gang rape. After the rape, Nan loses his potency, his fiancée, and all hopes for his future, a rare case of an individual suffering as a result of committing such a crime.

35. See also Gill, which draws attention to honor as underlying "so many forms of gender-based violence across the world" (478).

36. Other narratives on honor-based violence in Asia and within Asian diasporic communities include Jasvinder Sanghera's *Shame* (2007), *Daughters of Shame* (2009), and *Shame Travels* (2012). Sanghera is the founder of Karma

Nirvana (est. 1993), the United Kingdom's first charity for survivors of honor-based violence. See also the British Pakistani writer Nadeem Aslam's *Maps for Lost Lovers* (2004).

37. See also the Canadian poet and multimedia artist Rupi Kaur, who in *milk and honey* (2014) and *the sun and her flowers* (2017) provides additional insights into Sikh diasporic experiences. Athwal's family and her community distort many aspects of Sikhism.

38. See Jisoo Kim's discussion of marriage, family, and Confucian patriarchy in fifteenth-century Korea and Sun Joo Kim and Jungwon Kim's translations of nineteenth-century Korean inquest records. Although both men and women were punished for committing adultery, women's sexual behavior was more stringently regulated (Kim and Kim 24). Adultery remains a criminal offense in some parts of the world; it was decriminalized in South Korea only in 2015, in India in 2018, and in Taiwan in 2020 and remains a felony or misdemeanor in about one-third of the United States.

39. For examples, see Hundal; Julios 43–68.

40. In contrast, Aslam's novel *Maps for Lost Lovers* depicts the honor killing of an unmarried diasporic Pakistani couple in the United Kingdom, the narrator commenting on the stark differences between British and Pakistani laws. See Mirza for depictions of Pakistani-Muslim masculinities in this novel.

41. A primary difference between the two cases, in addition to the race and ethnicity of the victim, was that Blackman's death was not orchestrated by her family.

WORKS CITED

Abrahams, Naeemah, et al. "Worldwide Prevalence of Non-Partner Sexual Violence: A Systematic Review." *Lancet*, vol. 383, 12 Feb. 2014, pp. 1648–54.

Adolfsson, Kerstin, et al. "Blame Attributions in Multiple Perpetrator Rape Cases: The Impact of Sympathy, Consent, Force, and Beliefs." *Journal of Interpersonal Violence*, vol. 35, nos. 23–24, Dec. 2020, pp. 5336–64.

Alekseyeva, Julia. "Comfort Women and the Human Rights Documentary." *Artistic Representations of Suffering: Rights, Resistance, and Remembrance*, edited by Mark Celinscak and Curtis Hutt, Rowman and Littlefield, 2021, pp. 185–97.

Ambai. "Trisanku." *A Kitchen in the Corner of the House*, by Ambai, translated by Lakshmi Holmström, Archipelago Books, 2019, pp. 167–79.

Aslam, Nadeem. *Maps for Lost Lovers*. Vintage Books, 2006.

Athwal, Sarbjit Kaur. *Shamed*. Virgin Books, 2013.

"Author Talks: Kim Soom." *The Korea Society*, 2023, www.koreasociety.org/arts-culture/item/1457-author-talks-kim-soom.

Begum, Lipi, and Ravinder Barn. "Crossing Boundaries: Bras, Lingerie and Rape Myths in Postcolonial Urban Middle-Class India." *Gender, Place, and Culture: A Journal of Feminist Geography*, vol. 26, no. 10, Oct. 2019, pp. 1324–44.

Begum, Poppy, and Mangai Natarajan. "Honor-Based Violence: A Review." *International and Transnational Crime and Justice*, edited by Natarajan, Cambridge UP, 2019, pp. 376–82.

Bowdler, Michelle. *Is Rape a Crime? A Memoir, an Investigation, and a Manifesto*. Flatiron Books, 2020.

Brownmiller, Susan. *Against Our Will: Men, Women, and Rape*. Fawcett Books, 1975.

———. "Making Female Bodies the Battlefield." *Newsweek*, 4 Jan. 1993, p. 37.

Chesler, Phyllis. "When Women Commit Honor Killings." *Middle East Quarterly*, vol. 22, no. 4, fall 2015, pp. 1–12.

———. "Worldwide Trends in Honor Killings." *Middle East Quarterly*, vol. 17, no. 2, spring 2010, pp. 3–12.

Cho, Kassy. "This Author Killed Herself after Writing a Novel about Her Alleged Rapist." *BuzzFeed News*, 16 May 2017, www.buzzfeednews.com/article/kassycho/author-commits-suicide-after-writing-about-alleged-rapist.

Choe, Sang-Hun. "A Brutal Sex Trade Built for American Soldiers." *The New York Times*, 2 May 2023, www.nytimes.com/2023/05/02/world/asia/korea-us-comfort-women-sexual-slavery.html.

———. "'The Only Exit': Where Soldiers Are Dying after Sexual Assaults." *The New York Times*, 15 Oct. 2021, www.nytimes.com/2021/10/15/world/asia/south-korea-military-sexual-assault-suicide.html.

Choi, Chungmoo. "The Politics of War Memories toward Healing." *Perilous Memories: The Asia-Pacific War(s)*, edited by Takashi Fujitani et al., Duke UP, 2001, pp. 395–409.

Chowdhury, Elora Halim. *Ethical Encounters: Transnational Feminism, Human Rights, and War Cinema in Bangladesh*. Temple UP, 2022.

Chua, Gabriel Clement, et al. "Honour Killing as Engendered Violence against Women in Amit Majmudar's *Partitions* (2011)." *The Southeast Asian Journal of English Language Studies*, vol. 22, no. 1, Mar. 2016, pp. 221–33.

Coomaraswamy, Radhika. *Report on the Mission to the Democratic People's Republic of Korea, the Republic of Korea and Japan on the Issue of Military Sexual Slavery in Wartime*. United Nations Economic and Social Council, 1996, hrlibrary.umn.edu/commission/country52/53-add1.htm.

Cooney, Mark. *Execution by Family: A Theory of Honor Violence*. Routledge, 2019.

Crenshaw, Kimberlé. "Mapping the Margins: Intersectionality, Identity Politics, and Violence against Women of Color." *Stanford Law Review*, vol. 43, no. 6, July 1991, pp. 1241–99.

Curtis, Paula R. "Taking the Fight for Japan's History Online: The Ramseyer Controversy and Social Media." *The Asia-Pacific Journal: Japan Focus*, vol. 19, no. 22, 15 Nov. 2021, apjjf.org/2021/22/Curtis.html.

Daiya, Kavita. "Reframing Partition: Gender, Migration, and Storytelling in Postcolonial Conflict." *Teaching Anglophone South Asian Women Writers*, edited by Deepika Bahri and Filippo Menozzi, Modern Language Association of America, 2021, pp. 41–51.

The Dancing Boys of Afghanistan. Directed by Najibullah Quraishi, Clover Films, 2010.

Desai, Kishwar. *The Sea of Innocence.* Simon and Schuster, 2013.

Dey, Arunima. "The Female Body as the Site of Male Violence during the Partition of India in Bapsi Sidhwa's *Ice-Candy-Man*." *Complutense Journal of English Studies*, vol. 26, 2018, pp. 27–45.

Di Li. "The Well." *Wild Mustard: New Voices from Vietnam*, edited by Charles Waugh et al., translated by Nguyễn Lien et al., Curbstone Books, 2017, pp. 49–55.

Đỗ Tiến Thụy. "Vết thương thành thị." *Vết Thương Thành Thị: Tập truyện ngắn*, by Đỗ Tiến Thụy, Nhà xuất bản Trẻ, 2009, pp. 166–93.

———. "Wounds of the City." *Wild Mustard: New Voices from Vietnam*, edited by Charles Waugh et al., translated by Nguyễn Hung and Waugh, Curbstone Books, 2017, pp. 105–18.

Fincher, Leta Hong. *Betraying Big Brother: The Feminist Awakening in China.* Verso, 2018.

Garland, Tammy, and April Bennett. "An Overview of Sexual Assault and Sexual Assault Myths." Reddington and Kreisel, pp. 3–25.

Gettleman, Jeffrey. "In India Tech City Shocked by Gang Rape, Vigilante Justice Gets Praise." *The New York Times*, 21 Dec. 2019, www.nytimes.com/2019/12/21/world/asia/india-rape-hyderabad.html.

Ghadery, Farnush. "#Metoo—Has the 'Sisterhood' Finally Become Global or Just Another Product of Neoliberal Feminism?" *Transnational Legal Theory*, vol. 10, no. 2, Apr. 2019, pp. 252–74.

Gieseler, Carly. *The Voices of #MeToo: From Grassroots Activism to a Viral Roar.* Rowman and Littlefield, 2019.

Gill, Aisha. "Honor Killings and the Quest for Justice in Black and Minority Ethnic Communities in the United Kingdom." *Criminal Justice Policy Review*, vol. 20, no. 4, Dec. 2009, pp. 475–94.

Goldstein, Matthew A. "The Biological Roots of Heat-of-Passion Crimes and Honor Killings." *Politics and the Life Sciences*, vol. 21, no. 2, Sept. 2002, pp. 28–37.

Gregory, Geraldine A., et al. "Honour-Based Violence: Awareness and Recognition." *Paediatrics and Child Health*, vol. 30, no. 11, Nov. 2020, pp. 365–70.

Ha Jin. "Man to Be." *Under the Red Flag: Stories by Ha Jin*, U of Georgia P, 1997, pp. 17–30.

Hanser, Robert. "Sexual Assault Definitions." Reddington and Kreisel, pp. 29–55.

Hasunuma, Linda, and Ki-young Shin. "#MeToo in Japan and South Korea: #We Too, #WithYou." *Journal of Women, Politics, and Policy*, vol. 40, no. 1, Jan. 2019, pp. 97–111.

Heineman, Elizabeth. "The History of Sexual Violence in Conflict Zones: Conference Report." *Radical History Review*, no. 101, spring 2008, pp. 5–21.

Holland, Mary K., and Heather Hewett, editors. *#MeToo and Literary Studies*. Bloomsbury, 2021.

Horvath, Miranda Angel Helena, and Liz Kelly. "Multiple Perpetrator Rape: Naming an Offence and Initial Research Findings." *Journal of Social Aggression*, vol. 15, no. 1, Mar. 2009, pp. 83–96.

Hosseini, Khaled. *The Kite Runner*. Riverhead Books, 2004.

Hundal, Sunny. "No Silence over Honour Killings." *New Statesman*, 13 Aug. 2012, p. 15.

Idriss, Mohammad Mazher. "Not Domestic Violence or Cultural Tradition: Is Honour-Based Violence Distinct from Domestic Violence?" *Journal of Social Welfare and Family Law*, vol. 39, no. 1, Jan. 2017, pp. 3–21.

India's Daughter: The Story of Jyoti Singh. Directed by Leslee Udwin, Assassin Films, 2015.

Itō Shiori. *Black Box*. Translated by Allison Markin Powell, Feminist Press, 2021.

———, speaker. The #MeToo Movement in Asia: How Can We Fight against Sexual Violence? Asia Society Japan Center, 12 Feb. 2021. Webinar.

Jones, Adam. *The Scourge of Genocide*. Routledge, 2013.

Julios, Christina. *Forced Marriage and "Honour" Killings in Britain*. Routledge, 2015.

Kang, Laura Hyun Yi. *Traffic in Asian Women*. Duke UP, 2020.

Kaur, Rupi. *milk and honey*. Andrews McMeel Press, 2015.

———. *the sun and her flowers*. Andrews McMeel Press, 2017.

Kim, Jisoo M. "From Jealousy to Violence: Marriage, Family, and Confucian Patriarchy in Fifteenth-Century Korea." *Acta Koreana*, vol. 20, no. 1, June 2017, pp. 91–110.

Kim Soom. *One Left*. Translated by Bruce Fulton and Ju-Chan Fulton, U of Washington P, 2020.

Kim, Sun Joo, and Jungwon Kim. *Wrongful Deaths: Selected Inquest Records from Nineteenth-Century Korea*. U of Washington P, 2014.

Kimura, Kan. Review of *Comfort Women Activism: Critical Voices from the Perpetrator State*, by Eika Tai. *Journal of Japanese Studies*, vol. 48, no. 1, winter 2022, pp. 154–57.

Kirti, Anand, et al. "The Face of Honour Based Crimes: Global Concerns and Solutions." *International Journal of Criminal Justice Sciences*, vol. 6, nos. 1–2, Jan.–Dec. 2011, pp. 343–57.

"KLF-2017: The Dawn of Freedom, The Pain of Partition (12.2.2017)." *YouTube*, uploaded by KarachiLitFestival, 27 Mar. 2017, www.youtube.com/watch?v=RHeCRnKfuNA.

Kurniawan, Eka. *Beauty Is a Wound*. Translated by Annie Tucker, New Directions Publishing, 2015.

Lee, So-Hee. "A Comparison of *Fox Girl* and *The Bridle*: Gender/Nation, Colonialism/Postcolonialism." *Hyŏndae yŏngmi sosŏl*, vol. 14, no. 1, Apr. 2008, pp. 149–92.

"Letter by Concerned Economists regarding 'Contracting for Sex in the Pacific War' in the *International Review of Law and Economics*." *Chwe.net*, 2021, chwe.net/irle/letter/.

Loney-Howes, Rachel, et al. "Digital Footprints of #MeToo." *Feminist Media Studies*, Feb. 2021, https://doi.org/10.1080/14680777.2021.1886142.

Lowe, Michelle, et al. "Attitudes toward Intimate Partner 'Honor'-Based Violence in India, Iran, Malaysia, and Pakistan." *Journal of Aggression, Conflict, and Peace Research*, vol. 10, no. 4, Nov. 2018, pp. 283–92.

Maguddayao, Merck. "Philippines: Release of Ex-Mayor Convicted for Rape, Murder Halted by Public Protest." *Green Left*, no. 1236, 6 Sept. 2019, www.greenleft.org.au/content/philippines-release-ex-mayor-convicted-rape-murder-halted-public-protest.

Mahathongdy, Phet. "Mother Love." *Troubling Borders: An Anthology of Art and Literature by Southeast Asian Women in the Diaspora*, edited by Isabelle Thuy Pelaud et al., U of Washington P, 2014, pp. 52–57.

Mam, Somaly. *The Road of Lost Innocence*. Random House, 2008.

Maniam, K. S. "The Kling-Kling Woman." Yamada, pp. 119–30.

Matsushita, Kayo. "Diverging Narratives: Exploring the Hidden Influence of Transquoting in Framing the Journalistic Portrayal of Shiori Ito." *Language and Intercultural Communication*, vol. 21, no. 3, May 2021, pp. 366–78.

Mirza, Maryam. "Ambiguous Pakistani-Muslim Masculinities in the Diaspora: A Study of Nadeem Aslam's *Maps for Lost Lovers*." *South Asian Diaspora*, vol. 9, no. 2, July 2017, pp. 193–206.

Misri, Deepti. "The Violence of Memory: Renarrating Partition Violence in Shauna Singh Baldwin's *What the Body Remembers*." *Meridians*, vol. 11, no. 1, Sept. 2011, pp. 1–25.

Muta, Kazue. "The 'Comfort Women' Issue and the Embedded Culture of Sexual Violence in Contemporary Japan." *Current Sociology*, vol. 64, no. 4, July 2016, pp. 620–36.

Nair, Anita. *Chain of Custody*. Bitter Lemon Press, 2016.

———. *Ladies Coupé*. St. Martin's Press, 2001.

Namishray, Mohan Das. "Our Village." Translated by Laura Brueck and Christi A. Merrill. *Words without Borders*, 1 Oct. 2018, wordswithoutborders.org/read/article/2018-10/october-2018-dalit-writing-our-village-mohan-das-namishray-brueck-merrill/.

Nicholls, Tracey. *Dismantling Rape Culture: The Peacebuilding Power of "Me Too."* Routledge, 2021.

O Chŏnghŭi. "Spirit on the Wind." *The Red Room: Stories of Trauma in Contemporary Korea*, translated by Bruce Fulton and Ju-Chan Fulton, U of Hawai'i P, 2009, pp. 25–121.

O'Dwyer, Shaun. "What Lies behind Shiori Ito's Lonely #MeToo Struggle." *Japan Times*, 26 Jan. 2020, www.japantimes.co.jp/opinion/2020/01/26/commentary/japan-commentary/lies-behind-shiori-itos-lonely-metoo-struggle.

Oh, Bonnie. Foreword. *One Left*, by Kim Soom, translated by Bruce Fulton and Ju-Chan Fulton, U of Washington P, 2020, pp. vii–xiv.

———. "The Japanese Imperial System and the Korean 'Comfort Women' of World War II." Stetz and Oh, pp. 3–25.

Paramaditha, Intan. "Vampire." *Apple and Knife*, by Paramaditha, translated by Stephen J. Epstein, Vintage Books, 2018, pp. 95–102.

Peletz, Michael G. *Gender, Sexuality, and Body Politics in Modern Asia*. Association for Asian Studies, 2011.

Phillips, Mark, et al. "Media Coverage of Violence against Women in India: A Systematic Study of a High Profile Rape Case." *BMC Women's Health*, vol. 15, no. 1, Jan. 2015, pp. 1–10.

Pillai, Shanthini. "In Gendered Chambers: The Figure of the Indian Immigrant Woman of Colonial Malaya." *Hecate*, vol. 30, no. 1, Jan. 2004, pp. 141–59.

Qiu, Peipei. *Chinese Comfort Women: Testimonies from Imperial Japan's Sex Slaves*. Oxford UP, 2013.

Ramseyer, J. Mark. "Recovering the Truth about the Comfort Women." *Japan Forward*, 12 Jan. 2021, japan-forward.com/recovering-the-truth-about-the-comfort-women/.

Reddington, Frances P., and Betsy Wright Kreisel, editors. *Sexual Assault: The Victims, the Perpetrators, and the Criminal Justice System*. Carolina Academic Press, 2017.

Sanghera, Jasvinder. *Daughters of Shame*. Hodder and Stoughton, 2009.

———. *Shame*. Hodder and Stoughton, 2016.

———. *Shame Travels*. Hodder and Stoughton, 2011.

Sedem, Mina, and Laura Ferrer-Wreder. "Fear of the Loss of Honor: Implications of Honor-Based Violence for the Development of Youth and Their Families." *Child Youth Care Forum*, vol. 44, no. 2, Sept. 2014, pp. 225–37.

Sehgal, Parul. "Blood Lines." *The New Yorker*, 2 and 9 Jan. 2023, pp. 64–69.

Sexual Violence and Armed Conflict: United Nations Response. United Nations Division for the Advancement of Women / United Nations Department of Economic and Social Affairs, Apr. 1998, www.un.org/en/preventgenocide/rwanda/pdf/sexual-violence-and-armed-conflict-1998-UN-report.pdf.

Shandilya, Krupa. "Nirbhaya's Body: The Politics of Protest in the Aftermath of the 2012 Delhi Gang Rape." *Gender and History*, vol. 27, no. 2, Aug. 2015, pp. 465–86.

Sharlach, Lisa. "Rape as Genocide: Bangladesh, the Former Yugoslavia, and Rwanda." *New Political Science*, vol. 22, no. 1, Mar. 2000, pp. 89–102.

Shusenjo: The Main Battleground of the Comfort Woman Issue. Directed by Miki Dezaki, First Run Features, 2018.

Soh, C. Sarah. *The Comfort Women: Sexual Violence and Postcolonial Memory in Korea and Japan*. U of Chicago P, 2008.

Stanley, Amy, et al. "'Contracting for Sex in the Pacific War': The Case for Retraction on Grounds of Academic Misconduct." *Asia-Pacific Journal: Japan Focus*, vol. 19, no. 5, 1 Mar. 2021, apjjf.org/2021/5/ConcernedScholars.html.

Stetz, Margaret D., and Bonnie B. C. Oh, editors. *Legacies of the Comfort Women of World War II*. Routledge, 2001.

Stevenson, Alexandra, and Zixu Wang. "Battling Violence and Censors, Women in China Become 'Invisible and Absent.'" *The New York Times*, 6 Sept. 2022, www.nytimes.com/2022/09/06/business/china-women-metoo.html.

Stokes, Katherine May. *Sexual Violence and the Authority to Speak: The Representation of Rape in Three Contemporary Novels*. 2008. McGill U, PhD dissertation.

Suzuki, Michiko. "Writing Women and Sexuality: Tamura Toshiko and Sata Ineko." *Handbook of Modern and Contemporary Japanese Women Writers*, edited by Rebecca Copeland, Amsterdam UP, 2023, pp. 97–112.

Thoma, Pamela. "'Such an Unthinkable Thing': Asian American Transnational Feminism and the 'Comfort Women of World War II' Conference." Stetz and Oh, pp. 101–27.

Ueno, Chizuko. *Nationalism and Gender*. Translated by Beverly Yamamoto, Trans Pacific Press, 2004.

Ullman, Sarah E. "Multiple Perpetrator Rape Victimization." *Handbook on the Study of Multiple Perpetrator Rape*, edited by Miranda A. H. Horvath and Jessica Woodhams, Routledge, 2013, pp. 198–213.

Urban, Lynn, and Sherri Dioguardi. "Sex Trafficking." Reddington and Kreisel, pp. 57–83.

Villanueva, Marianne. "The Mayor of the Roses." Yamada, pp. 254–62.

Violence against Women Prevalence Estimates, 2018: Global, Regional and National Prevalence Estimates for Intimate Partner Violence against Women and Global and Regional Prevalence Estimates for Non-Partner Sexual Violence against Women. World Health Organization, 2021.

Wilkerson, Isabel. *Caste: The Origins of Our Discontents*. Random House, 2020.

Yamada, Teri Shaffer, editor. *Virtual Lotus: Modern Fiction of Southeast Asia*. U of Michigan P, 2002.

Yamamoto, Beverly. "Translator's Introduction." *Nationalism and Gender*, by Ueno Chizuko, Trans Pacific Press, 2004, pp. vii–xxxi.

Yang, Hyunah. "Revisiting the Issue of Korean 'Military Comfort Women': The Question of Truth and Positionality." *Positions*, vol. 5, no. 1, spring 1997, pp. 51–71.

Yasir, Sameer. "She Told Relatives She'd Been Raped. They Paraded Her and the Suspect." *The New York Times*, 31 Mar. 2021, www.nytimes.com/2021/03/31/world/asia/india-rape-paraded.html.

Yoda, Tomiko. "Feminine Aspiration, Feminine Malaise: Kirino Natsuo's *Grotesque* and the Tōden OL Debates." *Boundary 2*, vol. 42, no. 3, Aug. 2015, pp. 185–99.

Yoon, Emily Jungmin. *A Cruelty Special to Our Species*. HarperCollins Publishers, 2018.

Yoon, Young-Shil [Miya Qiong Xie]. "'Places' in East Asia and Deterritorialization of Modern Korean Literature—Focusing on Narratives of Korean Comfort Women." *The Journal of Korean Fiction*, no. 60, Aug. 2017, pp. 79–120.

Yun Ko-Eun. *The Disaster Tourist*. Translated by Lizzie Buehler, Counterpoint, 2020.

6. Perpetuating and Interrupting Cycles of Family Violence

While Sarbjit Kaur Athwal's primary focus in the memoir *Shamed*, discussed in the previous chapter, is honor-based violence, Athwal also reveals that both she and her sister-in-law were subjected to considerable family violence, generally understood as physical, sexual, psychological, emotional, verbal, and financial abuse within families. Severely impacting individuals of every gender, age, race, ethnicity, and education and socioeconomic level, family violence is widespread in Asia and its diasporas, as in most communities around the world. Child abuse is particularly common: writing in 2016, Susan Hillis and colleagues estimate that at least 64% of children in Asia aged two to 17 experienced violence in the previous year, including physical, emotional, and sexual abuse, as well as bullying and witnessing violence (6).[1] Globally, half the world's children between two and 17 experience some form of violence annually (1). Violence against children, which increased with the COVID-19 pandemic, imposes significant and enduring economic, emotional, health, and social consequences, making prevention, rapid response, and elimination especially urgent (*Global Status Report* 1–2).

Elder abuse, which also increased during the COVID-19 pandemic, is another widespread form of family violence. Already affecting millions of individuals globally, albeit with substantial variation among communities, cultures, and nations, the numbers of elders abused is expected to grow quickly as the world's population ages more rapidly than ever before (Pillemer et al. S194, S202; Yan et al.). This is particularly true of Asia, where by 2050, nearly 25% of the population will be at least age 60 (Yan et al. 199). Violence against the elderly can include emotional, financial, physical, psychological, and sexual abuse as well as abandonment, neglect, and affronts to dignity; individuals who experience elder abuse are twice as likely to die prematurely as those who do not ("Abuse"). At the same time, understandings of what constitutes elder abuse differ among cultures. For example, unlike many Western societies, many Asian societies believe disrespecting elders is a serious form of abuse. On the other hand, some Asian societies tolerate or even expect what some Western societies might consider financial exploitation of elders (Yan et al. 200–01). Research points to adult sons and daughters-in-law as the primary perpetrators of elder abuse in Asia (215), even as in some communities, including Athwal's, daughters-in-law are themselves frequently subjected to family violence.

Although all genders experience family violence, with transgender and nonbinary individuals the most vulnerable, girls and women, particularly those who are already marginalized, are the largest groups at significant risk (Bhattacharya 1). Girls face feticide, sex-selective abortion, and infanticide; physical abuse, rape, incest, and neglect within their natal homes; and violence perpetrated by their in-laws after marrying and moving in with their husband's family.[2] Elderly women tend to be at greater risk than their male counterparts ("Women"). Family violence is frequently intergenerational and multidirectional. Individuals who directly experience or witness violence within the home, particularly as children or young adults, suffer disproportionately from cognitive, developmental, and behavioral challenges (Nelson et al. 212). They are also at greater risk of later becoming perpetrators of violence, including against family members (e.g., their mothers, younger siblings) who have also been abused by other family members (Lansford et al.; Meyer et al. 477–78; Widom 187, 196). Family violence often intersects with other forms of gender-based violence, including reproductive violence, stranger and social violence, and intimate partner violence, discussed in chapters 4, 5, and 7, respectively.

This chapter focuses on four powerful narratives published between 1995 and 2015 by courageous women from across Asia and Asian diasporas on the subjectivities of girls and women grappling with intergenerational violence, intersectional family violence, or both. Three of these narratives depict individuals traumatized by family violence who take justice into their own hands by themselves perpetrating violence, highlighting the intergenerational impacts of trauma and offering insights into the inner lives and motivations of those who perpetuate family violence. The Bangladeshi diaspora writer and gender scholar Tisa Muhaddes's shocking short story "Over and Over Again" (2009) is narrated by a wealthy young Bangladeshi woman who is plagued by memories of being molested by her uncle and who retaliates by murdering his young daughter.[3] The Indian writer Kishwar Desai's daring novel *Witness the Night* (2010) lays bare the horrors of an Indian teenager accused of murdering thirteen members from three generations of her affluent and well-educated family, which has a long history of feticide, infanticide, and violence against girls and women.

"Over and Over Again" and *Witness the Night* draw attention to the devastating impacts family violence can have on children, driving some to participate in unspeakable violence that further intensifies their own and their family's trauma.[4] The semi-autobiographical family novel *Bloodline* (*Bainian xuemai*, 百年血脉, lit. *Hundred-Year Bloodline*, 2015), by the award-winning Uyghur-Hui-Han Chinese writer Patigül (1965–), discusses family violence, primarily but not entirely against women, of even greater scale. Covering a century in the life of her Uyghur-Hui-Han Chinese family, the first-person narrator describes multiple cycles of family violence against and committed by children, siblings, parents, spouses, in-laws, elders, and individuals suffering from both mental and physical illnesses. Notably, although Patigül's narrator explicitly denounces violence among different ethnic groups, giving a privileged view into her own family dynamics, she goes so far as to justify violence within individual families, suggesting that family violence cannot be mitigated without diminishing interethnic violence.

In contrast with Muhaddes's, Desai's, and Patigül's narratives, other contemporary Asian narratives focus on individuals subjected to family violence who deliberately interrupt cycles of abuse. These include the short story "Motijan's Daughters" ("Matijānera Meyerā," মতিজানের মেয়েরা, 1995), by the acclaimed Bangladeshi writer Selina Hossain (1947–), which features a Bangladeshi woman who defies the demands of her abusive mother-in-law and seeks justice by empowering her young daughters, even while the third-person narrator accentuates the woman's vulnerability. The narratives discussed in this chapter aesthetically highlight diverse and singular experiences of family violence in Asia and beyond. They creatively draw attention both to social structures that perpetuate family and other forms of violence within and across generations and to the impacts of this abuse on individuals, exposing how thoroughly amelioration and justice are compromised.

Escalating Violence: Tisa Muhaddes's "Over and Over Again" (2009)

Most research on child sexual abuse and exploitation in Bangladesh focuses on reducing and ultimately eliminating child trafficking and child marriage. These abuses disproportionately affect girls and are often enabled if not arranged by family members, not unlike the collaboration of local families in procuring so-called comfort women, exposed in writings that include scholarship by C. Sarah Soh and the South Korean novelist Kim Soom's *One Left*, discussed in chapter 5. Research also centers on improving the bleak conditions of girls serving as domestic workers, who frequently are abused by their employers, regardless of gender, not unlike the plight of the migrant reproductive workers examined in chapter 3.[5] The *National Children Policy 2011* published by the Bangladesh Ministry of Women and Children Affairs declares "elimination of all forms of child abuse and discrimination" a fundamental principle (4). The policy also calls for eliminating discrimination between boys and girls and ensuring gender equality in the family (11–12). Yet it says nothing about child sexual abuse and exploitation perpetrated by family members. In Bangladesh, as in many parts of the world, this type of violence often goes unreported, shrouded in cultures of silence and shame (Islam and Akhter). Narratives such as Muhaddes's "Over and Over Again" creatively help break silences surrounding such abuses and their aftermaths.[6]

"Over and Over Again" is narrated in the first person by a young woman overwhelmed by memories of being molested as a child by her pedophile uncle and of her ayah (nanny) forcing her to apologize to him. Desperate to "make the world all right again," the narrator pushes her young cousin Anju (her uncle's daughter) to her death off the roof of the family home. The sight of her uncle clutching a picture of his deceased daughter and "attempting to fathom the injustice of his loss" causes the narrator to sigh vengefully "with a relief that seemed twenty years too late" (Muhaddes 101). Yet the following and final sentence of the story suggests that the narrator already regrets her actions. Through its narrative and aesthetic strategies, including multilingualism, "Over and Over Again" highlights the devastating and exponentially multiplying long-term impacts of incest and other forms of child sexual assault—both on the individual who has been abused and on other vulnerable people.

The narrator of Muhaddes's short story reveals that even years after her uncle stopped molesting her, there is no escaping the trauma of his abuse. She describes "shards of memory" as not unlike forced sexual penetration. Speaking explicitly, she writes that these "shards" "rear their heads from the depths of an abysmal darkness, pricking and piercing me mercilessly with their truth. . . . Random scenes unfold like parts of a film that I cannot piece together, yet am forced to replay over and over again in my mind" (Muhaddes 98). The narrator shares one particularly painful memory: "He had me pinned against the bed. . . . His free hand was roaming, meandering its insistent way over my sullied skin. He gently lowered his body on top of mine. . . . He placed a hand gently over my mouth and whispered '*Eita shudhu ador* . . . this is only affection' over and over again" (100). After he rapes her, with her nanny banging on the door, he repeats, "[E]*ita shudhu ador* . . . this is only affection . . ." (100–01). In Bengali, the word *ador* (*ādar*) often refers to cuddling, as a family member would cuddle a small child, although *ador* can also refer to sexual touching among adults. Attempting to mislead the narrator into thinking his actions innocent, the uncle clarifies in English his Bengali utterance.[7] Moreover, entering the room, the narrator's nanny chastises her and demands she apologize to her uncle "for ruining his afternoon nap." Even after she spots "the crumpled bed, the milky puddle, and [the narrator's] frozen state," the nanny says nothing (101). "Over and Over Again" contrasts Anju's "catatonic father," Anju's "desperately" pleading mother, and the "caravan of women" who commiserate with one another over Anju's death and proclaim it a "tragedy . . . a dreadful tragedy" (98) with the complete indifference toward the narrator's trauma.

After revealing both her uncle's abuse and her nanny's complicity, the narrator remarks that she "cannot remember other episodes, or even if there were any more" (Muhaddes 101). This differs from her statement in the opening paragraphs of "Over and Over Again" that she was "six when he started" and that the molestation "was never in a dark room" (98), utterances that suggest repeated assaults. Yet even this one episode has left indelible scars across and within her body, the narrator asserting that "his stench, his kisses on my shoulders, on my chest, on my arms, on my legs, in my secret crevices—those I cannot clean away" (101). The continuously replaying "shards of memory" that prick and pierce the narrator from within cannot exit her body, smothered as she is by her uncle's stench. Intensifying the narrator's pain is the knowledge that she has killed an innocent girl, whose frail cocooned body still lies in a corner of the bedroom.

The story's title phrase, "over and over again," first refers to the memories of abuse that mercilessly assault the narrator (Muhaddes 99) and then to her uncle's repeated "whispering" justification of his abuse (100). Similarly, the novel's final phrase—"whispering silently, 'It wasn't my fault, it wasn't my fault' over and over again" (101)—finds the narrator paradoxically attempting to justify her own heinous crime. Bookending Muhaddes's story as its first and final words, the phrase "over and over again" points to both the repetition of abuse and the repeated silencing of abuse. At the same time, narrated in the first person, "Over and Over Again" reveals the voice of the narrator as no longer "mute" and "smothered in the embers of unspoken thought" (98), no longer "whispering silently," but instead as unveiling the severe and reverberating impacts of child sexual assault.

Manipulating Violence: Kishwar Desai's *Witness the Night* (2010)

Similar to Muhaddes's "Over and Over Again," Desai's *Witness the Night*—the first novel in the Simran Singh trilogy, the second and third of which are discussed in chapters 4 and 5, respectively—movingly depicts a young woman, Durga Atwal, who violently retaliates against family violence.[8] Yet the scale of violence has increased significantly from Muhaddes's short story. *Witness the Night* explicitly links the abuse to which Durga has been exposed and subjected to generations of violence against girls and women in her own affluent family in Punjab (northern India) and in families of all socioeconomic levels across India (e.g., female feticide, sex-selective abortion, infanticide, and child abuse as well as intimate partner violence). Moreover, Durga herself is charged with murdering thirteen of her family members (her parents, grandmother, two brothers, aunts, and cousins), most if not all of whom were abusers. To be sure, unlike the unnamed narrator of "Over and Over Again," Durga has a fierce advocate, a social worker named Simran who is asked by the inspector general of Punjab to help police assess Durga's mental health. Recognizing that Durga has been pushed into the "dark world" both by her family and by outsiders seeking to take advantage of her vulnerability, Simran facilitates Durga's release from an abhorrent mental health facility and is determined to help her become "a normal independent working woman" (Desai 240). Yet just as in Muhaddes's short story, the novel ends ominously, with Durga deeply traumatized and feeling anything but "normal," despite Simran's best efforts.

Child abuse is common in India: surveys reveal that at least half of the nation's children experience emotional, physical, or sexual violence (Seth 707). Even greater numbers of children are neglected, largely a result of adverse socioeconomic circumstances (707). Violence against girls is particularly extreme and begins in utero with sex-selective abortions. India's ratio of boys to girls age six and under has been rising steadily, from 102.4 males per 100 females in 1961 to 108.8 males per 100 females in 2011, in large part a result of increasingly accessible ultrasound technology. In some northwestern states the imbalance is as high as 118 males per 100 females

(Punjab) and 120 males per 100 females (Haryana; Seth 709). Often, violence against girls within the family continues throughout childhood and ultimately a woman's entire life. As Rashmi Dube Bhatnagar and colleagues argue, "[T]he modern holocaust of femicide" in India "signifies not only the serial killing of female fetuses but also girl-child murder by negligence through discriminatory practices such as uneven food allocation . . . access to medical care, family resources, and minimum survival needs" (3). Moreover, "[t]he victims of female infanticide are not only the aborted female fetus" but also "the girl child, the birthing mother, and the infanticide survivors who grow up with the knowledge that they and their female siblings survived attempts to murder them" (3).[9]

Desai published *Witness the Night* in 2010, shortly after the Indian government began taking a more active role in reducing female feticide and child abuse more broadly. To give several examples, the 1994 Pre-Natal Diagnostic Techniques (Regulation and Prevention of Misuse) Act was amended in 2003 as the Pre-Conception and Pre-Natal Diagnostic Techniques (Prohibition of Sex Selection) Act. India established the National Commission for Protection of Child Rights in 2007, and in 2009 the Indian government set up the Integrated Child Protection Scheme, recognizing that "child protection is a primary responsibility of the family, supported by community, government and civil society" (Seth 711). In 2012 India passed the Protection of Children from Sexual Offences Act, India's first comprehensive law regarding the sexual victimization of children. The act aimed to help Indians "overcome the traditional inimical attitudes of silence and shame and take appropriate educative measures to prevent CSA [Child Sexual Abuse]" (Seth and Srivastava 953). Through its focus on a single family and particularly a vulnerable teenage girl within this broader context, Desai's novel highlights both the necessity of eradicating child abuse and the structural barriers impeding eradication.

Witness the Night alternates between first-person italicized passages from Durga's diary, which open each chapter; Simran's first-person narrative in roman type, which comes in the middle of each chapter; and emails between Simran and Binny (Durga's sister-in-law, who lives in the United Kingdom), which end each chapter. Unlike Muhaddes's "Over and Over Again," in which the narrator tells her own story despite initially describing her voice as "smothered in the embers of unspoken thoughts" (98), Desai's narrative structure prioritizes Simran's voice over the voices of the two other women, allowing Simran to selectively curate what the reader learns about Binny and especially Durga.

At the same time, Durga is a powerful writer who in her diary graphically exposes a long family history of horrific abuse and its deep impact on generations of individual girls and women. She writes compellingly about her older sister Sharda, who five years earlier had been sent to a psychiatric hospital for becoming pregnant at 16 outside marriage by the family's tutor, Harpreet, explicitly connecting attempted infanticide with Sharda's current confinement: "They tried to do everything they had done to her when she had been born" (Desai 94).

Durga later places Sharda's abuse in larger context, describing in her diary how she had gradually discovered

> the most savage part of my family history, how my great grandmother had been told that she would have to leave the main house when she gave birth to the sixth daughter in a row. A great tradition of culling out girl children that we maintain till today for ourselves and for others through the clinics we run, where tests are conducted, and babies are aborted. They are buried without fanfare in the fields around the house. (Desai 161)

Soon thereafter, Durga asks rhetorically about her own story, before describing what happened to her as an infant: "What had been my story? I imagined myself—a tiny child, as yet not even able to suckle—being fed opium. . . . I can still feel the earth being shoveled onto me" (181). Even as she writes (part of) her story, Durga asks about her story, pointing to years of (attempted) silencing and how close she came to dying after being buried alive, only slightly more fortunate than generations of female infants who preceded her and with whom she draws a direct parallel.

Durga also speaks about the abuse experienced by her mother, who despite being able to "discuss the suffragette movement and women's votes in a posh English accent had been beaten into submission. . . . It was the way things were . . . and how they would remain forever" (Desai 180). Here Durga echoes the protagonist of Meena Kandasamy's *When I Hit You; or, A Portrait of the Writer as a Young Wife* (2017), discussed in chapter 7, who speaks explicitly of the impotence of Western feminist theory in addressing gender-based violence. She also reveals deep pessimism regarding possibilities for change. Notably, the greatest enabler of Durga's father was his mother, Durga's grandmother, who had discarded her own infant daughters in the Beas River and, like Athwal's mother-in-law in *Shamed*, discussed in chapter 5, and the mother-in-law in Hossain's "Motijan's Daughters," discussed below, "did not conceal her deep dislike for her daughter-in-law's inability to produce the male heir" (Desai 180).

Binny corroborates Durga's portrayal of her family, emailing Simran, "No one ever spoke to her [Durga]. Her father was incredibly cruel to her. She was made to feel like a complete idiot" (Desai 109). Later in the novel, in another email to Simran, Binny remarks, "The moment I arrived in Jullundur I realized what an obsession these people have with their sons" (155). And she fears for her unborn child: "The pressure was already building on me to abort the baby as my father-in-law spoke about the need for a small compact family. My mother-in-law tried to tell me how it would be nice for my parents as well if the firstborn were a son" (159). Refusing to visit the local clinic, Binny escapes back to her home in Southall, West London. Simran explains, "Not so long ago, the midwives used to take away newborn girls from their mothers, seal them in earthen pots and roll the pot around till the baby stopped crying. Or they would simply suffocate them. Or give them opium and then bury them. . . . In a recent incident, a woman confessed to having had seven abortions in the hope of a boy" (63). Indeed, little has changed, despite the fact that women now hold leadership positions. Simran wonders, "Shouldn't I be more upbeat? We had had a woman prime minister, we had a woman president, we had women representatives everywhere. But had things really changed? . . . This morning I had yet again read about a woman being stripped naked and branded a witch paraded around a village in Uttar Pradesh" (63–64). Later, Simran reflects on a recent conversation with her mother, who had shared that she, like many women, had been encouraged to starve her baby daughter, "because if a child dies of malnutrition you can't be charged with murder. You just say, she refused to feed, what can I do?" (149). Simran observes, "Now things were more sophisticated than during my mother's pregnancy. In the twenty-first century, female children were killed as part of a package deal, while within the womb, during the pre-natal checkup" (149).

With legal measures wholly inadequate to counteract entrenched cultural norms, India's criminal justice system further victimizes survivors of abuse. From the beginning, Simran believes the evidence against Durga "too obvious" (Desai 5), and the more she investigates, the more she becomes convinced that Durga, who was herself poisoned, raped, and tied up the night her family was killed, could not have committed thirteen murders alone (185). And indeed, Simran's sleuthing ultimately reveals that Harpreet, the family's tutor, had orchestrated the slaughter of

Durga's family. He had groomed Durga to "avenge the cruelties inflicted on Sharda. . . . The helpless child who pined for affection [Durga] fell into the trap as she was twisted and turned like a plastic doll and bent into shape by the gentle lover. . . . [Harpreet] pushed and pushed at her until she reached the point of complete submission to his demands" (224–25). At the same time, there is no justice for Durga. As Desai highlights in the author's note on the novel's final page, although the characters in *Witness the Night* are "entirely fictional," the events described are not: "There is a complicity of corruption between the police, the judicial system, politicians, media and the uncivil society. . . . [G]ender issues are still treated with contempt" (243).[10]

Witness the Night concludes ominously. To be sure, Durga and Sharda move in with Simran and her mother, and Simran's mother is no longer so adamant about Simran getting married. Simran is determined to help Durga heal and follow her childhood dream of having a meaningful life and career. Simran also provides Sharda with a therapist who sees her daily, no small feat in a nation with fewer than three psychiatrists per million and where patients in mental health facilities are regularly "abused, beaten, chained, and tortured" and "given electric shocks without anesthesia" (Desai 120). Yet Durga's final diary entry reveals that although being encouraged to forgive herself, love herself, and "start this new life" (235), she remains consumed by gruesome memories and by rage that makes her want "to slash and tear and hurt and wound . . . in exactly the same way in which those poor little babies were wounded" (235–36). Moreover, Harpreet has just reached out to her, and his "soft voice still echoes in my ears. . . . I know you say I was very young but I wanted it all, I wanted him and, yes, I think I even wanted them all dead. Can I ever tell you that? Will you listen?" (237). Durga admits in her diary aspects of herself she cannot vocalize and shares her doubts that others will listen to her. In the novel's final lines, Binny emails Simran, writing that Harpreet has come to her home in Southall and that Binny and her infant daughter are smitten with him. For much of *Witness the Night*, except for Simran's reference to the Billie-Jo Margaret Jenkins case (11), England—as former colonial power—is framed as "a site of refuge" quite distinct from India (Morgan 725).[11] But Harpreet's email to Durga and arrival in Southall as well as Durga's final diary entry are sober reminders that no space is safe from violent family members and that just as in Athwal's *Shamed*, family violence is not deterred by national borders or systems of justice.

Imploding Violence: Patigül's *Bloodline* (2015)

As with Desai's *Witness the Night*, Patigül's semi-autobiographical *Bloodline* graphically describes decades of horrific intergenerational and intersectional brutality, although this time against all genders in a Uyghur-Hui-Han family.[12] In so doing, the novel reveals seldom studied aspects of women's lives in China's Muslim Uyghur and Muslim Hui communities, two of China's 56 ethnic groups, as well as the particular challenges faced by the small minority of individuals who are of mixed heritage.[13] To be sure, in recent years, the international media have reported frequently on intensifying Han Chinese oppression of Uyghurs, particularly in the Xinjiang Uyghur Autonomous Region (northwestern China); increased Islamic insurgency and the revival of Uyghur nationalism; Uyghur attacks on Han Chinese, both police and civilians; and alleged Uyghur connections with the Taliban, al-Qaeda, and the Islamic State (Zang 1). Moreover, considerable research has been done on family violence in Islamic societies (25). In addition, there is a growing corpus of scholarship on family violence in China (Niu and Laidler 93; Wan et al. 1299–300). But only limited attention has been given to intimate partner violence, child abuse, and other forms of family violence in late-twentieth- and early-twenty-first-century China's Uyghur communities (Zang 25, 46). The situation is similar for research on the Hui (Niu and Laidler 93).[14]

An unfortunate side effect of *Bloodline*'s exposé of Uyghur and Hui family and intimate partner violence is that such an exposé reinforces Han Chinese stereotypes of ethnic minorities. The Chinese state has long depicted these communities as "backward" and "primitive," inferior to Han Chinese because of their "lower level of development" (Zang 139). Uyghurs are particularly disadvantaged for having "jealously guarded their linguistic and cultural traits of distinction from the Han" (Friedrichs 59).[15] At the same time, Patigül's narrator does not leave Han Chinese unscathed, instead depicting violence against women as endemic across ethnicities. Moreover, the narrator points to hardships faced by Hui and particularly Uyghurs because of Han Chinese ethnic policies; intergroup inequalities are depicted as exacerbating Hui and Uyghur violence against women.[16]

Covering a tumultuous century of her multiethnic family's life across China, the narrator of *Bloodline*, born in the mid-1960s, first focuses on 1993 and 2013 (parts 1 and 2), then moves back to 1960–85 (parts 3 and 4) and then to 1910–60 (part 5), before finishing in 2014, the present (part 6 and afterword). This narrative strategy draws attention to the painful consistency of gender-based and other forms of violence throughout the twentieth and into the twenty-first century. It also compels readers to amend their assumptions and highlights the importance of understanding historical contingencies. *Bloodline* opens with the narrator leaving Qochek, a small town near China's border with Kazakhstan, where she has worked as a journalist for the last decade. While in a drunken haze, she is groped by her colleague Su Feng. The narrator reveals that earlier, she and Su Feng had collaborated on a story about a local village chief's attempted rape of a Hui Muslim girl and that Su Feng had made her so uncomfortable that she had done her best to avoid being alone with him. Just as the narrator is thanking Su Feng for driving her to Ürümqi (the capital of Xinjiang), he attacks and rapes her, the narrator revealing her dehumanization: "I felt like I was being torn to pieces; ripped up like a piece of paper" (Patigül, *Bloodline*).[17]

The brutality of this encounter, which resonates with what fellow journalist Itō Shiori exposes in *Black Box*, discussed in chapter 5, pales in comparison with the violence the narrator describes as taking place within her family. When the narrator was a child, her maternal grandmother, channeling her hatred for her son-in-law, declared the narrator "as ugly as your Pa [given his Uyghur facial features]. . . .You look like a feral cat. . . . I wish I could gouge out your [yellow] eyes, and put black ones in their place" (Patigül, *Bloodline*). For as long as she can remember, the narrator joined her father and siblings in calling her mother not "Ma" but "Pockface Ma," given how smallpox had ravaged her mother's appearance. Her mother also suffered from serious mental illness, and from earliest childhood the narrator imitated other family members in verbally disparaging and physically beating her. Even after her father died and the narrator took over her mother's care, the only one of her siblings willing to do so, she was caught in a cycle of intergenerational violence that she explicitly justified: "At any time and in any place, I was liable to a fit of the temper passed down to me by my father. . . . I was punishing her *on behalf of father*. . . . Beating her was right and proper." The beatings continued until her mother disappeared in the early 1990s. This violence is particularly noteworthy given the narrator's obsession throughout with bloodlines, and fear that, after her brother Simayil, she would be next to succumb to mental illness, not unlike Durga in Desai's *Witness the Night*.

On top of assaulting the narrator's mother and the many other women with whom he had had relationships (some believe him to have had sixteen wives, all of whom he abused), the narrator's father also regularly beat the narrator and her three siblings:

> [My mother] had fed me, and in return I'd beaten her. But I was destined to behave that way, because that was the family I'd been born into. It might be hard for an outsider to understand but, in our family, we were cruel to one another. Our father thrashed us with his leather whip, and my brothers and I slapped our mother to vent our unhappiness. And so, right from the start, we learnt these barbaric ways of interacting, and no one ever stepped into teach us any different. (Patigül, *Bloodline*)[18]

Here, too, the narrator rationalizes this family violence as part of a longstanding pattern of abuse.[19] She also, particularly in the Chinese version of *Bloodline*, points to the very different heritages of China's Han and Muslim ethnic minority populations (Patigül, *Bainian xuemai*), even as family violence is prevalent in both communities.

In addition to describing the violence within her natal family, the narrator speaks of her cruelty toward Su Feiya, her daughter with her abusive ex-husband, Mi Fu.[20] Su Feiya had been separated from her mother for much of her childhood, Mi Fu and his family falsely claiming that the narrator was unable to care for her. When Su Feiya was finally reunited with her mother, who had moved with her abusive second husband and former rapist, Su Feng, to Zhejiang Province (southeastern China), the narrator's attempts to have Su Feiya reject the Mi family backfired spectacularly: "[Su Feiya's] pain stemmed entirely from my inability to forgive [the Mi family]. . . . It was a vicious cycle. She was no angel, and I was certainly no saint. It was demon pitted against demon—the same blood running in our veins" (Patigül, *Bloodline*).[21] The narrator knew she should have more empathy for her daughter, given the narrator's own earlier difficulties transitioning from life in the West of China to life in the Southeast, but instead, "I had become a mean and vindictive person, wielding insults like weapons. . . . We were two lab mice, biting each other after receiving electric shocks. The stronger the current, the more vicious our combat. I felt no pity as I watched her struggle. She had no way to escape and I knew that better than anyone, because it was I who had caged her."[22] Here, as in many narratives, including Desai's *Witness the Night* and Kim Soom's *One Left*, discussed in chapter 5, animal metaphors highlight the dehumanization of more vulnerable individuals, particularly women and girls. The narrator also occasionally beats Mardan, her son with Su Feng. These attacks are far less frequent than the narrator's abuse of Su Feiya, and Mardan criticizes the narrator for being so relentless with his half-sister.

Significantly, Mardan is the only member of the family who has fully assimilated into Han culture:

> Mardan was a poster boy for cultural assimilation. He adapted easily to life in the south, the language, the customs, the food. . . . A few short generations and here was Mardan, taking to mainstream Chinese culture like a duck to water. He wasn't conflicted like we'd been. I no longer worried that he'd inherit the unstable traits of my mother and elder brother. . . . From my great-grandfather, my grandfather, and my mother, all the way down to me, there'd been such struggles to reconcile matters of ethnicity, religion, and where we came from. But that all ended with Mardan. He was balanced and straightforward in his affections, and he extended that warmth to his sister too.
>
> (Patigül, *Bloodline*)[23]

Mardan is very different from Su Feiya's other half-brother, Mi Fu's son with his second wife, Ma Fen. Both young men are attracted to Han women, but while Mardan enjoys a lighthearted relationship with his Han girlfriend, Su Feiya's other half-brother torments the Han woman who is "head-over-heels in love" with him but whom he is prohibited from dating. *Bloodline* suggests it is precisely Mardan's ease in navigating multiple cultures that enables him to reject violence and experience joy. He is unlike the other members of his family, including the narrator, who had fallen in love with a Han Chinese man only to be physically attacked by her father, who insisted she marry Mi Fu. Mardan by no means rejects his cultural heritage. Proclaiming "They'll be luckier than us! There's nothing to regret," he suggests to his half-sister Su Feiya that they send their respective future children to Kashgar to live with their extended family, so that the children can become fluent in both Uyghur and Mandarin. Yet he evades the staggering mental toll on individuals who cannot or will not assimilate.

The narrator's maternal grandmother had warned her that after marriage "your blood mixes. . . . It stays in your body, cutting through your flesh like a knife. Boring into you like nails" (Patigül, *Bloodline*).[24] And the narrator's father had been determined that his children forcibly assimilate themselves to Chinese language and culture, like "nails hammered into a plank of wood." This type of forced assimilation, accentuated by the family's figurative language, differs considerably from the integration Mardan experiences, not to mention what he hopes for his children. It also is very different from the assimilation experienced by the narrator's maternal grandfather, born Han and adopted into a Hui household, something the narrator is told only very belatedly. In the novel's afterword, Patigül steps in and underscores the importance of recognizing that "we are all parts of the same body. When one of us suffers, we all suffer. . . . We are all interconnected, and affect one another with our actions." Patigül speaks of her great-grandfather adopting the child of his Han enemy as "an example of humanity transcending ethnicity." She argues that as gaps between cultures in China are "steadily narrowing," "compassion and virtue should not be trapped behind fences." But neither Patigül nor her first-person narrator addresses what happens in the absence of compassion, particularly toward children, the elderly, and those grappling with mental or physical illness. For its part, *Bloodline* reveals that these individuals are even more vulnerable to the violence of family members who share their blood than to the violence of people of other ethnicities.[25]

Defying Violence: Selina Hossain's "Motijan's Daughters" (1995)

As exposed in Athwal's *Shamed*, discussed in chapter 5, in some families, daughters-in-law are the most vulnerable, and the most violent abusers are their parents-in-law.[26] Conflicts between daughters- and parents-in-law, especially mothers-in-law, are common in many parts of the world, regardless of culture, ethnicity, education, socioeconomic status, or other factors. But, as evident in *Shamed* and in Desai's *Witness the Night*—in which Durga's grandmother abuses her daughter-in-law, Durga's mother, and in which Binny hurries back to Southall before her in-laws can force her to have an abortion—the risk that these struggles will turn violent increases significantly in communities where women are believed considerably inferior to men, where women's families are expected to provide dowries, and in patrilocal communities where women move in with their husband's family after marriage. Geetanjali Gangoli and Martin Rew's observations regarding mother-in-law abuse of daughters-in-law in India—namely, that this type of female-on-female violence "not only serves male interests in dividing women, but also uses older women to control younger ones in the family" (422)—generally hold true for Bangladesh. As Rew and colleagues argue, violence against daughters-in-law "is often legally subsumed under the label of dowry violence . . . minimizing and often rendering invisible the impact of the specific roles that women play in perpetuating patriarchal power and control in all aspects of household affairs" (156).

In "Motijan's Daughters," Hossain spotlights some of the roles women play in perpetuating patriarchal power.[27] The third-person narrator does not specify when or where this story takes place, but "Motijan's Daughters" reflects attitudes and practices prevalent in Bangladesh when the story was published in 1995. As the 1993 document *Human Rights Briefs: Women in Bangladesh* articulates, "Bangladeshi women are valued less than both children and property." Girls were frequently forced into arranged marriages as teenagers and were chastised for giving birth to daughters; female infants, toddlers, and young girls were given less food than their male siblings, were at increased risk of malnutrition and disease, and were less likely than boys to receive medical care; women's literacy was only 20%, and women's job opportunities were extremely limited; and violence against women—including rape, sexual exploitation, abduction, and kidnapping—was high, despite the 1983 Cruelty to Women Act (*Human Rights Briefs*).[28]

Hossain's perceptive story "Motijan's Daughters" centers on Motijan, a young woman forced into marriage by her father and then abused both by her husband, Abul, and, even more severely, by Gulnoor, her mother-in-law. Gulnoor became a widow when her son was just a toddler and managed the family and their property alone with an "iron" ("śakta"/"shakta"; lit. "strong" or "tough") hand for more than two decades ("Motijan's Daughters" 98; "Matijānera Meyerā"). She is known in the village as a "hard" ("śakta"/"shakta") woman, a designation in which she takes great pride ("Motijan's Daughters" 98–99). The term "śakta," also written as "shakta," appears frequently in the Bengali version of "Motijan's Daughters" and can have both a negative (as in "rigid" or "stubborn") and positive (as in "hardy" or "capable") connotation. Moreover, as Aniket De has noted, "[i]n Bengali, it is not uncommon to describe women's character in the ecological idiom of 'soft soil' (*naram mati*) and, its opposite, 'hard' (*shakta*) soil." Livid that Motijan's father has not delivered the promised dowry—a wristwatch and a cycle, items Motijan knows her father cannot afford—Gulnoor transitions from attacking her daughter-in-law by yelling "sharp words" that "often scorched [Motijan's] soul" ("Motijan's Daughters" 98) to dragging Motijan by her hair, throwing her to the ground, placing a rope around her neck, and tying her leg to a post (101).[29] In the evening, having deprived Motijan of food all day, Gulnoor drags her with the rope to the pond where she earlier had been forced to wash dishes and orders her to eat the grass, as though she were a cow (102). As with the narrator in Muhaddes's "Over and Over Again," there is no one to protect Motijan: she has virtually no contact with her birth family, and her husband, Abul, is rarely home and violent when he is at home, preferring cannabis and the company of other women and beating Motijan when she remonstrates with him (101).[30]

The third-person narrator of "Motijan's Daughters" describes how Motijan responds by herself growing resilient ("śakta"/"shakta"). At first, although she longs "to be as hard ["śakta"/"shakta"] as her mother-in-law" (99), Motijan is perpetually frightened, "scared to put her foot down anywhere, scared even to sneeze" (99–100). But anger at her father for forcing her into marriage to spare himself from losing face and for being "utterly humiliated" for having an unmarried daughter makes Motijan determined to "become a hard ["śakta"/"shakta"] woman" herself (101). And the more her mother-in-law abuses her, the more Motijan resolves to "turn into a hard ["śakta"/"shakta"] woman" (102). Gradually, through force of will, she does become more defiant. Her first act of resistance is to ignore Gulnoor's rebuke for her "unmannerly mirth." Instead, she continues laughing (103). However small, this act strengthens her resolve. Later that day, when Gulnoor again refuses to give her anything to eat, Motijan defiantly walks into the kitchen and consumes the meal her mother-in-law has made for her son. Immediately, Motijan feels "within her heart a surge of victory as though the waves of the Mahananda were tearing a path through a curtain of thick mist" (104).[31] Gulnoor is temporarily stunned into silence but, the surge of victory remaining figurative rather than actual, soon thereafter begins to berate Motijan for not yet giving birth.

Motijan responds by entering a clandestine relationship with her husband's friend Lokman and ultimately having a daughter with him. Not surprisingly, having warned Motijan that she "must bear a boy, or you'll suffer the consequences," Gulnoor refuses to acknowledge her granddaughter, and she is furious at how delighted Motijan is with her baby girl (Hossain, "Motijan's Daughters" 108). Yet the more Gulnoor rages, the more defiant Motijan becomes, the narrator describing how "she no longer remained silent but shouted back" (108). A year later, Motijan gives birth to her second daughter with Lokman. Caring for her children and doing all the household chores leaves her "nearly always overcome with fatigue and exhaustion" (109). One day, Gulnoor screams at Motijan in front of their neighbors, "the curses flying out of her mouth like fireworks," and declares that she will throw Motijan out of her house and find another wife for her son to continue the family line. In response, Motijan—holding her daughters close—laughs mockingly at her and reveals that Abul is not their father (109). Gulnoor stares at her daughter-in-law with "dilated, unbelieving eyes," and the story concludes, "From the safety of their mother's breast, Motijan's daughters glared at everyone before them" (109). Unbelieving stares at one are countered with glares at all by daughters supported by their mother.[32]

Motijan's strength is of a notably different type from that of her mother-in-law. Despite the severe abuse to which she is subjected, Motijan does not become violent. Moreover, she transforms her own family's indifference toward her, and her mother-in-law's hatred of her and her daughters, into deep love for her own children. She defies cycles of family violence and in so doing empowers her daughters. At the same time, Motijan's inner life, her story, is told for her; she is not the author of her own narrative. Moreover, Motijan's future is precarious, as is that of her daughters. To be sure, Gulnoor is likely to intensify her demand that her son divorce Motijan, liberating her from her abusive marriage. But it is doubtful Motijan can return to her impoverished natal family, given both social stigmas and economic realities.[33] And there is no mention of Lokman taking responsibility for his children or of the community stepping in to assist Motijan; the gathering crowd limits itself to softly murmuring. Motijan had once dreamed of earning her own living working with a friend at the village cooperative, but it is unclear whether this possibility remains. Even as "Motijan's Daughters" depicts cycles of family violence as being interrupted, the story stops short of depicting its protagonist as having defied gender injustice. Instead, just as in Urmila Pawar's short story "Justice," discussed in the introduction to this book, "Motijan's Daughters" points to the persistent vulnerability of girls and women.[34]

Muhaddes's "Over and Over Again," Desai's *Witness the Night*, Patigül's *Bloodline*, and Hossain's "Motijan's Daughters," in addition to several narratives discussed in earlier chapters, such as Dạ Ngân's *An Insignificant Family* (chapter 1) and Athwal's *Shamed* (chapter 5), are only a handful of the countless works of Asian and Asian diaspora literatures, not to mention other literatures from around the world, that spotlight family violence.[35] Many of these stories, including the first three discussed in this chapter, depict cycles of abuse as repeating relentlessly, generation after generation. Traumatized girls and women—regardless of education or socioeconomic status—themselves traumatize more vulnerable individuals, impeding if not curtailing improved futures. Other narratives, including Hossain's, Dạ Ngân's, and Athwal's, offer possibilities, however tenuous, for interrupting cycles of abuse and attaining limited justice. Each of these narratives, as is true of much creative production, highlights the individual voices, subjectivity, humanity, and dignity of victims and survivors through personal perspectives, figurative language, and other aesthetic and narrative techniques. Together, these trenchant narratives underscore the need for Asian societies, and societies around the world, to continue efforts to mitigate child, in-law, and elder abuse as well as the abuse of those suffering from serious health conditions, both within and outside families. Other narratives from Asia and its diasporas engage more directly with questions of justice surrounding intimate partner violence, the focus of the next and final chapter.

NOTES

1. The numbers are 56% for North America, 50% for Africa, 34% for Latin America, and 12% for Europe (Hillis et al. 6). As with other forms of family and gender-based violence, much child abuse goes unreported.

2. Disparate rates of infanticide were the case even in parts of eighteenth-century Japan that relied on this practice to keep family size to two to three children and in principle aspired to alternate the genders of their children (Drixler 91–92, 95).

3. Similarly, the novel *The Bird* (*Sae*, 1996), by the South Korean writer Oh Jung-hee (O Chŏnghŭi), is narrated by an impoverished girl who is engulfed by memories of her father abusing her mother, who is herself abused and abandoned by her father and other family members, and who in turn abuses her younger brother (Thornber 207–10).

4. See also the Indonesian writer Eka Kurniawan's *Man Tiger* (*Lelaki Harimau*, 2014), in which Margio, a young man who is a "child of domestic rape" (104) and is possessed by a female white tiger, kills his neighbor, who had impregnated Margio's mother. Margio's father brutally beat his children and abused and raped his wife (103–04). Cheah discusses the novel's attempts to "regularize the event" (102).

5. As Islam describes, in the past in Bangladesh, "girl children were discriminated and degraded from very birth," with girls sometimes married off at birth (239). Conditions for girls and women have improved in the past decades. Yet serious problems persist, with lifetime prevalence of gender-based violence at more than 53% and child marriage at 45% for girls ages 15–19 (*Global Gender Gap Report 2023* 102).

6. Muhaddes earned an MA in gender studies from the School of Oriental and African Studies, University of London (Hasan 3126). She has contributed to the Violence against Marginalized Women in Bangladesh research project

and published in the *Journal of Interpersonal Violence*, while her creative work appears in a range of literary magazines in Bangladesh and in several anthologies (Ghuznavi, "Contributors" 190–91).

7. Thank you to Aniket De for this insight.

8. For background on Desai, as well as conditions women face in India, see also chapter 4.

9. As Amaral and Bhalotra demonstrate, the demographic imbalance has led to increased violence against women in India overall (2). See also Hvistendahl.

10. Indian crime fiction writers frequently "alter generic conventions to draw attention to other problems such as impunity or corruption" (Meyer 112).

11. Billie-Jo Margaret Jenkins was a 13-year-old British girl who was stabbed to death in 1997. Her foster father, whom his wife had accused of molesting Billie-Jo, initially was found guilty and imprisoned for the murder but was acquitted in 2006. The case remains unsolved.

12. Patigül was born in Xinjiang Province to a Uyghur father from Xinjiang and a Hui mother from Gansu Province. Her creative work, including *Bloodline*, has received numerous awards. In the essay "Daliangpo: Egg, Water, and Milk" ("Hunxue de cunzhuang," lit. "Hybrid Village," 2014), Patigül describes her hometown as long populated by multiple ethnic groups (Han, Uyghur, Hui, Kazakh), all speaking their own languages and eating their own cuisines yet understanding, sharing with, and relying on one another (92–94).

13. At 1.3 billion people, Han Chinese are China's and the world's largest ethnic group. China's Uyghur population is about 13 million, and its Hui population around 10 million. Uyghurs are China's most endogamous ethnic group, at 99.47%; intermarriage between Uyghurs and Hui is a mere 0.06%, and intermarriage between Uyghurs and Han is almost nonexistent (Friedrichs 69).

14. One exception is Wan et al., which reveals that ethnic minority children, particularly girls, are at greater risk of being maltreated than their Han peers, in part because of different understandings of violence and in part because of unequal opportunities and resources.

15. China's Hui population is more broadly distributed across the nation, is more sinicized, and is religiously moderate. Hui people therefore are believed to be "closer to the Han civilizational center" than Uyghurs (Friedrichs 55, 59–60).

16. Zang summarizes twentieth- and early-twenty-first-century relations between Han Chinese and Uyghurs (7–10).

17. The *Kindle* version of *Bloodline* is the only English-language version available.

18. *Bloodline* is replete with similar discussions of family violence. See, for instance, the chapter "A Test of Loyalty." The English translation tempers many of the Chinese-language version's depictions of family violence.

19. The Chinese reads as follows: "We are destined to get along with mother this way, like a group of little animals and without ethical relations and heavenly

principles. It seems unbelievable to an outsider, but we see it as the cruel way of being close to family members" (我们注定以这样的方式与自己的母亲相处，像一群小动物，没有人伦天理，在外人看来不可思议，在我们看来则是与家人亲热的残酷方式; Patigül, *Bainian xuemai* 24).

20. Since *Bloodline* was published in 2015, it has become more difficult to obtain a divorce in China; the nation's rising divorce rates prompted more stringent requirements, including a 30-day "cooling off period," putting abused spouses, primarily women, at greater risk (Tang; Wee). Michelson describes how China's legal practices have led to a "sizable population of female marital-violence refugees" ("Decoupling" 325). Xiao analyzes Chinese cultural representations of divorce. See also Michelson, *Decoupling*; He.

21. Here, too, the English translation omits some of Patigül's graphic language and sense of inevitability, translating the original Chinese, "We can't stop this vicious cycle and can only let it bite us and tear us apart" (不能停下这恶性循环，听任它撕咬; Patigül, *Bainian xuemai* 121), as "It was a vicious cycle."

22. In the essay "Life of a Mimic" ("Mofengzhe de shenghuo," 2012), Patigül notes that unlike in the ethnically diverse community in which she was raised, in South China "I really am missing part of my identity" (261).

23. The Chinese source text speaks of Mardan not as "adapt[ing] easily to life in the south" but rather as "losing all resistance to the dialect, the customs, the food" in his new home (他对姚城方言、习俗、饮食全然没有了抵抗; Patigül, *Bainian xuemai* 167). In addition, in the Chinese source, the narrator is no longer worried that Mardan will inherit the "schizophrenic" (精神分裂的), as opposed to the "unstable," traits of her mother and elder brother (167). And the final lines read more literally: "but all those conflicts became smoothed out in Mardan. There is no more restlessness. Mardan hopes to embrace his sister with his warm love" (那种冲突到了儿子身上变得平缓了，不再有浮躁，儿子希望用他的温暖的爱去包容姐姐; 168).

24. The Chinese source reads literally: "piercing into your bones like an awl" (像锥子在骨头里锥; Patigül, *Bainian xuemai* 240).

25. Patigül does not seem to have publicly addressed whether or how much of the violence described in *Bloodline* is autobiographical. Thank you to Fangdai Chen for this insight.

26. Cf. the Indian writer Mridula Garg's Hindi-language *Country of Goodbyes* (*Kathgulab*, 1996), which speaks about the violence to which some women are subjected by their brothers-in-law. Smita, the eponymous narrator of the opening section, "Smita," is raped by her brother-in-law, moves to the United States, is taken advantage of by her therapist, and is furious with the god that killed her rapist prematurely, believing "he took my revenge from me" (30).

27. Hossain is one of Bangladesh's most accomplished feminist writers, having published more than 20 novels and more than 10 short story collections.

Written in Bengali, her award-winning creative work has been translated into multiple European and Asian languages, including many Indian languages.

28. Conditions for women in twenty-first-century Bangladesh have improved in some respects but in many ways remain forbidding (Islam 243–44; Kabir and Chowdhury 80). Shehabuddin cautions against seeing women in Bangladesh solely as "victims of Islamic doctrine rather than [of] domestic and international corporate greed" (274) and calls out accounts such as Susan Brownmiller's in *Against Our Will* (1975), which drew global attention to the "hit-and-run" rapes of 1971, when hundreds of thousands of Bangladeshi women were raped by West Pakistanis (211). Brownmiller provides an unfortunately one-dimensional image of Bangladeshi women as "extraordinarily vulnerable" victims (211).

29. In the Bengali version of the story, Gulnoor ties Motijan's neck, not her leg, to a post, exhibiting greater violence (Hossain, "Matijānera Meyerā").

30. From the beginning, Abul insists that Motijan refrain from speaking to him about his mother. Claiming that "I know nothing and can do nothing. Mother . . . keeps my heart trampled under her feet" (Hossain, "Motijan's Daughters" 99), Abul suggests that he, too, has been mistreated by his mother.

31. The Mahananda is a tributary of the Ganges River.

32. The Bengali source reads slightly differently, the daughters' eyes shining, not glaring: "From inside their mother's breast, Motijan's daughters looked at everyone with shining eyes" (মায়ের বুকের ভেতর থেকে জ্বলজ্বলে চোখে সবার দিকে তাকায় মতিজানের মেয়েরা।; Hossain, "Matijānera Meyerā").

33. For background on conditions in Bangladesh, see *Human Rights Briefs* and *Bangladesh*.

34. More extreme is the Pakistani writer Neelam Ahmed Bashir's Urdu-language "A Manly Act" ("Mardon-wālā kalām," 2008), in which a young woman, Hameedan, is tormented by her mother-in-law, Amma, and then by other relatives and neighbors for failing to produce a child with Amma's son Shera. Yet Shera ultimately falls in love with another woman, and before Hameedan has the opportunity to share with him that she is finally pregnant, he arranges for her murder (76).

35. Other examples from Asian literatures include Farah Ghuznavi's "Getting There" (2010), A Yi's "Attic" ("Gelou," 2012), Djenar Maesa Ayu's "The Leech" ("Lintah," 2001) and "Painting a Window" ("Melukis Jendela," 2001), Minato Kanae's *Confessions* (*Kokuhaku*, 2008), Kirino Natsuo's *What Remains* (*Zangyakuki*, 2004), Shimoda Harumi's *A Person Begging for Love* (*Ai o kou hito*, 1992), Yū Miri's "Full House" ("Furu hausu," 1997), Choi Eunyoung's (Ch'oe Ŭnyŏng's) "Shoko's Smile" ("Syok'o ŭi miso," 2016), Dương Bình Nguyên's "Wild Mustard" ("Cải lạc loài," 2006), and Hồ Thị Ngọc Hoài's "Thung Lam" ("Thung Lam," 2007).

WORKS CITED

"Abuse of Older People." *World Health Organization*, 13 June 2022, www.who.int/news-room/fact-sheets/detail/elder-abuse.

Alston, Margaret, editor. *Women, Political Struggles and Gender Equality in South Asia*. Palgrave Macmillan, 2014.

Amaral, Sofia, and Sonia Bhalotra. "Population Sex Ratios and Violence against Women: The Long-Run Effects of Sex Selection in India." *ISER Working Paper Series 2017–12*, Institute for Social and Economic Research, 2017, pp. 1–57.

Bangladesh: Information on Arranged Marriages, Including Information on the Matching Process and the Role of the Matchmaker. Immigration and Refugee Board of Canada, 1998.

Bashir, Neelam Ahmed. "A Manly Act." *Half the Sky: Stories by Women Writers of Pakistan*, edited by Nirupama Dutt, Unistar Books, 2004, pp. 60–76.

Bhatnagar, Rashmi Dube, et al. *Female Infanticide in India: A Feminist Cultural History*. State U of New York P, 2005.

Bhattacharya, Anindita. "'The Day I Die Is the Day I Will Find My Peace': Narratives of Family, Marriage, and Violence among Women Living with Serious Mental Illness in India." *Violence against Women*, vol. 28, nos. 3–4, Mar. 2021, pp. 1–25.

Cheah, Pheng. "Worlding Literature: Living with Tiger Spirits." *Diacritics*, vol. 45, no. 2, 2017, pp. 86–114.

De, Aniket. Personal correspondence with the author. 14 Feb. 2022.

Desai, Kishwar. *Witness the Night*. Penguin Books, 2010.

Drixler, Fabian. *Mabiki: Infanticide and Population Growth in Eastern Japan, 1660–1950*. U of California P, 2013.

Friedrichs, Jörg. "Sino-Muslim Relations: The Han, the Hui, and the Uyghurs." *Journal of Muslim Minority Affairs*, vol. 37, no. 1, Jan. 2017, pp. 55–79.

Gangoli, Geetanjali, and Martin Rew. "Mothers-in-Law against Daughters-in-Law: Domestic Violence and Legal Discourses around Mother-in-Law Violence against Daughters-in-Law in India." *Women's Studies International Forum*, vol. 34, no. 5, July 2011, pp. 420–29.

Garg, Mridula. *Country of Goodbyes*. Kali for Women, 2003.

Ghuznavi, Farah. "Contributors." Ghuznavi, *Lifelines*, pp. 188–92.

———, editor. *Lifelines: New Writing from Bangladesh*. Zubaan, 2012.

Global Gender Gap Report 2023. World Economic Forum, 2023, www3.weforum.org/docs/WEF_GGGR_2023.pdf.

Global Status Report on Preventing Violence against Children 2020. Executive Summary. World Health Organization, 2020.

Hasan, Tanvir, et al. "Prevalence and Experiences of Intimate Partner Violence against Women with Disabilities in Bangladesh: Results of an Explanatory Sequential Mixed-Method Study." *Journal of Interpersonal Violence*, vol. 29, no. 17, Nov. 2014, pp. 3105–26.

He, Xin. *Divorce in China: Institutional Constraints and Gendered Outcomes*. New York UP, 2021.

Hillis, Susan, et al. "Global Prevalence of Past-Year Violence against Children: A Systematic Review and Minimum Estimates." *Pediatrics*, vol. 137, no. 3, 1 Mar. 2016, www.ncbi.nlm.nih.gov/pmc/articles/PMC6496958.

Hossain, Selina. "Matijānera Meyerā." *Galpersamy.com*, 19 Mar. 2018, galpersamay .com/2018/03/19/মতিজানের-মেয়েরা/.

———. "Motijan's Daughters." *Galpa: Short Stories by Women from Bangladesh*, edited by Firdous Azim and Niaz Zaman, translated by Sagar Chaudhury, Saqi, 2005, pp. 98–109.

Human Rights Briefs: Women in Bangladesh. Immigration and Refugee Board of Canada, 1993, www.refworld.org/docid/3ae6a8398.html.

Hvistendahl, Mara. *Unnatural Selection: Choosing Boys over Girls, and the Consequences of a World Full of Men*. PublicAffairs, 2011.

Islam, Farzana, and Gulshan Ara Akhter. "Child Abuse in Bangladesh." *IMC Journal of Medical Science*, vol. 9, no. 1, Jan. 2015, pp. 18–21.

Islam, Mahmuda. "Women, Politics, and Patriarchy: A Case of Bangladesh." Alston, pp. 238–53.

Kabir, Rokeya, and Omar Tarek Chowdhury. "Women in Bangladesh: Invisible Heroes in the Economy and Society." Alston, pp. 72–82.

Kurniawan, Eka. *Man Tiger*. Translated by Labodalih Sembiring, Verso, 2015.

Lansford, Jennifer E., et al. "Early Physical Abuse and Later Violent Delinquency: A Prospective Longitudinal Study." *Child Maltreatment*, vol. 12, no. 3, Aug. 2007, pp. 233–45.

Meyer, Neele. "Challenging Gender and Genre: Women in Contemporary Indian Crime Fiction in English." *Zeitschrift für Anglistik und Amerikanistik*, vol. 66, no. 1, Mar. 2018, pp. 105–17.

Meyer, Silke, et al. "The Intergenerational Transmission of Family Violence: Mothers' Perceptions of Children's Experiences and Use of Violence in the Home." *Child and Family Social Work*, vol. 26, Aug. 2021, pp. 476–84.

Michelson, Ethan. *Decoupling: Gender Injustice in China's Divorce Courts*. Cambridge UP, 2022.

———. "Decoupling: Marital Violence and the Struggle to Divorce in China." *American Journal of Sociology*, vol. 125, no. 2, Sept. 2019, pp. 325–81.

Morgan, Holly Jennifer. "Kishwar Desai's Simran Singh Series: Crime, Detection, and Gender." *The Journal of Commonwealth Literature*, vol. 57, no. 3, May 2020, pp. 722–37.

Muhaddes, Tisa. "Over and Over Again." Ghuznavi, *Lifelines*, pp. 98–101.

National Children Policy 2011. Bangladesh Ministry of Women and Children Affairs, Feb. 2011. *Bangladesh ECD Network*, ecd-bangladesh.net/document/documents/National-Children-Policy-2011-English-04.12.2012.pdf.

Nelson, S., et al. "Mental Health Problems and Medically Unexplained Physical Symptoms in Adult Survivors of Childhood Sexual Abuse: An Integrative Literature Review." *Journal of Psychiatric and Mental Health Nursing*, vol. 19, no. 3, Apr. 2012, pp. 211–20.

Niu, Xuan, and Karen A. Joe Laidler. "Understanding Domestic Violence against Muslim Women in China." *Feminist Criminology*, vol. 10, no. 1, Jan. 2015, pp. 92–112.

Patigül. *Bainian xuemai*. Beijing shidai Huawen shuju, 2014.

———. *Bloodline*. Translated by Natascha Bruce, Kindle ed., Aurora Publishing, 2019.

———. "Daliangpo: Egg, Water, and Milk." *Chinese Women Writers on the Environment: A Multi-ethnic Anthology of Fiction and Nonfiction*, edited by Dong Isbister et al., McFarland, 2020, pp. 87–94.

———. "Life of a Mimic." *To the Goat-Dipping*, edited by Li Jingze and Shi Zhanjun, translated by Jim Weldon, Foreign Languages Press, 2015, pp. 247–74.

Pillemer, Karl, et al. "Elder Abuse: Global Situation, Risk Factors, and Prevention Strategies." *The Gerontologist*, vol. 56, supp. 2, Apr. 2016, pp. S194–S205.

Rew, Martin, et al. "Violence between Female In-Laws in India." *Journal of International Women's Studies*, vol. 14, no. 1, Jan. 2013, pp. 147–60.

Seth, Rajeev. "Child Abuse and Neglect in India." *Indian Journal of Pediatrics*, vol. 82, no. 8, Aug. 2015, pp. 707–14.

Seth, Rajeev, and R. N. Srivastava. "Child Sexual Abuse: Management and Prevention, and Protection of Children from Sexual Offences (POCSO) Act." *Indian Pediatrics*, vol. 54, no. 11, Dec. 2017, pp. 949–53.

Shehabuddin, Elora. *Sisters in the Mirror: A History of Muslim Women and the Global Politics of Feminism*. U of California P, 2021.

Tang, Qiaomei. "Marriage Disputes and Legal Judgments in Early and Medieval China." 12 Aug. 2021, Seoul National University.

Thornber, Karen Laura. "Comparison and Gender Injustice: Opportunities in Worlds of Pandemics." *Comparative Critical Studies*, vol. 20, nos. 2–3, 2023, pp. 201–21.

Wan, Guowei, et al. "Child Maltreatment in Western China: Ethnic Disparities, Poverty-Related Adversity and Policy Deficiency." *Journal of Child and Family Studies*, vol. 30, no. 5, Mar. 2021, pp. 1299–313.

Wee, Sui-Lee. "Her Husband Abused Her. But Getting a Divorce Was an Ordeal." *The New York Times*, 16 Sept. 2020, www.nytimes.com/2020/09/16/world/asia/china-domestic-abuse.html.

Widom, Cathy Spatz. "Long-Term Impact of Childhood Abuse and Neglect on Crime and Violence." *Clinical Psychology Science and Practice*, vol. 24, no. 2, June 2017, pp. 186–202.

"Women and Elder Abuse." *Nursing Home Abuse Guide*, 2023, nursinghome abuseguide.com/women-and-elder-abuse/.

Xiao, Hui Faye. *Family Revolution: Marital Strife in Contemporary Chinese Literature and Visual Culture*. U of Washington P, 2014.

Yan, Elsie, et al. "A Systematic Review of Prevalence and Risk Factors for Elder Abuse in Asia." *Trauma, Violence, and Abuse*, vol. 16, no. 2, Apr. 2015, pp. 199–219.

Zang, Xiaowei. *Uyghur Conceptions of Family and Society*. Routledge, 2017.

7. Intersecting Responsibilities for Intimate Partner Violence

In most communities, intimate partner violence occurs even more frequently than the interconnected forms of gender-based violence highlighted in the previous three chapters. Furthermore, given long-standing beliefs regarding accepted behaviors in intimate partner relationships, individuals experiencing this type of violence are even less likely to obtain justice.

Defined by the World Health Organization as "behaviour by an intimate partner or ex-partner that causes physical, sexual or psychological harm, including physical aggression, sexual coercion, psychological abuse and controlling behaviours," intimate partner violence often intersects with other forms of violence. Although violence occurs in all types of intimate relationships, intimate partner violence most commonly takes the form of male-on-female violence, with 27% of women aged 15–49 globally who have been in a relationship having been harmed by a male intimate partner or ex-partner ("Violence").[1] Given the severe economic, social, financial, and mental and physical health consequences both for those who are abused and for societies more broadly, in the last few decades the World Health Organization, national and local public health agencies, NGOs, and particularly feminist organizations and other activist groups and individuals have struggled to change attitudes and behaviors surrounding intimate partner violence.[2] These groups and individuals have demanded that violent actions deemed prosecutable crimes outside an intimate partner relationship also be prosecutable crimes when they happen within that relationship and that nonconsensual sex be acknowledged as rape, even when a couple is married (i.e., being married does not give a person liberty to have nonconsensual sex with their spouse).

Today, marital rape has been criminalized in all of Europe and Oceania, in most of the Americas and Southeast Asia, in more than half of Africa, and in all of East Asia, except for China and North Korea. In contrast, marital rape remains legal in much of the Middle East and in most of South Asia, except for Nepal and Bhutan (Natarajan and Rodriguez-Spahia 374).

Yet in most parts of Asia and the world, skepticism and denial persist regarding the criminality or even injustice of abusing an intimate partner as well as about society's responsibility for ensuring that individuals are not subjected to violence within their most personal relationships. In many families and communities, individuals witness intimate partner violence from early childhood. Regardless of legal prohibitions, such behaviors are presented as normal and appropriate. Not surprisingly, intimate partner violence intensified during the COVID-19 pandemic, creating a shadow pandemic even in many nations that deem such behavior a prosecutable offense ("Facts").[3]

Although intimate partner violence has often been perceived as an inappropriate topic for literature, creative narratives are particularly valuable in drawing attention to the glaring complicity of family, friends, neighbors, health professionals, and bystanders in perpetuating and exacerbating this violence, not unlike narratives on the forms of gender-based violence discussed in chapters 4–6. These writings—as is true of Itō Shiori's *Black Box* (chapter 5), Kishwar Desai's *Origins of Love* and *Witness the Night* (chapters 4 and 6), and many others—also highlight the vital roles individual members of society could play not only in condemning, ameliorating, and preventing future intimate partner violence but also in understanding, supporting, and acknowledging the humanity of those subjected to this violence. This chapter focuses on five works of fiction published between 1983 and 2017 by writers from across Asia that skillfully spotlight the importance of broad community commitment to creating a just environment where an individual's traumas are acknowledged and intimate partner violence is censured: *When I Hit You; or, A Portrait of the Writer as a Young Wife* (2017), a work of autofiction (a combination of autobiography and fiction, distinct from memoir) by Meena Kandasamy (1984–) narrated in the first person by an Indian woman who has escaped an abusive marriage; the short story "An Episode at Dusk, 2" ("Chŏmun nal ŭi saphwa 2," 저문날의삽화2, 1987), by Pak Wansŏ (1931–2011), narrated in the first person by a South Korean woman who only reluctantly acknowledges that the neighbor she idolizes is abusing his wife; the short story "Teacher

Shortage" (2008), by Shabnam Nadiya, narrated in the first person by a Bangladeshi woman recalling the intimate partner violence to which a childhood friend's mother was subjected; the novella *The Butcher's Wife* (*Shafu*, 殺夫, lit. *Husband Killing* or *Killing the Husband*, 1983), by Li Ang (Shih Shu-tuan, 1952–), about an impoverished Taiwanese woman sold into marriage by her uncle to an exceptionally abusive man whom she ultimately murders; and the short story "Men's Rights" ("Sitthiburut," สิทธิบุรุษ, 2006), by Duanwad Pimwana (Dū'anwāt Phimwan, Pimjai Juklin, 1969–), about a Thai husband so furious that his wife was unfaithful that he nearly murders her.

These narratives not only speak explicitly and personally about intimate partner violence against women, including marital rape. They also reveal just how swiftly family, friends, neighbors, health professionals, and bystanders alike dismiss stories and signs of intimate partner violence, signs and stories that if acted upon might have prevented further abuse. The writings discussed in this chapter additionally highlight how readily, rather than seek justice for those subjected to intimate partner violence, members of society hold women at least partially responsible for the abuse they experience. And they expose how often broader social expectations and structural violence nearly guarantee that families, friends, neighbors, health professionals, and bystanders become complicit in intimate partner violence, failing to intervene and in fact going so far as to blame the individual who is abused or to deny the significance and even the occurrence or nature of the abuse.

This is not at all to liberate from responsibility individuals who assault their partners. Rather, it is a reminder of the importance of ensuring the emotional and physical safety of the person being subjected to intimate partner violence and of holding the actual perpetrator responsible, even when this individual is a family member, friend, neighbor, colleague, or trusted professional. One of the most disturbing aspects of the narratives discussed in this chapter is their depictions of how little it ultimately would have taken for those closest to the women who are abused to acknowledge their suffering and temper the abuse. Although they deploy different aesthetic techniques, are set in very different places and times, and focus on women from very different economic, educational, ethnic, and social backgrounds, these compelling feminist narratives from India, Korea, Bangladesh, Taiwan, and Thailand all portray intimate partner violence as an open secret, one that ensures futures marked by continued violence and a notable absence of justice.

Failures of Family, Friends, Health Professionals, Courts, and Bystanders: Meena Kandasamy's *When I Hit You; or, A Portrait of the Writer as a Young Wife* (2017)

Statistics vary on precisely how many Indian women have been subjected to intimate partner violence, but the numbers are striking. As of the first decade of the twenty-first century, approximately 40% of Indian women had been physically, sexually, or psychologically abused by their husbands, resulting in high mental and physical morbidity (Kalokhe et al.; Yoshikawa et al.). The United Nations Population Fund has reported that more than two-thirds of married women in India between the ages of 15 and 49 have been beaten or raped by their husbands (Press Trust). This abuse is rarely brought to the attention of authorities, and even when it is, justice is only very rarely obtained. A 2014 study revealed that less than 1% of sexual violence by husbands is reported, in part because India has been loath to acknowledge the existence of abuse within marriage (Nair). Until October 2017, Indian law did not consider rape in marriage a crime if the wife was older than 15. That month, the Delhi (India) High Court raised the cutoff to age 18, appalling activists by arguing that criminalizing marital rape when the wife is over age 18 "may destabilise the institution of marriage apart from being an easy tool for harassing the husbands" (qtd. in Nair).

Activists were also horrified by the central government's argument for Indian exceptionalism:

> The fact that other countries, mostly western, have criminalized marital rape does not necessarily mean India should also follow them blindly. This country has its own unique problems due to various factors like literacy, lack of financial empowerment of the majority of females, mindset of the society, vast diversity, poverty, etc., and these should be considered carefully before criminalizing marital rape. (Nair)

India is a nation of tremendous diversity and inequality. The most populous nation in the world, home to more than 1.42 billion people, thousands of languages and dialects, and an immense range of religions and other cultural practices and expectations, it is a notoriously difficult country to characterize. Even though conditions vary widely within and among regions of India, the central government is correct that, in general, poverty and limited financial opportunities remain serious concerns, especially for women. To be sure, health, education, and living standards increased significantly in India between the mid-2000s and the mid-2010s, with rates of multidimensional poverty cut in half, from 54.7% to 27.5% of India's population. Between 2005 and 2016, 271 million Indian citizens escaped multidimensional poverty ("271 Million Fewer Poor People").[4]

Yet in 2023, the World Economic Forum ranked India 127th of 146 nations in filling its overall gender gap, 142nd in health and survival, and 142nd in economic participation and opportunity (*Global Gender Gap Report 2023* 11, 17, 18). In addition, as evidenced by the 2017 Delhi High Court decision, little has been done to increase safety for women, including within marriage. As Kandasamy, a prominent and highly controversial English-language Dalit Indian poet, fiction writer, Tamil-English translator, and outspoken feminist and anti-caste activist, explained in a 2018 interview, "I come from a culture where if a woman says her husband is hitting her, people will say: 'Well, that's one side of the story and the other side of the story is: what did you do to make him hit you?' If a woman is raped, they'll say: 'What did the woman do to make him rape her?'" ("And").

As in Itō's *Black Box*, blaming women for the violence committed against them happens regardless of privilege and education. Indeed, as exposed in *When I Hit You*, published in the mid-2010s amid India's swirling debates regarding marital rape, even well-educated women from relatively comfortable backgrounds whose parents allow them to marry whom they want and when they want are not immune to intimate partner violence. Moreover, as the first-person narrator of *When I Hit You* highlights, there is little protection in being well-versed in Western feminisms and understanding marital rape and intimate partner violence as abstract concepts. This is in no small part because of the apathy of friends, family, physicians, and bystanders toward gender-based violence.

The title of Kandasamy's novel references the Irish writer James Joyce's novel *A Portrait of the Artist as a Young Man* (1916). Each novel is a *Künstlerroman* (German for "artist novel"), a novel on the formation of an artist, a subset of the bildungsroman, a literary genre focused on the protagonist's coming-of-age. Yet while Joyce's artist is a young man ashamed of his sexual desires who ultimately leaves his natal home in search of greater freedom, Kandasamy's artist is a young wife in an abusive relationship who ultimately flees back to her natal home for safety, only to be forced to leave. The title, *When I Hit You*, initially suggests that the narrator inflicts physical violence. But as quickly becomes apparent, the reference is to writing that enables the narrator to aesthetically hit back against all who have betrayed her and thwarted her search for justice. Although Kandasamy draws from personal experience in *When I Hit You*, especially her brief yet horrifically abusive first marriage, she has insisted that hers is a work of autofiction: "We can't dismiss it as just some woman's problem. . . . [This goes] beyond just one person's story, and therefore I choose fiction" ("Indian Feminist Poet Meena Kandasamy" 02:43–02:59). The literariness of Kandasamy's work—including what one critic describes as "ferocity of craft . . . Not just the beauty of the prose . . . but the labour that the structure of the book performs" (D.)—enables deeper insights into shared suffering and highlights the dignity and subjectivity of individuals who are too often silenced and dismissed both in literature and in life.

The first-person narrator of *When I Hit You* is an unnamed writer in her 20s from Chennai (southeastern India) with a master's degree from a college in Kerala (southwestern India).[5] She describes how five years earlier, after a failed love affair with an unnamed politician, she married a college lecturer and onetime underground revolutionary and Maoist guerrilla. The narrator followed him to his hometown of Mangalore, more than 400 miles from her parents. There he took advantage of her isolation from family networks in Chennai and her circle of artist friends in Kerala as well as of her unfamiliarity with local languages. He became an ardent communist who degraded and isolated her under the pretense of re-education, ultimately physically abusing and nearly killing her. The narrator endured four months and eight days of escalating violence before escaping and filing for divorce. Yet after a brief reprieve with her parents in Chennai, her father ordered her to leave and not return.

Kandasamy's narrator not only describes her own experiences and the backlash she faced from loved ones and strangers alike but also speaks explicitly to the experiences of women in India more generally. Particularly noteworthy about *When I Hit You*, in addition to its sophisticated poetic and aesthetic style, is the narrator's courageous exposure of families, friends, health professionals, and bystanders as some of the greatest enablers of intimate partner violence.[6] For the most part, what motivates these individuals is not outright malice toward (other) women but instead ingrained expectations concerning a woman's proper role in marriage and in society more broadly, expectations that have remained stubbornly consistent despite other changes in society—for instance, the fact that women now have greater access to higher education and are more frequently allowed to choose whom they marry. As is generally true in India and many countries around the world, rather than do what they can to curtail abuse and assist those who have been abused, people who hear about or witness intimate partner violence in *When I Hit You* are more inclined to ignore or dismiss what has happened, and they do not hesitate to blame the woman who is abused. At no time is the abuser held accountable for the abuse, even by eyewitnesses.

The narrator of *When I Hit You* reveals that her parents are her husband's most immediate enablers. She informs them of the escalating abuse in real time, but rather than take their daughter seriously, her parents alternate between dismissing her concerns and holding her responsible. Both believe their daughter's husband is abusing her "for [her] own good," a shopworn mantra, the narrator observes, that in years past justified other forms of abuse, including "my teenage neighbor putting his fingers inside my eight-year-old vagina to check for forest insects and bed bugs and evil imps" (Kandasamy, *When* 60). Here Kandasamy's narrator echoes the childhood abuses experienced by Kim Jiyoung, Itō Shiori, the narrator of Tisa Muhaddes's "Over and Over Again," and other characters discussed in previous chapters. The narrator of *When I Hit You* describes the common tendencies not just to dismiss women's concerns but also to believe their suffering is necessarily justified and they are most to blame.

Even after the narrator confides to her parents that her husband's beatings are becoming increasingly violent, that every day "I inch closer to death, to dying, to being killed" (Kandasamy, *When* 155), her mother and father "take turns convincing [her] to stay" (156), not unlike Tiệp's parents in the Vietnamese writer Dạ Ngân's *An Insignificant Family*, examined in chapter 1. The narrator boldly underlines their complicity, transcribing some of their instructions. Her father urges her to listen to her husband, have patience and tolerance, learn how to obey, and think about how others will mock her father if she breaks off her marriage. Her mother advises that her daughter needs to give her husband time (158); that the first year is the worst year (157); that she, too, experienced abuse, but eventually "you forget all the sadness" (158); and that "finding the perfect man is a myth" (160). The narrator's mother also declares, "[I]f he's beating you, it only shows he has run out of arguments. Just be patient, dear. Buy yourself time" (198). The burden here is solely on the narrator. It is only when she repeats to her parents, word for word, her husband's threat to "scalp" her that they implore her to flee (209). As Kandasamy's narrator observes, again linking her experiences to those of women more broadly, "In the eyes of the world, a woman who runs away from death is more dignified than a woman who runs away from her man" (209).

Eyewitnesses also enable abuse by failing to intervene. The narrator describes a visit to a medical center for a pelvic ultrasound. No one comes to her aid when her husband, in plain view of a room filled with patients, attempts to force water down her throat and then slaps her for drinking too slowly: "The people in the waiting room either watch or avert their eyes. To them, this is just an overexcited man eager to be a father. They do not know what I live through. Or maybe they all know, and everyone takes it for granted" (Kandasamy, *When* 199). And the eyewitnesses remain silent even when the narrator vomits and her husband berates her and demands, "Hold it in. Behave yourself" (200). Moreover, the narrator reports, "the doctor compliments me on having such a loving husband; on being married to such a devoted, doting man. . . . At no time does he give me an opportunity to talk to him. At no time does he ask me how I am. Even if he had, how could I open up to strangers who buy the fiction performed for their benefit?" (200).

Not surprisingly, those further removed from the abuse, even close friends, are even less inclined to offer the narrator the support she needs. Instead, they challenge and blame her. The narrator's friends ask why, if things were so terrible, she did not simply leave. They pummel her with questions, including "How much of this wasn't really consensual?" (Kandasamy, *When* 218). The narrator again generalizes her experiences, explaining, "It does not cross their mind that a woman who is being beaten is intimidated into feeling, believing, knowing that to ask for help from others will only put her at greater risk" (220). Even a year after the narrator has bolted from her marriage, she, like many women, feels compelled "to lend an appropriate colour of goodness to [my] abuser" (225).

The narrator of *When I Hit You* also places her experiences in broader context by referring to specific instances of India's horrific mistreatment of victims of abuse. One of the most illustrative is the 1996 Suryanelli rape case, where a 16-year-old schoolgirl from a lower-class family in rural Suryanelli, Kerala, was abducted by 42 men, some of whom were well-known and well-connected; for 40 days, 35 of the 42 raped her. The Suryanelli case attracted considerable media attention, and groups of concerned women, some of whom explicitly identified as feminists, publicly protested, demanding justice (Subrahmanian 8). Even though 35 men were found guilty in 2000, five years later, nearly a decade after the rapes, all but one of the accused were acquitted. It was not until the 2012 Delhi rape case, where, as mentioned in chapter 5, a 23-year-old physiotherapy intern was gang-raped and tortured on a private bus in Delhi and died two days later in a hospital in Singapore, that India's Supreme Court reassessed the Suryanelli case and convicted 24 of the rapists (Dey 363).

In staccato sentences followed by a series of aggressive questions, Kandasamy's narrator summarizes initial responses to the Suryanelli case, which echo her own experiences: "The police do not investigate her case. The high court questions her character. The highest court in the land asks the inevitable. Why did she not run away? Why did she not use the opportunities that she had for escape? Why did she stay if, indeed, the conditions were as bad as she claims? How much of this wasn't *really* consensual?" (Kandasamy, *When* 219). No wonder, as the narrator pronounces earlier, "[t]he shame of rape is the shame of the unspeakable. Women have found it easier to jump into fire, consume poison, blow themselves up as suicide bombers, than tell another soul about what happened" (169–70). As with many narratives featured in this book, *When I Hit You* is a courageous intervention that attempts to break silences surrounding gender-based violence.

Without question, Kandasamy's work of autofiction depicts as most culpable those who commit intimate partner violence. The novel also explicitly implicates the structural violence of Indian society that makes possible widespread intimate partner violence. But *When I Hit You* also makes clear throughout, especially through the narrator's repeated linking of her own experiences with those of women across India, that family, friends, neighbors, health professionals, courts, and bystanders are all responsible for creating safer spaces, acknowledging the humanity of those subjected to intimate partner violence, and ultimately striving for justice.

Bursting Fantasies:
Pak Wansŏ's "An Episode at Dusk, 2" (1987)

The 1980s were a turbulent decade in South Korea, with frequent and sometimes deadly protests against the dictatorship of President Chun Doo-Hwan, who came to power in a military coup in 1980 and left office in 1988.[7] This was also an era of increasing feminist consciousness: in 1986 activists from 33 organizations formed the Korean Women's Associations United, and in 1987 activists created the Korean Women Workers Association, both of which fought against gender discrimination. But with several notable exceptions—including the Korea Women's Hot Line (an activist group established in 1983 that "identified patriarchy and the unequal treatment of women as the root causes of spousal abuse and violence against women" [Han and Chun 245])—reducing violence against women was seen even by many women themselves as secondary to struggles for democratization, reunification, social transformation, and human rights more broadly (Jung 10; Palley 287).

Pak published "An Episode at Dusk, 2" in the final tumultuous year of Chun's presidency, as South Korea was in the throes of nationwide demonstrations demanding a democratic election.[8] Yung-Hee Kim, Pak's English-language translator, has described the story as "an unvarnished and telling exposé of lopsided husband-wife relationships, the viciousness of spousal abuse, and most of all, the hypocrisy of the husband—an egotistic, self-promoting antigovernment activist, who, in his treatment of his wife, duplicates the very violence of the military regime he opposes" ("Pak Wan-sŏ" 152). A revolutionary like his counterpart in *When I Hit You*, the husband in "An Episode" is also very abusive. Equally important, like Kandasamy's novel, "An Episode" additionally emphasizes both how readily evidence of intimate partner violence is overlooked and, even if this violence is acknowledged, how women continue to be held accountable for the violence committed against them. Yet unlike *When I Hit You*, Pak's short story is narrated in the first person by the neighbor and former teacher of a woman subjected to intimate partner violence, Kim Ch'ang-hŭi, not by the woman most directly confronting this violence, Min Kayŏn. Although Kayŏn's story is heavily filtered, the narrative strategy of "An Episode," and particularly the narrator Ch'ang-hŭi's extensive self-reflections, shine greater attention on the twisted dynamics of evading responsibility.

The signs of intimate partner violence are there from the beginning, but Ch'ang-hŭi, as is true of so many individuals, repeatedly and determinedly misinterprets them. "An Episode" depicts Ch'ang-hŭi as assuming that Kayŏn's children are responsible for the objects that have fallen from Kayŏn's balcony onto her (Ch'ang-hŭi's) veranda. Ch'ang-hŭi also believes that the children are the source of the cacophony, including a shouting male voice, that emanates from Kayŏn's apartment. After Kayŏn informs Ch'ang-hŭi that she does not yet have children, Ch'ang-hŭi does not question whether Kayŏn's husband is therefore the one shouting and throwing objects. Instead, Ch'ang-hŭi seemingly does her best to avoid acknowledging the violence that surrounds her and reminisces about her previous apartment, where she likewise had misinterpreted the source of the loud noises penetrating her walls.[9] To be sure, Ch'ang-hŭi is "utterly scandalized" when she discovers that Kayŏn's husband will not allow his wife to participate in the paid workforce (Pak 144). And after learning that Kayŏn's husband often vents his "anger from the outside by smashing and throwing their scanty home furnishings," she knows that she cannot advise the young woman simply to put up with his behavior. But still, she despairs at losing "the object of my hope—Kayŏn's husband," whom she barely knows but still adores because of his revolutionary activities (145).[10]

Ch'ang-hŭi's attitude toward Kayŏn's husband changes dramatically when Kayŏn reveals that he has been physically abusing her and shows Ch'ang-hŭi her bruises. Describing herself as (finally) facing up to reality, Ch'ang-hŭi springs into action and, through her personal connections, lines up a job interview for her neighbor. When Kayŏn responds that she will not be able to participate in this interview, Ch'ang-hŭi criticizes what she sees as Kayŏn's cowardice, naively telling her, "First, you need to get on your own feet mentally and then tell him your intention to rely on yourself. Everything will then turn out ok. . . . Nobody dares to hit a free person who is able to stand on her own" (Pak 147). Ch'ang-hŭi rapidly transitions from chastising Kayŏn for seeming to snub her former teacher to sympathizing with Kayŏn's husband to empathizing with Kayŏn to placing the burden of preventing violence on her vulnerable young neighbor. "An Episode" ends with Ch'ang-hŭi's imploring Kayŏn to "stand on your own. . . . You should get up on your own feet. . . . You can't put off your independence any longer" (148). Ch'ang-hŭi speaks of pleading with Kayŏn and hoping her neighbor will feel her friendship, but she does not seem to know how to actually assist Kayŏn.

"An Episode" can certainly be read "as a counsel against the injudicious, sentimental, over-idealization or adulation of the student activists of the 1980s . . . [and] as a scathing indictment of the rampant, toxic sociopolitical culture of violence of 1980s Korea" (Kim, "Pak Wan-sŏ" 153–54). And there is little question that, as Kim also observes, "Pak Wan-sŏ's pro-woman position is unequivocally put into words in the narrator's advice to Kayŏn at the end of the narrative. . . . [F]inancial independence and self-reliance [are prerequisites] for a truly liberated woman to be on equal footing with a man" (153–54). At the same time, as the story's aesthetic strategy reveals, Ch'ang-hŭi does not seem to understand that becoming independent and self-reliant, much less escaping violence, requires far more than simply being commanded to do so, no matter one's education or social status. It requires, at the very least, recognition of the humanity, dignity, and very real barriers facing individuals subjected to intimate partner violence. The narration of "An Episode" brings to the fore just how pernicious assumptions can be and just how infrequently individuals subjected to abuse are truly heard, much less obtain justice.

Several years after the publication of "An Episode," the Korea Sexual Violence Relief Center (est. 1991) was founded as a site for achieving a "gender-equal society" (Jung 28). Following the election of Kim Young-Sam as president in 1993 and the transition to a civilian-led democracy, reducing violence against women became a central focus and unifying agenda for South Korean women's groups (16–17). And after a 1997 survey revealed that rates of intimate partner violence were much higher than expected, this form of violence "was suddenly considered as one of the most urgent issues in South Korea" (Kim et al. 1554). But in general, rates of marital violence, which continues to be understood in Korea as a private family matter rather than a social problem or crime to be prosecuted, remain high (Chung and Ok 83; Lee et al.), making Pak's story as relevant today as it was in the late 1980s.[11]

Dismissing Abuse: Shabnam Nadiya's "Teacher Shortage" (2008)

Western media reports on Bangladesh have since the turn of the twenty-first century drawn attention to a particularly egregious form of intimate partner violence in that country—acid attacks against women, the majority of which are perpetrated by men angry that a woman has refused marriage or a relationship but which also sometimes occur within relationships (*Combatting* 3).[12] Work by feminist and other activist groups has mitigated the failure of state institutions to provide women with the protection they are now guaranteed by law (Chowdhury 19, 21). But as in most nations, intimate partner violence in Bangladesh also encompasses far less publicized forms of abuse that involve far more women: more than 50% of urban women and more than 60% of rural women in Bangladesh report lifetime experience with sexual or physical intimate partner violence (Ziaei et al. 349), with less privileged women at greater risk than their wealthier counterparts (VanderEnde et al.). Studies have highlighted that even if they oppose intimate partner violence in principle, many Bangladeshis believe it inevitable in practice (Sato et al.; Islam et al. 442). In "Teacher Shortage," the Bangladeshi writer and translator Shabnam Nadiya highlights a primary consequence of this belief and one echoed in both *When I Hit You* and "An Episode," namely the failure of family, friends, and the broader community to assist victims of intimate partner violence.

While *When I Hit You* and "An Episode" describe events of the present and recent past, the adult first-person narrator of "Teacher Shortage" reflects on the intimate partner violence to which a childhood friend's mother was subjected. She begins by contrasting the adults, who feigned ignorance, with the children, who "had known, of course; kids always do" (Nadiya, "Teacher Shortage" 3). The narrator's friend Mitul had spoken frequently and matter-of-factly about the violence her father, Sharif Uncle, a teacher at the school, inflicted on her mother, Sharif Aunty, also a teacher at the school, including slamming her against the walls of their home, pushing a chair into her ribs, and throwing hot food at her face.[13] Mitul also shared with her friends the intergenerational violence taking place in her household: Mitul's grandparents did not intervene in Sharif Uncle's abuse of Sharif Aunty because her grandfather himself hit her grandmother. The narrator's mother and her friends at first denied the abuse, claiming, "Such things don't happen *here*, for goodness sake" (4). But when they could deny it no longer, some decided action must be taken. The narrator's mother, for instance, complained to her husband, "Aren't you going to do anything about this? We all know what happens in that house. It's been going on long enough" (6). Her husband quickly absolved himself of all responsibility, his questions confirming his biases: "It's so easy to judge from the outside, isn't it? I mean, do we really know what goes on in that house? I mean, it's between the husband and the wife, right? What business do we have there?" (6).

Sharif Aunty eventually found the courage to leave her husband. She sought refuge at the narrator's home, where she asked to stay for a few days while she arranged for her own housing at the school; she revealed to the narrator's family that none of her three brothers, all of whom enjoyed considerable wealth, would take her in. The narrator's family similarly refused to do anything to help her, despite the narrator's mother being disgusted with Sharif Uncle's abuse. So Sharif Aunty left town with her children and was "never heard from again" (Nadiya, "Teacher Shortage" 17). As though to absolve itself from responsibility, the campus community continued to speculate—despite the lack of evidence—that there must have been another man, "otherwise how could Sharif Aunty have disappeared so quickly and effectively?" (18).

Depicting even close friends and sympathetic neighbors as completely unwilling to provide any type of succor to an individual subjected to repeated intimate partner violence, the narrative structure of "Teacher Shortage" emphasizes just how readily this abuse is normalized, justified, and pushed aside, part of the informal education reinforced by both the school and society. That the narrator describes conditions from some years earlier makes clear that this violence is not forgotten. But not forgetting is not the same as preventing future abuse, and early in "Teacher Shortage" the narrator speaks explicitly of women in situations like that of Mitul's mother who even today rarely leave their abusers. This is in part because, Nadiya's story suggests, the hostility they face outside the walls of their home makes conditions inside, as horrific as they are, in some cases preferable.

In the article "Why Do So Many Men Rape?" (2017), Nadiya deplores the prevalence of rape in Bangladesh and declares that so many women are raped "because our society makes it easy for the rapist," a phenomenon aesthetically interrogated in her short story "Teacher Shortage."

She continues: "the whole dynamic of sexual behavior that is normalized in our society is one where the role of men is to aggress and for women to submit. . . . Whenever a rape becomes public, the first admonishing fingers are invariably raised against the victims." Moreover, Nadiya notes, Bangladeshi law does not acknowledge marital rape as rape; marrying a woman (or girl) to her rapist remains a common practice, with "rape mediations" overseen by police and local officials. The complicity of the campus community in "Teacher Shortage" is not as extreme, but it is no less destructive, revealing the paucity of options, not to mention absolute dearth of justice, even for educated women of relative means.

Without Recourse: Li Ang's *The Butcher's Wife* (1983)

The narratives examined above—Kandasamy's *When I Hit You*, Pak's "An Episode," and Nadiya's "Teacher Shortage"—all underscore the pervasiveness of intimate partner violence and identify family, friends, neighbors, health professionals, and the broader community as directly complicit in abuse. Their emphasis on the vulnerability of even educated women, and in Kandasamy's and Nadiya's cases employed women of some privilege, reveals the refusal of societies in South Asia, as in many other parts of the world, to dismantle ingrained hostility toward women's safety, health, and well-being.

The Taiwanese social activist, feminist, and writer Li Ang's celebrated and controversial *The Butcher's Wife*—the focus of considerable scholarship, including ecocriticism (K. Chang 169–70)—focuses on a woman in even more desperate circumstances than the women featured in the above narratives. Chen Lin Shi, the novella's protagonist, comes from an educated family. But her father, who had tuberculosis, sold his land to pay his medical bills. When he dies, he leaves his widow and daughter with just the family home, which one of Lin Shi's uncles soon commandeers, rendering Lin Shi and her mother homeless. Some years later, this uncle sells Lin Shi in marriage to Chen Jiangshui, a butcher who abuses her violently and repeatedly. Far from receiving assistance from her neighbors, Lin Shi instead is viciously maligned and ostracized, not unlike Sharif Aunty in Nadiya's "Teacher Shortage." Lin Shi becomes so desperate that, not unlike Durga in Desai's *Witness the Night* and the first-person narrator of Muhaddes's "Over and Over Again" (chapter 6), both of whom murder abusive family members, she takes justice into her own hands and kills her husband.

Li Ang published *The Butcher's Wife* in 1983, 15 years after the 1968 educational reforms, a decade after the rise of the relatively elite second wave of Taiwan's autonomous women's movement (1972), and seven years after Lu Hsiu-lien (Annette Lu), the leader of the first stage of this second wave and the eventual first female vice president of Taiwan, established Taiwan's first 24-hour hotline for victims of sexual assault and domestic violence (D. Chang 11–13, 87).[14] In 1983 Taiwan was also in its last years before the lifting of martial law (1987), which ushered in the far more inclusive third wave of the autonomous women's movement (12–13). Just as Lu launched one of the first major challenges against the Taiwanese Nationalist government's assumption of "the guardianship of tradition and cultural heritage" and encouragement of women "to play supportive and subservient roles both at home and in society" (Ng 180), so, too, did *The Butcher's Wife* challenge conventional Chinese-language writing and especially writing by women (183).[15] In addition to asserting itself as a "serious feminist work" (183), Li Ang's novella also reminded readers of the presence, and the extreme vulnerability, of the millions of women who were essentially invisible to Taiwan's women's movements, both autonomous and state-controlled.

The Butcher's Wife additionally exposed how little had changed for most women since the early twentieth century. As Li Ang notes in the preface, she based the novella on a news report from 1930s Shanghai describing a woman who declared that she had murdered her husband "only to escape his abuses" and that "she was innocent of any extramarital involvements" (Preface ix). This woman countered what Li Ang describes as a "demeaning attitude toward the moral character of women" that "has been held by Chinese for thousands of years," namely that "any woman guilty of killing her husband is a promiscuous woman, and no other interpretation is possible" (ix). Li Ang moved the story from Shanghai to her hometown in central Taiwan, which she describes as "just another small town that retained the flavor of 'old Taiwan'" (ix). This allowed her to create "a story of old Taiwanese society" (x). The novella itself explicitly obscures the timing of the events it describes, opening as it does with a section titled "News Report #1," which begins with "Date: _____, 19__," followed by "On the morning of __________" (Li, *Butcher's Wife* 3). In so doing, Li Ang's novella deprives this "old Taiwanese society" of an end date.

In the preface to the novella, Li Ang admits that she "approached the writing of *The Butcher's Wife* with a number of feminist ideals, wanting to show the tragic fate that awaited the economically dependent Taiwanese woman living under the rules of traditional Chinese society," rules that were stubbornly intact even in the 1980s (Preface x). But in writing the novella, Li Ang found herself "becoming more and more concerned with larger issues of humanity, such as hunger, death, sex" (x). And, she writes, "what I want to emphasize here is that the ultimate concern of a piece of 'feminist literature' is after all, human nature" (x). Without question, the feminist concerns *The Butcher's Wife* addresses are also those of human nature, including both the desperation of people subjected to unrelenting abuse, desperation that can lead to murder, and the lack of empathy and feelings of responsibility communities have for those who are abused. As Elizabeth Flock has argued, in much of the world, women who kill intimate partners in self-defense or following repeated abuse often make headlines. At the same time, they rarely receive sympathy, much less leniency, from either the criminal justice system or their communities.

This is precisely what unfolds in *The Butcher's Wife*. The novella opens with two undated news reports on Lin Shi. Abandoning objectivity, and revealing the power of long-standing assumptions, "News Report #1" declares that Lin Shi's claim of abuse "defies reason and logic, for, since ancient times, a murder of this sort has always been the result of an adulterous affair" (Li, *Butcher's Wife* 3). The reporter insists, "The authorities must treat this case with the utmost severity in order to stem the public outcry and restore healthy social tendencies" (3). For the reporter, as for so many in Taiwan and societies around the world, women's safety is not included within the rubric of "healthy social tendencies."

"News Report #2" relates that even though no secret lover has been discovered, Lin Shi has been sentenced to death for killing her husband. The reporter omits all mention of Lin Shi's defense, instead asserting that this punishment is a "necessity," a "warning against immorality," an act that will surely cause Taiwanese women to "take heed and refrain from imitating foreign women, who are always clamoring for equality and the right to attend Western schools. . . . We hope that the parade [of the condemned Chen Lin Shi through the streets] will inspire concerned citizens to redouble their efforts in the fight to stop the decline in womanly virtues" (Li, *Butcher's Wife* 4). "News Report #2" can be read in part as a satire of government-affiliated women's organizations, led by Chiang Soong May-ling (Soong Meiling, Madame Chiang), the wife of Chiang Kai-shek, the leader of the Republic of China in mainland China (1928–49) and then Taiwan (1949–75). As in prewar and wartime China, during the early postwar decades in Taiwan, these organizations generally prioritized national goals over women's rights and interests (D. Chang 66).

Paradoxically, as *The Butcher's Wife* makes clear, Lin Shi can hardly be said to have attempted to emulate "foreign women." Unlike Kandasamy's narrator, it is doubtful whether Lin Shi even knew about these women, or if she did, that she aspired to even a basic education.[16] That the reporter should so readily equate a woman's desire to escape abuse with her desire to emulate "foreign women," "leave house and home," and in so doing "destroy our age-old concepts of womanhood" (4) reveals not only a total lack of appreciation for the trauma of abuse but also a deep fear of any change to the status quo. It was at least in part Lin Shi's inability to "leave house and home" (e.g., her lack of education and marketable skills) that culminated in her husband's murder.

Following the two news reports, *The Butcher's Wife* elaborates on the events leading up to mariticide, the third-person narrator weaving in the story of Lin Shi's early years. Resonating with the narratives discussed in chapters 4–6 of *Gender Justice*, Li Ang's novella addresses Lin Shi's traumatic childhood, the abuse to which her starving mother was subjected by her family and the community for having sex with a soldier for food, and then the abuse to which Lin Shi's uncle subjected her after he drove her mother out of town, essentially orphaning Lin Shi and making her entirely dependent on him. *The Butcher's Wife* highlights the apathy of the neighborhood women who are said to have sympathized with her for being motherless but ultimately give her little support. Eventually, looking to sell her off, Lin Shi's uncle declared her as sexually ravenous as her mother had been and sold her in marriage to Jiangshui, who raped her repeatedly, beginning on their wedding night. Lin Shi resisted but was no match for his strength. After she overheard the neighbors, goaded by Auntie Ah-wang, criticizing her for her screams—which they believed inappropriate cries of pleasure—she endured Jiangshui's sexual abuse in silence, which further infuriated her already volatile husband. As with *When I Hit You*, *The Butcher's Wife* graphically describes this abuse: "He hit, he choked, he pinched, he prolonged the time he was inside her, but she just gritted her teeth and bore it all in silence—except for the panting hisses that escaped . . . like the gasps of a tiny animal in the throes of death" (109). Whenever he was home, Jiangshui "tried his best to make her scream every single time, prolonging his tormentings as much as possible" (118). One night, after her husband had fallen asleep, Lin Shi picked up the knife with which he had threatened her and butchered him to death.

Notable in *The Butcher's Wife* is how readily the women in Lin Shi's new neighborhood disregarded her abuse and how easily they turned against her, in a way that is even more striking than the women who turn against Sharif Aunty in Nadiya's "Teacher Shortage." Particularly egregious is the local gossip Ah-wang, who, based on an ancient superstition, chastised Lin Shi for having sex during the seventh month. When Lin Shi protested that "I am not the one who wants it. What can I do?" (Li, *Butcher's Wife* 48), Ah-wang called her a "simpleton" and claimed she could prevent her husband's advances by faking a long period (49). Moreover, Ah-wang publicly disparaged Lin Shi. She accused the "greedy Lin Shi" of being insatiable, claiming, "She can't get enough. She wants it day and night. I don't know how anyone can be so shameless! Who ever heard of anyone doing things like that in broad daylight. . . . She makes so much noise that people three miles away can hear her" (102). Later, after her husband denied her access to food, Lin Shi visited several neighboring households, offering to do anything for a meal, but she was repeatedly turned away, Ah-wang having poisoned the townspeople against her (131). And after Lin Shi murdered her husband Jiangshui, the busybody Ah-wang, who had been spying on her and alerted the authorities to what she had done, repeated to ordinary citizens and investigators alike:

> You know the old saying "There's no murder without adultery." . . . In my opinion, Lin Shi didn't have enough sense to count her blessings. Just think, by marrying Pig-Butcher Chen she had no parents-in-law to lord it over her, no brothers- or sisters-in-law to care for, and no need to go to sea or work in the fields. . . . She didn't know a good thing when she had it, and that's why she wound up like she did. . . . All a woman has to do is put up with it a while, and it'll pass. Who ever heard of someone yelling and carrying on until everybody in the neighborhood knows and no other woman is willing to speak up for her? (141–42)[17]

Ah-wang cites the old saying about adultery being the sole trigger for murder but makes no claim that this is what happened with Lin Shi. Nor does she suggest that Lin Shi has been polluted with "Western" ideas, as does the second news report at the beginning of *The Butcher's Wife*. Instead, she focuses on how much Lin Shi's life has allegedly improved since her marriage and how she, as is true of women everywhere, should simply "put up with it a while."

As Sheung-Yuen Daisy Ng has argued, Lin Shi and her mother "are doomed victims of the sexual double standard prevalent in society. . . . Lin and her mother are victimized by a society that refuses to listen to women's sufferings. . . . [T]hey are made to bear the blame for their suffering. . . . Women are oppressed not only by men, but also by other women" (192). Although many critics have hailed *The Butcher's Wife* as feminist protest and applauded its exposure of women's subjugation and rebellion, some have censured the novella for not being feminist enough, arguing that it "contains no progressive ideas that can advance [the] women's movement" (Wu 63), that it only exposes "the injustice that women suffer in traditional Chinese society" (64) instead of imagining "a relation of women to power" (63), and that the battered wife Lin Shi lacks "subjectivity, self-awareness, and agency" (68). At the same time, one of the major contributions of *The Butcher's Wife* is its stark revelation of the major roles family and community play in propagating intimate partner violence.

In October 1993, a decade after the publication of Li Ang's novella, Deng Ruwen's murder of her long-abusive husband, Lin A-qi, inspired feminists in Taiwan to fight for formal domestic violence policies and legislation. Taipei's first spousal abuse treatment center opened later that year ("Domestic Violence" 1). In 1998, Taiwan passed the Domestic Violence Prevention and Control Act (Huang and Lin 302; Wang 2429). This measure, the first in Asia to declare family violence a crime, prompted more than 16,000 women to bring forth cases of intimate partner violence between June 1999 and January 2001, resulting in more than 10,000 injunctions (D. Chang 131; Haj-Yahia and Shen 1041). Yet more than 20 years later, intimate partner violence remains endemic in Taiwan. The patriarchal family system and "an unwillingness among people to intervene outside of their own homes" have been identified as key factors in perpetuating this violence (White), making *The Butcher's Wife* as relevant today as it was four decades ago.

Justice for Whom?
Duanwad Pimwana's "Men's Rights" (2006)

Thai activists have been fighting vigorously against domestic violence since the 1980s. The Foundation for Women, an NGO established as the Women's Information Centre in 1984, opened Bangkok's first women's shelter for victims of domestic violence in 1986. The following year marked the publication of the prizewinning "A Pot That Scouring Will Not Save" ("Mǭ Thi Khūt Mai Oǭk," หม้อที่ขูดไม่ออก, 1987), by Anchan (Anchalee Vivatanachai [1952–]).[18] This short story was a "benchmark" in women's writing in Thailand in its exposure of intimate partner violence, a topic many deemed inappropriate for literature, and particularly for literature written by women (Kepner, "Anchan" 200). But it was not until 2007 that marital rape was criminalized in Thailand. Moreover, entrenched beliefs concerning women's roles in society, combined with the belief in Thailand, as in much of the world, that intimate partner violence is an "internal family matter," have meant that physical and sexual intimate partner violence against women in Thailand has been underreported and continued apace (Chuemchit et al. 315). One recent study found that more than 40% of women in Thailand's capital of Bangkok and more than 47% of Thai women in rural Nakornsawan have experienced intimate partner violence. Additionally, more than 21% of women in Bangkok and close to 23% of women in Nakornsawan report being currently abused by a romantic partner—physically, sexually, or both (Garcia-Morena et al. 1264; see also Chuemchit et al.). Rape and other forms of sexual violence are a staple of *lakhon*, popular Thai primetime television dramas (Townsend).[19]

Published a year before marital rape was criminalized in Thailand, the prizewinning Thai writer Duanwad Pimwana's provocatively titled "Men's Rights" underscores the dangers of focusing solely on the "rights" of men without considering the implications for women. While the other narratives examined in this chapter center primarily on the stories of wives subjected to intimate partner violence, Pimwana's short story daringly juxtaposes the abuse of a wife, Namfon, with the experiences, thoughts, and emotions of her abusive husband, Wasu. Wasu's perspective in fact dominates this narrative. By revealing the devastating costs to Namfon of Wasu's belief that he has the right to murder his wife for being unfaithful, not unlike the honor-based violence Sarbjit Kaur Athwal discusses in *Shamed* (chapter 5), "Men's Rights" piercingly undermines conventional justifications of intimate partner violence in Thailand and many parts of the world. As with other narratives analyzed in this chapter, Pimwana's short story highlights broad complicity in this abuse by depicting the relative apathy of both friends and neighbors.

"Men's Rights" opens with Wasu exhausted yet unable to sleep, agonizing over his wife's absence. Believing her a "whore" and a "slut" who is having an affair, and finding such behavior "beyond contempt," he hatches a violent plan to kill her (Pimwana, "Men's Rights" 71).[20] Later that morning he brutally attacks her, Pimwana's narrative graphically describing the gruesome assault. Wasu ultimately spares his wife's life, but he declares that "if he ever caught her cheating again, he would bury a knife in her gut" (71). Their neighbors know about that morning's attack, word of the beating having made the rounds, and they are described as "eager to know what had caused the outburst" (72).[21] One neighbor asks

Wasu a more pointed question: "This morning—what happened? Why'd you have to lay hands on her?" (73).[22] Wasu explains, "Fon, my wife, has run off with her lover," to which the neighbor replies, "My goodness! How could she? The baby's not even weaned. And who's this other man? Where's he from, Ratom?" (73). The neighbor's focus quickly changes from the more accusatory "Why'd you have to lay hands on her?" to the empathetic "How could she?," echoing the entrenched belief that women who are unfaithful deserve to be beaten. As is true of the women subjected to abuse depicted in the other narratives discussed in this chapter, Namfon has nowhere to turn; those closest to her almost immediately turn against her.

Meanwhile, Wasu feels himself sinking deeper into despair. "He realized," declares the narrator, with not a little irony considering what has happened to Namfon, "that there was no justice in this world. At random, a person could be forced to endure hardship all alone. Yes, that was the truth. This was what reality looked like. He saw it now, with painful clarity" (Pimwana, "Men's Rights" 76).[23] To be sure, Wasu also resolves to attack his wife's lover (his good friend Boonleua), and the two men come to blows. But their fight rapidly dissipates, both men eager to downplay their own culpability, reflecting the different standards to which men and women are held: while women are expected to be monogamous, men are at liberty to have multiple lovers.[24] The narrator speaks briefly of Namfon, describing her as sitting "lifelessly on the bench. Her face was badly bruised, her eyes on the verge of tears" (84). But the spotlight quickly returns to Wasu and Boonleua. "Men's Rights" concludes shortly thereafter, with the two men "linked at the shoulders" (84), neither Boonleua nor his wife, who is sitting with Namfon and their children, acknowledging that Namfon has been abused.

In a recent interview, Pimwana noted that in Thailand her writing has never been described as feminist, but that exploring the relationships between men and women in her narratives in fact "brings out the feminism in my stories." For Pimwana, feminism is not about opportunism or rendering men powerless. Instead, it is about "claiming basic rights"; it is about "humans being equal."[25] Yes, Pimwana continues, unwittingly echoing Li Ang, as cited above, this is feminist, but "it's a feminism under the umbrella of human rights" (Pimwana and Poopoksakul). "Men's Rights" underlines just how frequently women are denied these rights and instead treated as property without agency and just how frequently those surrounding them fail to hold abusers accountable for intimate partner violence, thwarting any chance at justice.

At the conclusion of the famed Bengali writer Selina Hossain's short story "Izzat" (1995), the narrator remarks that Maleka—a 26-year-old woman who is decapitated by her husband and becomes a headless ghost who haunts him, their family members, and other villagers—wishes she could be alive once more so that she could "kick honour out" (8). Discarded in death as she was in life, Maleka continues to question the double standard facing women: why, she asks, does a man's respectability increase with the number of wives, but the woman who "wants to arrange her life a little differently—is all the fault hers?" (4). Yes, her husband, her brothers, and her neighbors all assert, echoing Athwal's family in *Shamed*, the fault *is* hers: "she besmirches the family honour, therefore she has to die" (4). Kandasamy's *When I Hit You*, Pak's "An Episode," Nadiya's "Teacher Shortage," Li Ang's *Butcher's Wife*, and Pimwana's "Men's Rights" all feature women who, unlike Maleka, survive intimate partner violence yet are left bereft of support. These five narratives and countless others from across Asia, Asia's diasporas, and the world reveal family, friends, neighbors, health professionals, and bystanders as being complicit in intimate partner violence, as failing to hold abusers accountable and failing to help those who are abused obtain justice, as accepting and normalizing this form of domestic abuse, and as going so far as to condition their daughters to expect and tolerate violence rather than protect them from such attacks.[26] Kandasamy's, Pak's, Nadiya's, Li Ang's, and Pimwana's narratives do not excuse the actual abusers, the men who beat and rape their wives. Nor do these narratives exonerate broader social structures and expectations that force wives into subservience and discount their experiences of abuse. Just as significantly, *When I Hit You*, "An Episode," "Teacher Shortage," *Butcher's Wife*, and "Men's Rights" also point to the important roles that most everyone could play in alleviating intimate partner and other forms of gender-based violence and, in so doing, in increasing opportunities for justice.

The COVID-19 pandemic has exacerbated gender inequities and gender-based violence across Asia and much of the world, particularly for marginalized and otherwise disadvantaged individuals. Extreme weather events brought on by climate change have been doing the same for decades: the connections between natural disasters and increased rates of gender-based violence are well-known (Rezwana and Pain). Already an exceptionally difficult challenge throughout Asia, Asian diasporas, and far beyond, attaining gender justice is likely to become even more elusive as the climate becomes increasingly unstable and environmental and humanitarian crises intensify.

Central to dismantling structures of injustice is engaging with stories of inequity and violence and not reflexively defending those inflicting abuse or holding responsible those subjected to abuse, as has been the case across Asia and much of the world for millennia. The multifaceted narratives analyzed in this book are a small yet significant subset of these stories, more of which need to be included in our teaching, learning, research, and activism. Boldly breaking a range of aesthetic and social silences and taboos, they depict individuals of diverse backgrounds and identities from across Asia and its diasporas facing persistent inequities; rigid familial, cultural, and social norms and demands; as well as unrelenting reproductive, non-partner, family, and intimate partner violence. *Gender Justice* not only partners with these narratives in placing individual, family, and community experiences in broader historical, cultural, educational (formal and informal), material, legal, social, statistical, feminist, and activist contexts. This book also brings these stories into dialogue with one another, revealing different forms of gender inequity and gender-based violence as pervasive across Asia, its diasporas, and the world.

Ultimately, the narratives analyzed in *Gender Justice*, as with so many stories of inequity and violence, are calls to action. They take us deep into fights for justice, highlighting individual and community dignity, agency, resilience, and resistance.[27] Their words have the capacity to inspire and strengthen us, giving us courage and sometimes explicit guidance on how we must actively recreate our worlds—if only we're brave enough to do so, to transform the dynamics of which the literature speaks, to transform what "just is" to "justice."[28]

NOTES

1. The World Health Organization estimates the lifetime prevalence of physical or sexual intimate partner violence as ranging from 19% (China) to 27% (Mongolia) in East Asia, 22% (Bhutan) to 46% (Afghanistan) in South Asia, and 14% (Philippines) to 25% (Vietnam) in Southeast Asia ("Global Database").

2. One of the more recently acknowledged mental and physical health consequences of intimate partner violence is chronic traumatic encephalopathy, more typically associated with American football (Behringer; Hillstrom; Valera and Kucyi).

3. Big data analyses in Bangladesh, India, Indonesia, Malaysia, Nepal, Thailand, the Philippines, and Singapore reveal that between late 2019 and late 2020 intimate partner violence cases notably increased (*Covid-19* 6–7). See also Ando.

4. The multidimensional poverty index is based on three key dimensions—health, education, and living standards—and 10 indicators ("271 Million Fewer Poor People"). See Singh and Taub et al.'s six-part series for more on the dearth of opportunities and violence facing women in India.

5. The narrator's level of education far exceeds that of most women in India; in 2010, only 11% of Indian women attended college (*Global Gender Gap Report 2010* 160).

6. Also significant in *When I Hit You* is the narrator's condemnation of conventional (mostly white, privileged) feminisms, echoing Kishwar Desai's *Witness the Night*, discussed in chapter 6. Schuller takes this argument a step further, revealing how "white feminist objectives work to liberate privileged women while keeping other structures of injustice intact" (4).

7. The deadliest of the student protests was the 1980 Gwangju Uprising, where hundreds if not well over 1,000 students and civilians were killed; in 1987, mass demonstrations ultimately forced Chun out of power.

8. Pak was one of South Korea's most prominent, prolific, and celebrated twentieth-century female writers. She focused on the painful legacy of the Korean War; injustice and corruption at all levels; gender relations and family dynamics, especially the challenges faced by middle-aged women; and the plight of many elderly individuals (Kim, "Pak Wan-sŏ" 149–52).

9. Thank you to Min Ji Choi for this observation.

10. The narrator's attachment to Kayŏn's husband also likely stems from her own son's confinement in a sanatorium, an important subplot of the story.

11. Park and Ko explore the support currently available to South Korean female victims of intimate partner violence. See also the South Korean novelist Han Kang's best-selling and widely translated *The Vegetarian* (*Ch'aesikchuŭija*, 2007), whose female protagonist Yeong-hye is raped repeatedly by her husband, who likens her to a "comfort woman" (30); raped by her brother-in-law (96); and hit (157) and force-fed (40) by her father, a Vietnam War veteran who also had abused her as a child. As is true of the Japanese American writer Ruth Ozeki's *My Year of Meats* (1998) and many other Asian and Asian diaspora ecofeminist writings, *The Vegetarian* connects violence against women with that against nonhuman animals. For more on the violence South Korean women face inside and outside the home, see chapters 1 and 5; for more on the comfort women, see chapter 5.

12. Globally, acid attacks are perpetrated by both men and women (Khoshnami et al.). See also the Indian film *Chhapaak* (*Splash*, 2020), on Laxmi Agarwal, who became a prominent activist after being attacked with acid by a man she had rebuffed.

13. In 2008, the year "Teacher Shortage" was published, only 55% of Bangladeshi women participated in the paid workforce, in contrast with 88% of Bangladeshi men; men occupied 90% of professional and technical positions and were 75% of legislators, senior officials, and managers (*Global Gender Gap Report 2008* 47).

14. The government quickly criticized this hotline for drawing attention to sexual violence against women in Taiwan. Doris Chang identifies the first wave of Taiwan's autonomous women's movement as occurring during the Japanese colonial period, which lasted from 1895 to 1945 (11).

15. See also Chien, who compares writing by Lu and Li Ang.

16. Taiwan's 1968 educational reform increased compulsory education from six to nine years. Tsai et al. reveal the significant impact of these reforms on female employment (757). At the same time, schools explicitly inculcated conventional gender expectations. It was not until the 1990s that teachers could choose textbooks that promoted gender equality (D. Chang 124).

17. The phrase translated as "She didn't know a good thing when she had it" reads more literally, "Who knew some women cannot guard what they have?" (哪知查某人不會守; Li, *Shafu* 202).

18. The expression "a pot that scouring will not save" refers to manners, nature, or traits that cannot change. Thank you to Cookie Kunarattanapruek for this insight.

19. Thank you to Cookie Kunarattanapruek for this insight.

20. The term in the Thai source is "rayum," which is stronger than "contempt" (Pimwana, "Sitthiburut" 164).

21. The Thai source translates more literally as "They want to know what the matter was, what the reason was" (พวกเขาจึงอยากรู้ว่ามันเรื่องใดเหตุใดกันหนอ; Pimwana, "Sitthiburut" 166–67).

22. The Thai source translates more literally as "This is distressing. What happened this morning that was so serious that you had to lay hands on her?" (นี่ระทม เมื่อเช้าน่ะ มีอะไรร้ายแรงถึงต้องลงไม้ลงมือ; Pimwana, "Sitthiburut" 167). In both versions, the neighbors believe that this violence is mandatory, but the Thai original acknowledges the distressing nature of the attack and suggests that to be justified, this violence must have been in response to something serious.

23. The Thai source speaks not of "hardship" but of "evil punishment" or "terrible punishment" (โทษทัณฑ์อันเลวร้าย) and not of "reality" but of truth that is "eternal," "absolute," and "dharmic" (สัจธรรม; Pimwana, "Sitthiburut" 170).

24. Boonleua claims he had an affair with Wasu's wife because Wasu had earlier "stolen" his girlfriend Moddang, who he asserts "belonged to me" (Pimwana, "Men's Rights" 83).

25. In 2006, when "Men's Rights" was published, men in Thailand outnumbered women in labor force participation 81% to 66% (*Global Gender Gap Report 2006* 130). Today, 59.23% of women participate in the labor force, compared with 75.22% of men (*Global Gender Gap Report 2023* 343).

26. One notable exception is the Afghan American writer Khaled Hosseini's novel *A Thousand Splendid Suns* (2007), in which Mariam, an older woman who had been married off to the abusive Rasheed, protects Laila, a younger woman whom Rasheed had taken as his second wife. Mariam ultimately kills Rasheed to save Laila and is publicly executed by the Taliban.

27. Inspired by Hune 11 and Rose 31.

28. The first half of this sentence is inspired by Ammons, who speaks of the power of words "to inspire us, to transform us, to give us strength and courage for the difficult task of *re*-creating the world" (14), while the second half echoes Gorman's "The Hill We Climb." Nguyen emphasizes the importance not just of reading but also of taking action based on what we have read (20).

WORKS CITED

Ammons, Elizabeth. *Brave New Words: How Literature Will Save the Planet*. U of Iowa P, 2010.

Anchan. "A Pot That Scouring Will Not Save." Kepner, *Lioness*, pp. 172–204.

Ando, Rei. "Domestic Violence and Japan's Covid-19 Pandemic." *The Asia-Pacific Journal: Japan Focus*, vol. 18, no. 18, 15 Sept. 2020, apjjf.org/2020/18/Ando.html.

Behringer, Allison, host. "Invisible Impact." *Bodies*, season 2, episode 5, 29 Apr. 2020.

Chang, Doris. *Women's Movements in Twentieth-Century Taiwan*. U of Illinois P, 2009.

Chang, Kathryn Yalan. "Ang Li's *The Butcher's Wife* (*Shafu*) and Taiwanese Ecocriticism." *East Asian Ecocriticisms: A Critical Reader*, edited by Simon Estok and Won-Chung Kim, Palgrave Macmillan, 2013, pp. 165–84.

Chhapaak. Directed by Meghna Gulza, Fox Star Studios, 2020.

Chien, Ying-Ying. "From Utopian to Dystopian World: Two Faces of Feminism in Contemporary Taiwanese Women's Fiction." *World Literature Today*, vol. 68, no. 1, 1994, pp. 35–42.

Chowdhury, Elora Halim. *Transnationalism Reversed*. State U of New York P, 2011.

Chuemchit, Montakarn, et al. "Prevalence of Intimate Partner Violence in Thailand." *Journal of Family Violence*, vol. 33, no. 5, July 2018, pp. 315–23.

Chung, Grace H., and Sun Wha Ok. "Marital Violence in South Korea." *Family Violence from a Global Perspective: A Strengths-Based Approach*, edited by Sylvia M. Asay et al., Sage, 2014, pp. 81–92.

Combatting Acid Violence in Bangladesh, India, and Cambodia. Avon Global Center for Women and Justice / New York City Bar Association / Cornell University Law School / Virtue Foundation, 2011.

Covid-19 and Violence against Women: The Evidence behind the Talk. UNFPA / UN Women / Quilt.ai, 3 Mar. 2021, asiapacific.unfpa.org/sites/default/files/pub-pdf/covid-19_and_vaw_insights_from_big_data_analysis_final.pdf.

D., Deepa. "A List of People Who Should Read Meena Kandasamy's *When I Hit You*." *The Wire*, 3 June 2017, thewire.in/books/list-people-read-i-hit.

Dey, Adrija. "'Others' within the 'Others': An Intersectional Analysis of Gender Violence in India." *Gender Issues*, vol. 36, no. 4, Mar. 2019, pp. 357–73.

"Domestic Violence." *Global Gender*, 2023, www.globalgender.org/upload/media/program/2011%20NGOs%20shadow%20report--domestic%20violence.pdf.

"Facts and Figures: Ending Violence against Women." *UN Women*, 21 Sept. 2023, www.unwomen.org/en/what-we-do/ending-violence-against-women/facts-and-figures.

Flock, Elizabeth. "A Violent Defense." *The New Yorker*, 20 Jan. 2020, pp. 20–26.

Garcia-Morena, Claudia, et al. "Prevalence of Intimate Partner Violence: Findings from the WHO Multi-country Study on Women's Health and Domestic Violence." *The Lancet*, vol. 368, 7 Oct. 2006, pp. 1260–69.

"Global Database on the Prevalence of Violence against Women." *World Health Organization*, 2021, vaw-data.srhr.org/map.

Global Gender Gap Report 2006. World Economic Forum, 2006, www3.weforum.org/docs/WEF_GenderGap_Report_2006.pdf.

Global Gender Gap Report 2008. World Economic Forum, 2008, www3.weforum.org/docs/WEF_GenderGap_Report_2008.pdf.

Global Gender Gap Report 2010. World Economic Forum, 2010, www3.weforum.org/docs/WEF_GenderGap_Report_2010.pdf.

Global Gender Gap Report 2023. World Economic Forum, 2023, www3.weforum.org/docs/WEF_GGGR_2023.pdf.

Gorman, Amanda. "The Hill We Climb." *Call Us What We Carry*, by Gorman, Viking Books, 2021, pp. 132–34.

Haj-Yahia, Muhammad M., and April Chiung-Tao Shen. "Beliefs about Wife Beating among Social Work Students in Taiwan." *International Journal of Offender Therapy and Comparative Criminology*, vol. 61, no. 9, July 2017, pp. 1038–62.

Han, Ju Hui Judy, and Jennifer Jihye Chun. "Gender and Politics in Contemporary Korea." *The Journal of Korean Studies*, vol. 19, no. 2, 2014, pp. 245–55.

Han Kang. *The Vegetarian*. Translated by Deborah Smith, Portobello Books, 2015.

Hillstrom, Christa. "The Hidden Epidemic of Brain Injuries from Domestic Violence." *The New York Times*, 1 Mar. 2022, www.nytimes.com/2022/03/01/magazine/brain-trauma-domestic-violence.html.

Hossain, Selina. "Izzat." *Different Perspectives: Women Writing in Bangladesh*, edited by Firdous Azim and Niaz Zaman, University Press, 1998, pp. 1–8.

Hosseini, Khaled. *A Thousand Splendid Suns*. Riverhead Books, 2007.

Huang, Lanying, and Yushen Lin. "Determinants of Police-Filed Petitions for Protection Orders in Taiwan: Comparing Predictive Factor Salience in Intimate Partner Violence Cases in the USA and Taiwan." *Asian Journal of Criminology*, vol. 9, no. 4, Sept. 2014, pp. 301–22.

Hune, Shirley. "Our Histories." *Our Voices, Our Histories: Asian American and Pacific Islander Women*, edited by Hune and Gail M. Nomura, New York UP, 2020, pp. 8–16.

"Indian Feminist Poet Meena Kandasamy on Resisting Patriarchy and the Caste System." *YouTube*, uploaded by FRANCE 24 English, 6 Mar. 2019, www.youtube.com/watch?v=elqAzL1DcxI.

Islam, Towfiqua Mahfuza, et al. "Correlates of Intimate Partner Violence against Women in Bangladesh." *Journal of Family Violence*, vol. 30, no. 4, Feb. 2015, pp. 433–44.

Jung, Kyungja. *Practicing Feminism in South Korea: The Women's Movement against Sexual Violence*. Routledge, 2014.

Kalokhe, Ameeta S., et al. "How Well Does the World Health Organization Definition of Domestic Violence Work for India?" *PLOS One*, 26 Mar. 2015, www.ncbi.nlm.nih.gov/pmc/articles/PMC4374684/.

Kandasamy, Meena. "And Finally: Meena Kandasamy." Interview conducted by Graeme Green. *New Internationalist*, 30 Apr. 2018, newint.org/features/2018/04/03/meena-kandasamy.

———. *When I Hit You; or, A Portrait of the Writer as a Young Wife*. Atlantic Books, 2017.

Kepner, Susan Fulop. "Anchan and 'A Pot That Scouring Will Not Save.'" Kepner, *Lioness*, pp. 199–204.

———, editor and translator. *The Lioness in Bloom: Modern Thai Fiction about Women*. U of California P, 1996.

Khoshnami, Mohammad Sabzi, et al. "Conceptual Model of Acid Attacks Based on Survivor's Experiences: Lessons from a Qualitative Exploration." *Burns*, vol. 43, no. 3, 2016, pp. 608–18.

Kim, Jae Yop, et al. "Prevalence and Trends in Domestic Violence in South Korea: Findings from National Surveys." *Journal of Interpersonal Violence*, vol. 31, no. 8, May 2016, pp. 1554–76.

Kim, Yung-Hee, translator. *Gendered Landscapes: Short Fiction by Modern and Contemporary Korean Women Novelists*. Cornell U East Asia Program, 2017.

———. "Pak Wan-sŏ (1931–2011)." Kim, *Gendered Landscapes*, pp. 149–54.

Lee, Minjee, et al. "Gender-Specific Differences in Risk for Intimate Partner Violence in South Korea." *BMC Public Health*, vol. 14, no. 1, May 2014, p. 415.

Li Ang. *The Butcher's Wife*. Li, The Butcher's Wife *and Other Stories*, pp. 1–142.

———. The Butcher's Wife *and Other Stories*. Translated by Howard Goldblatt, Cheng and Tsui, 1995.

———. Preface. Li, The Butcher's Wife *and Other Stories*, pp. ix–x.

———. *Shafu*. *Shafu: Lucheng gushi*, by Li, Lianhe baoshe, 1983, pp. 75–207.

Nadiya, Shabnam. "Teacher Shortage." *Lifelines: New Writing from Bangladesh*, edited by Farah Ghuznavi, Zubaan, 2012, pp. 1–18.

———. "Why Do So Many Men Rape?" *Dhaka Tribune*, 7 Oct. 2020, www.dhakatribune.com/magazine/weekend-tribune/225787/why-do-so-many-men-rape.

Nair, Shalini. "Don't Criminalise Marital Rape, May Disturb Institution of Marriage: Government." *The Indian Express*, 30 Aug. 2017, indianexpress.com/article/india/dont-criminalise-marital-rape-may-disturb-institution-of-marriage-government.

Natarajan, Mangai, and Diana Rodriguez-Spahia. "Domestic Violence: A Global Concern." *International and Transnational Crime and Justice*, edited by Natarajan, Cambridge UP, 2019, pp. 370–75.

Ng, Sheung-Yuen Daisy. "Feminism in the Chinese Context: Li Ang's *The Butcher's Wife*." *Modern Chinese Literature*, vol. 4, nos. 1–2, spring-fall 1988, pp. 177–200.

Nguyen, Viet Thanh. Introduction. *The Displaced: Refugee Writers on Refugee Lives*, edited by Nguyen, Abrams Press, 2018, pp. 11–22.

Ozeki, Ruth. *My Year of Meats*. Penguin Books, 1998.

Pak Wansŏ. "An Episode at Dusk, 2." Kim, *Gendered Landscapes*, pp. 129–54.

Palley, Marian Lief. "Feminism in a Confucian Society: The Women's Movement in Korea." *Women of Japan and Korea, Continuity and Change*, edited by Joyce Gelb and Palley, Temple UP, 1994, pp. 274–94.

Park, Sihyun, and Yejung Ko. "Victims of Intimate Partner Violence in South Korea: Experiences in Seeking Help Based on Support Selection." *Violence against Women*, vol. 27, nos. 3–4, 2021, pp. 320–38.

Pimwana, Duanwad. "Men's Rights." *Arid Dreams: Stories*, translated by Mui Poopoksakul, Feminist Press, 2019, pp. 69–84.

———. "Sitthiburut." *Samphanthaphap*, by Pimwana, Sāmānchon, 2006, pp. 163–79.

Pimwana, Duanwad, and Mui Poopoksakul. "Duanwad Pimwana and Mui Poopoksakul with Andrea Scrima." *The Brooklyn Rail*, Apr. 2019, brooklynrail.org/2019/04/books/Duanwad-Pimwana-and-Mui-Poopoksakul-with-Andrea-Scrima.

Press Trust of India. "Marriage Sacred in India, so Marital Rape Cannot Be Applied." *The Indian Express*, 30 Apr. 2015, indianexpress.com/article/india/india-others/concept-of-marital-rape-cannot-be-applied-in-india-govt/.

Rezwana, Nahid, and Rachel Pain. "Gender-Based Violence before, during, and after Cyclones: Slow Violence and Layered Disasters." *Disasters*, vol. 45, no. 4, Oct. 2021, pp. 741–61.

Rose, Jacqueline. *On Violence and On Violence against Women*. Farrar, Straus and Giroux, 2021.

Sato, Kimi N., et al. "Familial Power and Women's Contradictory Responses to Attitudinal Questions about Intimate Partner Violence in Rural Bangladesh." *Violence against Women*, vol. 21, no. 10, Oct. 2015, pp. 1171–93.

Schuller, Kyla. *The Trouble with White Women: A Counterhistory of Feminism*. Bold Type Books, 2021.

Singh, Manvir. "Lives in the Balance: Why Do 'Dowry Deaths' Persist?" *The New Yorker*, 19 June 2023, pp. 24–29.

Subrahmanian, Maya. "The Autonomous Women's Movement in Kerala: Historiography." *Journal of International Women's Studies*, vol. 20, no. 2, Jan. 2019, pp. 1–10.

Taub, Amanda, et al. "India's Daughters: Chapter 1: To Take Control, She Had to Run." *The New York Times*, 21 Oct. 2023, www.nytimes.com/2023/10/21/world/asia/indias-daughters-women-careers.html.

———. "India's Daughters: Chapter 2: Chasing Dreams at a Steep Cost." *The New York Times*, 28 Oct. 2023, www.nytimes.com/2023/10/28/world/asia/india-daughters-women-marriage-economy.html.

———. "India's Daughters: Chapter 3: Bargaining for Time." *The New York Times*, 4 Nov. 2023, www.nytimes.com/2023/11/04/world/asia/india-women-jobs.html.

———. "India's Daughters: Chapter 4: The Wedding." *The New York Times*, 11 Nov. 2023, www.nytimes.com/2023/11/11/world/asia/india-daughters-wedding.html.

———. "India's Daughters: Chapter 5: An Unlikely Escape Route." *The New York Times*, 18 Nov. 2023, www.nytimes.com/2023/11/18/world/asia/indias-daughters-wedding-engagement.html.

———. "India's Daughters: Chapter 6: Struggle and Hope." *The New York Times*, 25 Nov. 2023, www.nytimes.com/2023/11/25/world/asia/india-daughters-women.html.

Townsend, Rebecca. "Prisoner of Love: Sexual Violence on Thai Television." *Critical Asian Studies*, vol. 48, no. 4, 2016, pp. 579–96.

Tsai, When-Jyuan, et al. "Does Educational Expansion Encourage Female Workforce Participation? A Study of the 1968 Reform in Taiwan." *Economics of Education Review*, vol. 28, no. 6, 2009, pp. 750–58.

"271 Million Fewer Poor People in India." *United Nations Development Programme*, 2023, www.in.undp.org/content/india/en/home/sustainable-development/successstories/MultiDimesnionalPovertyIndex.html.

Valera, Eve, and Aaron Kucyi. "Brain Injury in Women Experiencing Intimate Partner–Violence: Neural Mechanistic Evidence of an 'Invisible' Trauma." *Brain Imaging and Behavior*, vol. 11, no. 6, Oct. 2016, pp. 1664–77.

VanderEnde, Kristin E., et al. "Community Economic Status and Intimate Partner Violence against Women in Bangladesh: Compositional or Contextual Effects?" *Violence against Women*, vol. 21, no. 6, June 2015, pp. 679–99.

"Violence against Women." *World Health Organization*, 9 Mar. 2021, www.who.int/news-room/fact-sheets/detail/violence-against-women.

Wang, Pei-ling. "Assessing the Danger: Validation of Taiwan Intimate Partner Violence Danger Assessment." *Journal of Interpersonal Violence*, vol. 30, no. 14, Sept. 2015, pp. 2428–46.

White, Edward. "Taiwan's Domestic Violence Epidemic: Abuse Reported Every Five Minutes." *The News Lens*, 19 June 2017, international.thenewslens.com/article/71187.

Wu, Yenna. *Li Ang's Visionary Challenges to Gender, Sex, and Politics*. Rowman and Littlefield, 2014.

Yoshikawa, Kayoko, et al. "A Lifetime Experience of Violence and Adverse Reproductive Outcomes: Findings from Population Surveys in India." *BioScience Trends*, vol. 6, no. 3, June 2012, pp. 115–21.

Ziaei, Shirin, et al. "Women's Exposure to Intimate Partner Violence and Child Malnutrition: Findings from Demographic and Health Surveys in Bangladesh." *Maternal and Child Nutrition*, vol. 10, no. 3, July 2014, pp. 347–59.

Index